Political Ideologies

of the Twentieth Century

DISCARD

P9-DMB-285

hARpeR ✦ ɔoRchBooks

*A reference-list of Harper Torchbooks, classified
by subjects, is printed at the end of this volume.*

Political Ideologies

of the Twentieth Century

by

Hans Kohn

Third edition, Revised

HARPER TORCHBOOKS ❦ *The Academy Library*
Harper & Row, Publishers, New York

POLITICAL IDEOLOGIES OF
THE TWENTIETH CENTURY

Copyright © 1949, 1957, 1966 by Hans Kohn.

Printed in the United States of America.

This book was originally published in 1949
by The Macmillan Company, New York,
under the title *The Twentieth Century*, with a
a second and enlarged edition in 1957. It is
here reprinted by arrangement with the author,
who has added a new Preface and a new
Chapter for the Torchbook edition.

First HARPER TORCHBOOK edition published
1966 by Harper & Row, Publishers,
Incorporated
49 East 33rd Street
New York, N.Y. 10016.

Library of Congress Catalog Card Number:
66–22369.

*This book is sold subject to the condition that it shall not, by way of
trade, be lent, re-sold, hired out, or otherwise disposed of without the
publisher's consent, in any form of binding or cover other than that
in which it is published.*

To Josef Korbel,
Scholar, Friend and Gentleman,
in happy recollection of my sojourn
at the University of Denver

CONTENTS

PREFACE TO THE TORCHBOOK EDITION

In the heydays of Victorian and Bismarckian peace and complacency, Friedrich Nietzsche warned that the twentieth century would be a war-like century of a nature which the world had not witnessed before. It has been, so far, a century of ideological wars, comparable therein to the sixteenth and seventeenth centuries, but on a world-wide basis and conducted with infinitely more deadly weapons. One frequently dates the onset of this century from the Great War of 1914. In reality, the war-like century began in 1898/99, in the year of the Dreyfus affair, of the Spanish-American war and the Boer war. One year before the fateful turning point, in 1897, Queen Victoria celebrated the sixtieth anniversary of her reign. The British empire was then at the zenith of its power. Its foundations appeared unshakable. Among the general jubilation Rudyard Kipling, who was regarded as Britain's "imperial" poet and was the first British recipient of the Nobel prize for literature, warned in a poem which he characteristically called "Recessional" against reliance on military power and the confidence in the durability of empire.

> Far-called our navies melt away;
>   On dune and headland sinks the fire:
> Lo, all our pomp of yesterday
>   Is one with Nineveh and Tyre!
> Judge of the Nations, spare us yet,
> Lest we forget—lest we forget!
>
> If drunk with sight of power, we loose
>   Wild tongues that have not Thee in awe,

Such boastings as the Gentiles use,
    Or lesser breeds without the Law—
Lord God of Hosts, be with us yet,
Lest we forget—lest we forget!

For heathen heart that puts her trust
    In reeking tube and iron shard,
All valiant dust that builds on dust,
    And guarding, calls not Thee to guard,
For frantic boast and foolish word—
Thy mercy on Thy People, Lord!

Half a century later Britain was no longer the leading empire of the world. The *pax Britannica* belonged to the past. The United States, which in 1898 established itself as the greatest imperial power in the Pacific and the Caribbean, inherited Britain's world-wide role, but with an infinitely greater military, technological and economic power at its disposal. Kipling's warning against pride and the illusion of omnipotence holds good today, too. At all times throughout history power, to use Lord Acton's famous phrase, has tended to corrupt, to distort vision and perspective, and to lead to self-righteousness.

The years from 1898 to 1914 mark the highest point in the confident growth of the imperial domination of most of the globe by the "white" man, a period, often nostalgically recalled as *"la belle époque"* in France, and as the "Edwardian afterglow" in Britain. Though these years were filled with "little" wars and alarms of war, to most "white" men the skies appeared serene and placid before 1914. To the Western world, the coming of the twentieth century seemed to promise an ever better ordering of the forces of nature and society, a growing accommodation among classes and nations, and a deepening humanization of the relations among men and peoples. The few warning voices were not listened to; the brutalities of war seemed confined to distant lands—the Philippine islands, Africa or the Balkans. The events of 1914 put an end to this widespread euphoria.

But after 1918 the "white" man, especially in the United States, still faced the future with complacency and, worse, with self-righteousness. Even Americans who had lived in Europe tended to regard the gathering clouds there with a feeling of non-involvement, fortified by the old myths of American superiority and purity. Thomas Wolfe wrote in his posthumous novel *You Can't Go Home Again*, which appeared in 1940, two years after his death, "America was young, America was still the New World of mankind's hope, America was not like this old and worn-out Europe which seethed and festered with a thousand deep and uncorrected ancient maladies." In an essay "Notes on the Next War" which won the prize for the best article for 1935, Ernest Hemingway spoke for most Americans: "But of the hell broth that is brewing in Europe we have no need to drink. Europe has always fought: the intervals of peace are only armistices. We were fools to be sucked in once in a European war, and we should never be sucked in again." Twenty years later the United States found itself worrying about the neutralism and pacifism of other lands and condemned them as immoral or unwise. In 1966, though we are still in the period of "little" wars and alarms of war, the twentieth century with its unprecedented armaments race, which few Americans expected in 1918 or in 1945, seems to bear out Nietzsche's prophecy. Peoples everywhere are full of apprehension, doubt and distrust.

This book was originally written in the hope that it may help to clarify some fundamental issues which dominate the tensions and conflicts of the twentieth century and challenge the historian as much as the statesman. It appeared first in mid-century, in 1949. Some of its material was reprinted, with the permission of the publishers, from four books published between 1937 and 1942 by the Harvard University Press and from several "idea" articles which I contributed to the *Encyclopaedia Britannica*. The background of this first edition was formed by the communist coup in Czechoslovakia, the threat to West Berlin, and the signing of the North Atlantic Treaty, creating NATO, the unexpected first step to a consolidation of the Western bloc; also in the background was the split between the Soviet communists under Stalin and the Yugoslav com-

munists under Tito, and the beginning of the unexpected affirmation of pluralism and diversity within the previously monolithic communist bloc.

A second edition, enlarged, appeared in 1957. After the death
of Stalin in 1953, Soviet communism and Soviet society began
to change. Stalin's successor went to Belgrade in 1955 to make
peace with Tito and to recognize the right of "national" communism to travel its own road to the goal of socialism. In
February 1956 Nikita Khrushchev delivered before the twentieth congress of the communist party of the Soviet Union a
long speech attacking Stalin and Stalinism. The greatest change,
however, happened outside the communist orbit. Between 1947
and 1957 most of Europe's former Asian colonies gained independence, and in 1957 Britain granted independence to Ghana,
a step which opened the period of Africa's entrance into contemporary history as a factor in its own right. As a result, the
United Nations changed its character and became more fully
representative of the diverse peoples and civilizations of the
earth.

In 1966, this new edition under a new title is appearing. By
now, a world-wide revolution has manifested itself in all do-
mains of life. Its course has coincided with the mature years
of the author's life; in his autobiography, *Living in a World
Revolution* (Trident Press, New York, 1964), he tried to illustrate
the meaning of its unique and unprecedented process. It has
given rise in the 1960s to a new situation which demands a
re-thinking of assumptions which were valid twenty years ago.
Western Europe, having regained much of its former self-confidence, asserts its independence from American leadership;
NATO lives through a crisis which threatens its very foundations; the fear of a re-armed Germany makes itself felt again;
the influence of Asian and African states in the United Nations
grows steadily; the monolithic character of world-communism
is a matter of the past and even in individual communist countries and parties voices of dissent are being raised more and
more; mankind is in the process of being unified and yet of
preserving its fundamental pluralism and diversity. The Roman Catholic Church, until very recently the most conserva-

tive, authoritarian and dogmatic among the West's great religions, has since the ascension to the papal throne of John XXIII in 1958 kindled a new light of hope for all mankind. Its head has become the spokesman for universal peace, conciliation, and intercourse.

The immediate effects of these factors should not be overestimated. Mankind has not become transfigured, the inertia of governments and masses has not been overcome. But winds of change are blowing which in 1914 or even 1945 few would have expected. The ideologies of the first part of the century are undergoing a subtle transformation without giving up their distinctive character. In this third edition, a new chapter has been added to give a brief account of the world of the late 1960s, which is so different from that of the 1930s and 1940s and in which ideologies count less than twenty years ago and national and imperial interests count more. The peoples of the earth are not divided into two irreconcilable camps, as the communists dogmatically stipulated, and as some in the West believe today when they confront the communist camp with a "Free World" in which dictators and all sorts of colorful governments of chaos and inefficiency are accepted as long as they are non-communist.

In reality, there are today some communist nations of great and growing diversity and a few democratic nations mostly in northern Europe and America. They show a wide variety in their political traditions and attitudes. Most other peoples are groping to find their identities and a place somewhere between communism and democracy, for they have been prepared for neither by their past experiences. We have to live with this diversity and to beware of all over-simplification. The twentieth century confronts us with a situation more complex and more dynamic than has ever before existed. We have to learn to think anew and not, to use Senator Fulbright's words in his speech before the Senate on March 25, 1964, "cling to old myths in the face of new realities."

H. K.

January, 1966

DISINTEGRATING FORCES IN NINETEENTH CENTURY CIVILIZATION

Les institutions humaines sont de leur nature si imparfaites, qu'il suffit presque toujours, pour les détruire, de tirer de leur principe toutes les conséquences.

—TOCQUEVILLE, *Pensées détachées.*

C'est sortir de l'humanité que de sortir du milieu: la grandeur de l'âme humaine consiste à savoir s'y tenir.

—PASCAL, *Pensées*, I, 9, 17.

I

MID-CENTURY: THE TURNING POINT

THE year 1848 was a focal point in modern European history; it marked also the true beginning of the nineteenth century. For the first decades after 1815, life in Europe continued in the same rural and slow-moving pattern as in the eighteenth century. By 1848, industrialization and technology, railways and telegraphs had made their appearance and changed the whole tempo of life. Nor were the spiritual and moral changes from 1815 to 1848 of great depth; the leading personalities and the people preserved the eighteenth century outlook. Metternich, as well as the liberals and radicals, was a good European; like Condorcet or Herder, the liberals cherished an optimistic faith in harmony and international solidarity, in man and in the people. To Metternich's Holy Alliance of monarchs to preserve European peace, the liberals opposed a Holy Alliance of peoples to maintain European solidarity. This eighteenth century spirit animated the revolutionaries at the beginning of 1848; the spring of this year promised to realize all the cherished and long deferred hopes of the eighteenth century philosophers and of the orators of 1789.

Rarely has the advent of an *annus mirabilis* been greeted throughout the Continent with such identical expectations. The air was saturated with the visions of the heavenly city of eighteenth century secularized Christianity. For some years Michelet and Mickiewicz, Lamennais and Mazzini had hailed with rapturous emotional fervor the people as a new messiah, the expected revolution as a divine revelation, Paris or Rome as the new Jerusalem for a regenerated mankind, and suffering nations

3

as the new Christ. The last two years were full of forebodings: 1846 saw the advent of a liberal Pope and the Polish uprisings in Cracow and Poznan; 1847, the civil war in Switzerland; January, 1848, the revolts in Milan and Naples. When the ice and snow of winter began melting, spring winds swept over Europe: on February 24, France was again a republic; on March 13, almost overnight, Metternich fled, and the seemingly all-powerful symbol of the recent past vanished.

The morning which followed was only a brief dawn. The dreams of the eighteenth century did not come to fruition on the Continent. The promises and hopes ended soon in bitter disillusionment. The cause of the people seemed everywhere defeated. True, the issues so bitterly fought and so miserably lost in 1848 were taken up a few decades later, and many were carried forward to apparent success. Yet this realization came in an entirely different moral and social climate, hardly familiar to Robert Blum or Herwegh, to Mazzini or Michelet. A new age had begun; and the very events of 1848 revealed, in their surprising and disappointing course, for the first time the pattern of the following century, which was dominated by the emergence and the impact of two new mass forces, of socialism and nationalism.

Both these forces predated 1848. They originated in late eighteenth century western Europe, in an atmosphere of humanitarian individualism and critical rationalism. In their youth they were animated by the prevailing hopeful outlook of general harmony which characterized the socialism of a Lamartine or Mazzini. Individual liberty and universal peace were proclaimed not only as the immediate goals, but also as the only admissible methods of socialism and nationalism. When in a brief flare-up the waves of national excitement ran high on both sides of the Rhine in 1840, Lamartine wrote his famous "Marseillaise de la Paix"; fifteen years later he still affirmed, "Homo sum, voilà ma patrie!" During the reign of Louis Philippe in France and of the Biedermeier in Germany, the tendencies of both nations were probably more peaceful than at any other time in modern history. At the same period, through men like Cobden and Bright, pacifism became a dominant creed in English political life. With the preservation of peace and the dissemination of pacifism in mind, the first proposals were then made for a close Anglo-American-French cooperation. A Western union of nations with similar traditions and aspirations was envisaged by some far-sighted lovers of peace. For that purpose George M. Gibbs suggested founding in Paris, in 1842, a daily paper in French, a project warmly supported by the London Peace Society and the American Peace Society. On June 28, 1843, the first international pacifist convention was held in London, and delegates from the United States, England, and France participated. With the cooperation of Elihu Burritt, the learned blacksmith from Connecticut, and of Cobden and Bright, a League of Universal Brotherhood was founded in London and a Société d'Union des Peuples in Paris. On September 20, 1848, the first international peace congress met in Brussels. Whittier greeted it with characteristic hopes:

Evil shall cease and Violence pass away,
And the tired world breathe free through a long Sabbath day.[1]

More important, however, was the second peace congress which met in August, 1849, in Paris and which was officially received by Tocqueville at the French foreign office. Victor Hugo was its president, Cobden its vice president. In typical pre-1848 style, the French poet declared in his opening address, on August 21, that universal peace was a practical and inevitable goal—"this religious thought, the union of all nations by a common bond, the gospel as a supreme law, arbitration taking the place of war." Pointing to the example of the French provinces which were at war some centuries ago and had since replaced the sword by the ballot box, he predicted that the nations of Europe would similarly fuse in a higher unit while preserving their distinct individualities. "A day will come," he proclaimed, "when we shall see these two immense agglomerations, the United States of America and the United States of Europe, facing each other and stretching out their hands across the seas in close cooperation." This, Hugo was convinced, would happen very soon, for railroads and technical innovations accelerated all developments. "What do we need?" he asked, and he answered with confident simplicity and to thundering applause: "to love each other." [2] But with the ebbing of the optimism of 1848, the movement quickly petered out. One more congress met the next year in the St. Paul Church in Frankfort on the Main. It showed neither the participation nor the animation of the Congress of Paris. The hopes for peace and brotherly love receded before the new messages of a struggle for survival and the proud realism of blood and iron. The spring of the peoples withered without blossoming forth into the hoped-for fruit; the miracle turned into a mirage.

Nor did republicanism prove the expected panacea. In 1848 the republic was greeted with mystical fervor. "In the eyes of the philosopher who contemplates a pure idea, the republic is a most perfect state, in which society which has entered the age of virile maturity, can find itself," wrote Mme. d'Agoult, who with George Sand is one of the few women who participated fully in the hopes and struggles of 1848, and who under the pen name of Daniel Stern published a well known history of the revolution of that year. "In the heart of the just and good man, the concept of the republic acquires an even higher character; it becomes the expression of the religious sentiment applied to the institutions of society." [3] The republic was seen not only as the fulfillment of the hope of the ages, but as a universal message destined for all peoples and guaranteeing the peace of mankind. The republicans throughout Europe in the spring of 1848 seemed a fraternal order above classes or nations. A typical poster calling the people of Berlin to a mass meeting on April 1, "in honor of the great European revolution," began in French and English with "Vive la République!" and "Hurrah for the Republic!" In the invitation it was announced that speeches were to be delivered in German, English, and French. The text announced the "resurrection of mankind" and proclaimed:

The hour of the last judgment has struck. Liberty rises from her tomb, and the works of Satan are swallowed up by eternal darkness.

. . . Frenchmen and Poles, Italians and Swiss, Irish and English, all peoples of Europe join hands fraternally to welcome freedom with a thundering voice. German fellow-citizens, you will show that you know how to esteem liberty, and that you are ready to help to make it the common property of the whole of mankind. Long live the European Revolution! Long live the new world!

The new world which emerged, however, was very unlike that which the republicans had hoped for. It was not a world of harmony and peace, but of conflict and violence. A new Europe came into being in which the West no longer set the pace. In 1848 socialism and nationalism were transplanted from western Europe to central and eastern Europe, sections with entirely different social conditions and political traditions. There, in the precapitalistic structure of society, socialism changed its emphasis and methods. Marx's expectation that the socialist revolution would come in the highly capitalistic countries proved wrong. It did not come in Britain or in the Low Countries, in Scandinavia or in the United States, where reform took the place of revolution and Marxism never became a fighting creed, a *Weltanschauung*. These countries of the West preserved even in the nineteenth century their conservative moral climate; only in the precapitalistic or backward countries could social revolution be imposed under the banner of Marxism as the new Bible. Nor did the nation state in central and eastern Europe mean what it meant in the West, a community of free citizens based on law established in a struggle for the constitutional liberty of the individual and for the tolerance of opposition. The new nationalism stressed collective power and unity far above the civil freedoms of the West: in the intermingling of ethnic groups, nationalism tended to mean independence from outside more than liberty inside; frequently, the temptations to assertion of one's own rule over ethnically disputed territory and populations were not resisted. Nationalism and socialism changed in the nineteenth century from liberal humanitarianism to aggressive exclusivism, from the emphasis on the dignity of the individual to that on the power of collectivities. What was true of the ethnic group was also true of the economic group. Both became invested with combative emotionalism. The rising era of wars of class against class and nation against nation frustrated the hopes of 1848.

The new pattern was revealed with astonishing speed in France. There the year of 1848 started with a united effort of students and artisans, bourgeois and workers, who easily overthrew the power of kingship and aristocracy. Lamartine was then the most popular man. But only four months later, at the end of June, barricades went up in Paris again, and the street fighting was infinitely more bloody and bitter than at any previous time. Yet the workers no longer fought king or noblemen; they fought the democratic republic, based upon universal suffrage, which had come into being only a short while ago with such general acclaim and hopeful expectancy. The workers had been foremost among those who welcomed the republic and general suffrage. "Political faith had found its refuge in the working class; there, it was alive and deep," Mme. d'Agoult wrote at about the beginning of the period. "The worker wished to be a citizen. On account of his ability, his sentiment of justice, and his patriotism, he had possessed for a long time the right to be a citizen. The worker in the cities desired the revolution with all his heart." His new uprising was not suppressed by king's men; it succumbed to a republican army under a republican general who himself had suffered under the monarchy for his republican convictions. These June days left an immense bitterness with the Parisian working class; and their memories are still rankling today, as does the fear in the hearts of the non-proletarian classes of a return of the chaos and terror of 1793. The brief civil war of June, 1848, left its indelible mark upon a whole century. It made itself immediately felt in the elections on December 10, 1848, when the French people for the first time elected in democratic freedom the president of the republic.

The man they chose, *l'élu du peuple*, was Louis Napoleon, who within three years put an end to the parliamentary republic in France. But he did not do it in the name of reaction; he overthrew liberty on behalf of true democracy and progress, of the will of the people which he claimed to embody and which he willingly consulted in plebiscites. The two new forces of nationalism and socialism helped him in his rise to power. He was the candidate of all those who lamented the peaceful, "antinational" policy of Louis Philippe and who longed for the glory of the advancing armies of 1793 and of Napoleon and for revenge for Waterloo and the treaties of 1815. But the author of the book *The Extinction of Poverty* gained the broad support of the masses also by his promises of social security and economic progress. Lamartine, the poet of peace and human rights, so popular in February, 1848, was in December of the same year the forgotten man. He got only 17,000 votes, less than half of one per cent of the number received by Napoleon. He was defeated by a new force, the authoritarian state backed by the masses and their emotional drives of nationalism and socialism.

The events of 1848 in France were only an adumbration of things to come later in the century. A small group of German exiles in London changed its eighteenth century name of "Bund der Gerechten" in November, 1847, to "Kommunistischer Bund" and replaced its eighteenth century slogan, "All men are brothers," in which the memories of Schiller and Beethoven lived on, with "Proletarians of all countries, unite." The emphasis shifted from the individual to the class. A few months later, in February, 1848, two young German socialists, Marx and Engels, published the *Communist Manifesto* as the program of the communist league. For it they shared the utopian hope of the early socialists of the West for a total transformation of human society, for a secularized kingdom of God here and now. But they based the expectation on entirely different methods, more in conformity with the new age which they anticipated and helped to shape. It would be as wrong to see Marx and Engels through Lenin's eyes only, as it would be to judge Frederick II or Bismarck as mere forerunners of Hitler. They were children of a different age and breathing in a very different moral climate. There was much in Marx of the German idealism and the Western humanism of the pre-1848 age. He shared their hopes. But he replaced the old methods of individual example and moral guidance by the proclamation of struggle and violence as the essence of history, the vehicle of progress, and the indispensable midwife assisting at the birth of the new humanity. He was an extremist in methods and goal. The expected revolution was to be a total revolution bringing a total salvation. As early as 1844, he wrote about Germany in terms which later seemed applicable to Russia. "The emancipation of Germany from medievalism is only possible as a simultaneous emancipation from the effects of an incomplete liberation from medievalism. It is impossible to destroy in Germany any form of slavery without destroying all its forms. Germany is too thoroughgoing to be able to make a revolution in any other way than from the very roots of society. The emancipation of Germany means the emancipation of mankind. Philosophy is the guiding impulse of this emancipation; its life blood is the proletariat." [4]

Marx did not leave the advent of this final salvation to the uncertain moral forces of man. It was the year in which Renan wrote his *L'Avenir de la science;* science was dethroning religion and philosophy as the guiding light of mankind. With great daring, Marx and Engels made science—no longer natural science but the new social science—the unassailable basis of their apocalyptic hopes. The Old Testament prophets had also proclaimed the messianic age, the end of all suffering on earth, the coming of the full glory, as the goal of history. But they expected its advent through the inscrutable will of God and the tenuous moral improvement of man. The *Communist Manifesto* replaced these rather unpredictable factors with the infallibility of science.

The intoxication with the new age of the machine and technology filled the air and inspired the visions of the Saint-Simonists. They were the first dream of a planned society guided by experts. In his *L'Avenir de la science,* which remained unpublished until 1890 but which expressed well the growing cult of science half a century before, Renan demanded a better "exploitation of the globe." Rouget de Lisle wrote a *Marseillaise industrielle* in which he spoke of the new goddess:

Deployant ses ailes dorées,
L'industrie aux cent mille pas,
Joyeuse, parcourt nos climats
Et fertilise nos contrées.

The product of this industrial advance was the new class of
factory workers. The year 1848 witnessed in the West the rise
of the proletariat, which discovered itself and grew conscious of
its situation and strength. Its misery aroused the sympathy of
many spokesmen of other classes. Disraeli published in 1845
his novel *Sybil, or the Two Nations*, which Lord Morley called
his "sincerest." In the discussion of the bill on public relief proposed by the Vicomte de Melun, Victor Hugo declared in the
French Assembly on July 9, 1849: "I do not belong to those
who believe that one can suppress suffering in this world; suffering is a divine law; but I belong to those who think and affirm
that one can destroy poverty (la misère). Poverty is a malady
of the social body as leprosy is a malady of the human body; it
can disappear as leprosy disappeared." [5] Marx went a step further. He did not only proclaim the end of poverty. He gave the
assurance that the suffering and humiliated proletariat was
called, by the irrefutable logic of history, to overthrow the world
of injustice and to establish on its ruins the reign of peace and
plenty for all. The pitiless war of the proletariat against its enemies became the infallible means toward universal salvation;
the adversaries of the proletariat or of Marx were by necessity
the enemies of mankind's progress and hopes. Humanity, united
before 1848, was thus divided in the nineteenth century into two
opposing battle camps. The new gospel, a heresy incredible to
the eighteenth century, insisted that truth and goodness depended upon the camp to which one belonged. Man mattered
less than class; the values and measures on which civilization
rested became relativized; individual reality was sacrificed to a
fictitious collectivity. The new social forces defeated the hopes
of 1848 in France.

These social forces then played hardly a role in central Europe. The social problem there, the emancipation of the peasant,
was solved, the one and only lasting achievement of the Austrian

parliament in Kremsier. For eastern Europe, as backward socially and politically in relation to central Europe as the latter
was to the West, the peasant problem, however, remained un-
solved in 1848. Nor did the problem of nationalism in eastern
Europe emerge in 1848 with the immediacy that it did in central
Europe. There the Austrian parliament was unable to solve this
problem. The awakening of the peoples began with a general
benevolence and harmony among nationalities as among social
classes. Sympathy for budding nationalities was as general and
as strong as for the proletariat. But by the end of the year nationalities faced each other in bitter combat. When the incipient
revolution released the Polish national leaders of 1846 from the
Moabit prison in Berlin, they marched in a procession through
the streets, welcomed by the German crowds, and their leader,
Ludwik Mieroslawski, carrying Polish and German flags, called
the Germans in French to a fraternal fight against the common enemy, Russia. But soon it became clear that the revolutions of 1848 throughout central Europe expressed less a fraternal longing for human liberty than a divisive nationalism.
Though their spokesmen demanded individual liberty and constitutional guarantees after the Western model, they desired,
above all, the realization of their national aspirations for collective unity and power. No appeal was stronger than that to ethnic
emotions and historical rights. The revolutionary fervor was
directed toward national goals rather than liberal ones. Wherever the two conflicted, nationalism prevailed.

This has been lately emphasized with regard to the German
liberals who met in May, 1848, in the first German parliament
in the Church of St. Paul in Frankfort on the Main. There was
among them much earnest desire to end German authoritarianism, to align the nation definitely with the West, and to transform it after the model of England or France; but their passions
were aroused by German demands against Denmark, Poland,
and Bohemia. Not the Prussian conservatives, but liberal writers
and intellectuals were the first in Germany to voice Pan-German
sentiments and to put forward claims to the source and the
mouth of the Rhine, to Alsace-Lorraine, and to the marches of

the East with their ethnographically mixed populations and
their historic ascendancy of German civilization. German liberal
leaders stressed the desire for national power and unity much
more than that for individual liberty. The German-Franco-Polish
fraternization of the spring of 1848 was dead four months later.
German-Polish relations concerning Poznań set the new pace.
"The discussion about Poland from July 24 to July 27 was one
of the most important turning points in the history of the German National Assembly," its most prominent German liberal
historian wrote. The Congress of Vienna gave the Grand Duchy
of Poznań, the historical cradle of the Polish nation, as a sovereign country to the king of Prussia and stipulated that national
institutions for the Poles should be created there. The Grand
Duchy remained outside the territory of the German Confederation.

German nationalism tried to change this arrangement of the
Prussian crown. The German liberals in Frankfort insisted on a
division of Poznań and on the incorporation of the western part
into Germany. The most impressive argument was put forward
by Wilhelm Jordan, who appealed to healthy national egoism
against rationalist or abstract justice, to the right of conquest
by plough and sword, and called all those who saw the justice
of the Polish point of view "traitors to their own people." The
few voices who were opposed to the inclusion of part of Poznań
into Germany, among whom Robert Blum and Arnold Ruge
were prominent, could not prevail against the emotional impact
of Jordan's powerful argument for a "sound patriotism." A new
faith in might was proclaimed; the decision was hailed as a
manifestation of patriotism; the majority of the National Assembly preferred nationalism to liberalism. At the beginning of
1848, the eighteenth century natural-right theory of equality, of
the brotherhood of peoples in a universal order of justice, was
still alive. By the end of 1848, it had given way to appeals based
upon historical rights, the "reality" of power, and the supposed
vital and strategic necessities of the nation.

The liberal German historian Dahlmann drew the consequences from the new attitude when, in his memorable speech to the Frankfort Assembly on January 23, 1849, he declared:

> The road of power was the only road which could satisfy and satiate the desire for liberty which was fomenting but which had not yet understood itself. For it does not mean liberty alone, it thirsts much more for power which has so far not been granted it. Germany must at last become one of the political great powers of the Continent. That can be achieved only through Prussia; neither can Prussia recover without Germany, nor Germany without Prussia.[6]

Looking back at the events of 1848, John Stuart Mill diagnosed the new evil with unusual perspicacity in 1849. He complained that nationalism makes men indifferent to the rights and interests "of any portion of the human species, save that which is called by the same name and speaks the same language as themselves." He characterized these feelings of exclusive nationalism and of appeals to historical rights as barbaric. He remarked bitterly that "in the backward parts of Europe and even (where better things might have been expected) in Germany, the sentiment of nationality so far outweighs the love of liberty that the people are willing to abet their rulers in crushing the liberty and independence of any people not of their race or language."[7]

This change of the character of nationalism in central and eastern Europe during 1848 was not only true of the Germans. All the other nationalities showed themselves in no way inferior in grasping and developing the new gospel of the rights of the nation. Oppressed nationalities, while appealing to the world against their own oppression, found it legitimate to oppress others when their supposed national interests seemed to demand it. Professors and writers were always at hand to produce historical and moral reasons for supporting the ambitions of their nation and to point out that their nation and its necessities represented a unique case to which the general rules did not apply. Success in war was hailed as the best proof of moral valor and historical worth. In the hopeful months which ushered in the year 1848, Pope Pius IX gained less popularity for his liberal reforms than for the words "God bless Italy," which he uttered on

February 19, 1848, and for the decision to send papal troops to join the Sardinian army in the war against Austria. And many years later, Carducci, the *vates* of Italy, as he called himself, sang rapturously "the smoke of blood rising from fields of battle"[8] and the ecstasy of the brief and insignificant victory of the Sardinian army at Goito on May 30, 1848. Thus it happened that outside the West, nationalism after 1848 meant first and foremost national power and collective independence, and less and less the insistence upon individual liberty and ethnic equality. The Rumanian patriot Nicolas Bălescu emphasized in 1848 that national rights took precedence over human liberty. He wrote:

> For my part, the question of nationality is more important than liberty. Until a people can exist as a nation, it cannot make use of liberty. Liberty can easily be recovered when it is lost [an optimism which seems rather dubious a century later], but not nationality. Therefore I believe that in the present position of our country we must aim rather at the preservation of our greatly menaced nationality and seek only as much liberty as is necessary for the development of our nationality.

Each people regarded itself, with little self-criticism, as "peace-loving" and its neighbors as aggressors. Herder's remark that the Slav peasant peoples best approximated Rousseau's ideal of an idyllic and pacific rural democracy naturally found a ready response among Slav intellectuals. Czechs and Poles who felt themselves menaced by the Germans assured the world that while the Germans inclined to oppress Slavs and other peoples, the Slavs were by their very nature incapable of such designs. As soon, however, as their longings for a nation-state of their own and for national power came true, they did not hesitate to claim expansion of their national territory, either by invoking historical rights or by advancing alleged national needs. Slavs, Hungarians, and Italians were entirely equal in that respect to the Germans. It was the insistence of the Polish democrats and radicals on the Polish frontiers of 1771 which made cooperation with the Russian democrats for common revolutionary action impossible in 1861. In the welter of conflicting ethnic claims and counterclaims, national passions became overheated, historical scholarship often became subservient to nationalist aspirations, and individual liberty was lost.

Pan-Germanism quickly found its rival and equal in Pan-Slavism. Both assumed, in the second third of the twentieth century, under national-socialist and communist leadership, an official character of racial aggressiveness and exclusiveness. In 1848 and in the following decades they did not receive any official recognition. They were intellectual movements rather than national policies. The first Pan-Slavic congress met in Prague simultaneously with the German parliament in Frankfort on the Main. But under the leadership of bourgeois Czech intellectuals, the Pan-Slavism of that day differed deeply from today's brand. The Slavs then gathered in Prague desired the westernization of their peoples, whom they wished to advance as integral parts of liberal Europe. They regarded the existence of the Habsburg Empire, within which they lived, as a necessary bulwark against the danger of Russian expansion, which they dreaded as much as all other Europeans. Even more clearly than Mazzini and other non-Slav liberals, they recognized that Russia not only wished to expand westward, but aspired to world leadership.

In that sense the Czech historian František Palacký,[9] the spokesman of his people and the president of the Slav congress, insisted in his letter to the German *Vorparlament* in Frankfort that Austria's preservation, integrity, and consolidation were essential not only to the Czechs, but to the security of Europe and the survival of Western civilization. He was convinced that Russian control of the Danube would constitute a threat of greatest magnitude to Europe. Only a union of the nationalities along the Danube could, in his opinion, thwart the Russian aspirations of establishing a world government and imposing the Russian way of life on all. He wrote on April 11, 1848:

You know what power it is that rules the entire huge East of our continent. You know that this power, now grown to vast dimensions, increases and expands of itself decade by decade in far greater measure than is possible for the countries of the West. You know that, secure at its own center against practically any attack, it has long become a menace to its neighbours. . . . You know too that every further step which it will take forward on this path threatens at an ever accelerated pace to establish a universal monarchy, an infinite and inexpressible evil, a misfortune without measure or bound, such as I, though body and soul a Slav, would none the less profoundly regret for the good of mankind, even though this monarchy be proclaimed a Slavic one.

The first Pan-Slavic congress in Prague in 1848 ended, as the German parliament in Frankfort did, without achieving anything. When it was dissolved in June, 1848, it found itself surrounded by an atmosphere of rapidly growing distrust separating the Czechs and Germans in Bohemia. Yet less than three months before, on March 21, the Prague writers and journalists, German as well as Czech, had unanimously and publicly proclaimed their determination to maintain a firm and permanent harmony between the two nations living in a common land. "Elated in their hearts by the feeling of liberty and unity manifested in these days among the German and Czech inhabitants of our homeland," they wrote, they would strive "that neither should Germans have preference over Czechs nor Czechs over Germans." Alas, these good intentions of the spring of 1848 were soon obliterated. The century which has since passed has brought little fruition to the hopes of liberty and harmony which blossomed in the short awakening of the peoples.

The pattern which began to manifest itself at the end of 1848 had by the end of the century imposed itself at an ever accelerated pace beyond the imagination of the most daring prophets. The teachings of Marx—in an interpretation which Marx and Engels might perhaps not have recognized—hold sway over the minds and bodies of a quarter of the globe's population who either live under the direct or indirect control of Russia or give their supreme allegiance to her as the embodiment, or at least the assumed embodiment, of the gospel according to Marx. The democratic dictatorship which Louis Napoleon started under the acclaim of universal suffrage has been revived in forms before which the humane and civilized world of Napoleon III would have shuddered. German, Slav, and Italian nationalisms, still liberal in 1848, have since developed in an ominous way. The liberals of Frankfort and Prague would probably repudiate their offspring, the Pan-Germanism of 1938 and the Pan-Slavism of a decade later.

In the century which has passed since 1848, humanitarian hopes, the heritage of Western civilization and of the eighteenth century, have, with the growing cult of violence and of the ready and willing acceptance of class war and national conflicts, lost more and more of their restraining power. In 1848 the foundations of Western civilization—intellectual belief in the objectivity of truth and justice, ethical faith in mercy and tolerance—were still unshaken. The men who prepared the climate of 1848 believed, like Condorcet, in moral progress, in a progress of spiritual forces, no longer pointing to a realization beyond earthly existence, but here on earth, within the frame of fragile human nature. What really happened in the century since was a breathtaking progress in technical discoveries and methods and an ever growing faith in them and in the functional manipulation not only of matter, but of souls and minds. Today mankind lives among the ruins which demagogy and class war, Pan-Germanism and Pan-Slavism, exclusive and militant nationalism and socialism have produced. But history has not only its saddening lesson; its perspective may bring comfort in fighting the battles of the grim day. In the spring of 1848 mankind was full of glowing hope, but the end of 1848 dashed the hopes, and the century which 1848 inaugurated appears to have led slowly but surely to decay and disaster. Today, in its wake, mankind faces the future with dark forebodings. But it may be that in the century ahead the road may take again, unexpectedly, another turn and lead slowly but surely to the reawakening of the concern for individual liberty and humanitarian morality.

II

NATIONALISM AND THE OPEN SOCIETY

It has been often remarked that the "one world" of the twentieth century offers the apparent paradox of an unparalleled intensity of economic and cultural intercourse between peoples—sometimes between those most widely separated geographically —and at the same time a completely novel bitterness in conflicts between nations. The development of science and of communication brought about not only a complete change in economic relationships, but a growing approximation at least outwardly, of all civilized life on the five continents to a similar pattern. A unified humanity with a common cultural design seemed to emerge at the beginning of the twentieth century, but at the same time the divisions within mankind became more pronounced than ever before; conflicts between them spread over wider areas and stirred deeper emotions. Cultural contact had engendered and intensified conflict between nationalities.

On the European continent political life in the modern sense of the word began with the French Revolution. It fused humanitarian cosmopolitanism of the eighteenth century with the new idea of the sovereign nation-state. Thus, though primarily a movement for the reformation of the French state, the Revolution at the same time carried a great and generous message of new liberty and dignity to all individuals and to all peoples. Using propaganda and the force of arms, it spread the universal message with missionary zeal; but it spread it as a French message establishing the superiority of French civilization in the eighteenth century tradition as the most rational, enlightened, and humane type of civilization. The new and deeper

19

renaissance to which continental Europe aspired in the eighteenth century was first realized in France. The eyes of Europe were turned toward the source from which the light came; it was contact with the ideas of the French Revolution which awakened the then dormant political life and thought in other European countries, especially in Germany and Italy. French centralizing nationalism, disregarding the foundation of self-government in the English-speaking nations, set the example for the unification of a nation; in Italy and Germany, French armies swept away most of the feudal encumbrances which impeded the process of national unification.

The combination of cosmopolitan individualism with French nationalism, which appeared natural to the French, could not, however, be accepted by the non-French peoples who came under the influence of the French Revolution. Within twenty-five years the French Revolution transformed the intellectual and social life of Germany and Italy. The idea that a tyrant might be expelled, the cult of liberty, the aspiration toward nationhood one and indivisible, the longing for a new national cohesion and a new national spirit, the idea of a state rooted in popular consent and enthusiasm—all these concepts of the French Revolution were eagerly learned from France. But the emphasis shifted; the tyrants to be expelled were French influence and French armies of occupation; the liberty worshiped was not so much individual freedom from authoritarian government as national freedom from foreign governments. An Italian nationalist of this period, Vicenzo Cuoco, summed up this shift in attitude in his *Saggio Storico* of the Neapolitan revolution of 1799. "Strange character of all the peoples of this earth!" he exclaimed. "The desire to give them an exaggerated liberty awakens in them a longing for freedom from the liberators themselves."

The new feeling of nationalism and of national pride spreading throughout Europe thus became opposed to the French nationalism from which it had received its first impulse. Each new nationalism looked for its justification to its own national heritage and strove for its glorification. Fighting against the preponderant influence of French authors, each extolled the beauty of its own language and literature in contrast to that of the French. Out of the myths of the past and out of dreams of the future, German and Italian writers created an ideal fatherland long before it became a political reality. The same was done a few decades later by the Slavs in contrast to their Western neighbors. The process of building a nation was reversed. In France, as in Great Britain and the United States, the struggle for a new political and social reality had preceded, or at least accompanied, the cultural rejuvenation of the nation; in Germany and Italy and among the Slavs, the cultural rejuvenation preceded, and was separated from the political and social transformation. The nationalism of the French Revolution was linked with individual liberty and rational cosmopolitanism. Nationalism in Germany and Italy, born under the influence of, and in the struggle against, France, tended for its own self-preservation and development to emphasize elements diametrically contrary to the very essence of French nationalism. This nationalism thus became not only anti-French, but could easily lead to a revolt against "French" rationalism and cosmopolitan tendencies. The German and Slav educated classes had, in the eighteenth century, willingly accepted French civilization; now the age of nationalism not only generated and deepened conflict between nations, but produced a cultural conflict which invested the struggle between nations with the halo of a semireligious crusade.

In the main, cultural intercourse followed the line of the cultural gradient and moved from the centers of greater cultural intensity in the West to those of lesser. In a dialectical process of action and counteraction, the French Revolution, at once political and cultural, shaped the development in Germany and Italy. Similarly, German literature in the time of Herder and of romanticism rejuvenated the intellectual life of the Slavs. Herder drew a picture of the pacific and democratic Slavs as victims of feudal warrior nations like the German. He says of the Slavs:

They were charitable, prodigally hospitable, lovers of rural freedom, but subservient and obedient, enemies of robbing and plundering. All that did not help them against oppression. On the contrary, it contributed to bring it about. Thus several nations, especially the German, sinned against them.[1]

He deplored the unhappiness of the Slavs of his day and he foresaw for them a glorious future of quiet industry, once they were awakened from their long slumber and liberated from their chains. And he insistently expressed the desire to see them cultivate their own language and their traditional arts. Slavic students who came to German universities or read German books received from German sources the inspiration for their own nationalism, for their own efforts to revive the Slavic languages and civilization. They were filled with a new sense of the future greatness of the Slavic race. This new conviction gave them a deep sense of obligation to liberate Slavic life from the cultural, and later on from the political, impact of Germany. By expanding Herder's characterization of the relationship between Slavs and Germans, the great Czech historian František Palacký arrived at a construction of Czech history which could serve as a foundation for Czech nationalism and as a justification of Czech opposition to Germany's cultural and political domination. Against the aggressive and conquering warrior spirit of German feudal society, he set the idyllic picture of the pacific and democratic Slavic community. The cultural contact between Germans and Slavs had aroused Slavic nationalism. This in turn rebelled against Germanic influences and sought its justification in a reconstruction of the past that would oppose German with Slavic ideas.

This process of cultural influence and resistance was not confined to Europe. When Thomas Macaulay in 1835 presented his Memorandum on education in India,[2] contact between the civilizations of Europe and Asia had for centuries been slight and superficial. In this Memorandum he proposed to spread a knowledge of European literature and science among the Indians and to promote English education and English ideals for India. The reform following the Memorandum created a new India, and its effects were felt throughout Asia. Through contact with England, a generation of Indian intellectuals imbued with English ideas of freedom and self-government grew up. Under the impact of English ideas and in imitation of English political methods, these intellectuals, with the help of English liberals, in 1885 created the Indian National Congress, the first representative organization of public opinion in Asiatic lands. The intellectual and moral stir in India, known as the Indian National Movement, was entirely a product of the cultural contact of India with Great Britain. The application of English ideas to Indian life awakened an Indian desire for nationhood, led to an agitation against the continuation of British domination over India. Soon this Indian nationalism, entirely a product of British influence, was bound to object not only to Britain's political domination, but to her cultural influence. India's self-realization as a nation, in order to be Indian, had to be different from that of England. Indian nationalism, which had originally been an insistence upon the right to demand constitutional liberties (in the wake of, and as a product of, English constitutional liberalism), was transformed into a moral obligation to protect national customs and the destiny of the country from foreign influence, and in particular from an imitation of English liberalism.

Legends of the past and dreams of the future combined to create a vision of India's peculiar and unique task in the service of mankind. A mission was discovered for India: to set Indian spiritualism and metaphysical profundity over and against Western materialism and physical (superficial) comfort. From the Orient the light was to shine over Occidental darkness. Indian religiosity was to save Europe from its permanent strife and chaos. This goal was set before Indian youth, sometimes with extravagant exuberance: "You shall help to create, to spiritualize an epoch, to Aryanize the world. And that nation is your own, that epoch belongs to you and your children, and that world is no mere tract of land, but the whole earth with its teeming millions."

The difference in the character of nationalism in western Europe and elsewhere can be partly explained by the fact that the growth to nationhood in England and France was to a large extent a process of internal or immanent growth, a product of indigenous social and political forces, whereas nationalism in central and eastern Europe and in Asia began its development under outside influence. It soon grew into two opposite branches. The one accepted the Western form of nationalism, with its implications, and wished to apply it to the newly awakened nations. It sought in the political form developed by Western nationalism, in British parliamentary institutions, and in the French middle-class republic, a universally applicable model. The modern industrial order, based upon individual initiative, which had developed simultaneously with bills of rights and with modern nationalism in western Europe, was welcomed and furthered as laying the social foundation for the desired form of nationhood. These nationalists, who may be called Westerners or liberals, were clearly the product of cultural contact and knew themselves as such. They could be found in Germany as well as in Russia and in India. In Germany, Kant, Friedrich Christoph Schlosser, Karl von Rotteck, Georg Gottfried Gervinus, Georg Herwegh, to name only a few, represented this tendency, which found its home in southwestern Germany especially. In the left wing of the Frankfort Parliament, it tried for the first time to shape a Germany according to the Western pattern. It was defeated in the spring of 1849. It was by no means dead then, but the hope of its renewed strength was cut short by Bismarck's successes and later on by the fact that in the tragic death of Emperor Frederick III the expectations of moderate liberalism were frustrated in Germany. William I was a representative of the *Vormärz*—the days of the reaction before March 1848; William II was a product of the Bismarckian empire. It was the tragedy of Germany and Europe that, partly through historical accident, not because of innate traits in the German people, the liberal generation of 1848 never had its day in Germany.

Stronger than this tendency toward Westernism in German nationalism—a tendency which was the direct result of cultural contact and knew itself as such—was the trait which emphasized German peculiarity and uniqueness and which set itself outside the influence of cultural contact with alien civilizations. It appealed to the differences in the historical past of Germany and western Europe rather than to their common development, to collective forces rather than to individual rights. The French historian Michelet, in the spirit of 1848, had expressed the conviction that with the growth of culture man becomes more and more independent of the bonds of nature and the past:

In this marvellous transformation the spirit has triumphed over matter, the general over the particular and the idea over reality, the barbarian periods represent almost nothing but the local, the particular, the material. Man still clings to the soil, he seems to be part of it. . . . Slowly the strength which is the real essence of man will detach him, will uproot him from this soil. . . . He will need, instead of his native village, instead of his town or his province, a great fatherland. The idea of this fatherland, an abstract idea which owes little to the senses, will carry him through a new effort to the idea of a universal fatherland, of the City of Providence.

German historiography stressed the peculiarity and the indelible natural character of each people. Liberalism and individual rights were regarded as products of the bourgeois West, unsuited to Germany. Germany had to find its own solution for its problems, and had to find it in its own past and its own character. Romantic historiography in Germany, which claimed to go back to the eternal principles and to the unchangeable nature of things, in reality often based its conclusions upon a hasty generalization from insufficient observation of contemporary events. It regarded the French Revolution as mere destructive chaos and the absolutism of Napoleon as characteristic of the persistent character of the French nation. Fichte, in his *Addresses to the German Nation,* defined, in 1807, German statecraft as an education of the individual for liberty, independence, originality; whereas the French, and the Romance people in general, according to Fichte, inclined to imitation, uniformity, dependence upon authority, and therefore to absolutism and one-man rule.[3] Fichte himself was a liberal, a disciple of Kant and of the French Revolution, and in spite of many seeming aberrations he remained fundamentally faithful to the ideas of his youth. But he shared the dominant German tendency to construct an irreconcilable opposition between Germanism and the West—with the latter seen as the principle of superficiality, the former as that of depth. This romantic nationalism glorified the precapitalistic political and social order, the municipal guilds, the patrimonial rule of an agrarian nobility, the immobility of the *Berufstände*. Middle-class liberalism and bourgeois democracy were looked upon as products of alien principles, conducive to conflict and chaos.

German romantic nationalism, produced by contact with Western modes of thought, bitterly conscious of Germany's inferiority as compared with the West and therefore flaunting its own alleged superiority defiantly and triumphantly, had its counterpart in Russian Slavophilism. Its origin and attitudes corresponded with those of German romantic nationalism; but Germany was included in the West which was rejected. Slavophilism soon outdid German romanticism in its opposition to Westernization. It saw in Peter the Great a destructive force which had turned Russia away from the strength that springs from a purely indigenous development and had instead opened her to cultural contact with the West. The Slavophiles rejected liberalism, individualism, and capitalistic economy. They believed the salvation of Russia to lie in strict adherence to its own foundations, its orthodox religious life, its autocratic form of government, and its traditional agrarian economy. The Slavophiles regarded the Russian as an *Urvolk*, a people of profound originality and unique mission, just as Fichte had regarded the Germans. They exalted the role Russia was to play in the salvation of mankind, and especially in that of the decaying West. Magnitsky, governmental censor and curator of the University of Kazan in the last years of Alexander I, saw in the Tatar yoke perhaps the greatest blessing of Russian history, for it had kept Russia isolated from Europe and had thus preserved her purity. Russia, which through her strength and faith had liberated Europe from the scourge of Napoleon, needed no cultural contacts with Europe; rather Europe needed to learn from Russia. Shishkov, minister of education in the reign of Czar Nicholas I, thought capital punishment fitting for anyone who would propose to introduce the Latin script into Russia. But Slavophilism was opposed in Russia by a long line of Westernizers and reformers—from the Decembrists in 1825 to the liberals in the provisional government of 1917. These saw the salvation of Russia as lying in acceptance of Western individualism and Western political constitutions—in Russia's adaptation to, and participation in, the general course of Western development.

The reaction to cultural contact, as represented by German romantic nationalism and by Slavophilism, has not been a development confined to Germany and Russia. It can be found in every part of the earth where national consciousness has been aroused by cultural contact with the West. The liberal Westernizers and social reformers in India found themselves opposed by the new nationalism of a Tilak and a Gandhi, for whom the very fact that the Indian people have remained so "uncivilized" was a thing of merit. In the first place Gandhi did not repudiate British political domination; he rejected European civilization. "One effort is required," he said, "and that is to drive out Western civilization. All else will follow." Western civilization seemed to him primarily economic and therefore materialistic. India's salvation lay for him in the revival of traditional forms of life. The renaissance of the spinning wheel became the center of Gandhi's hopes. But Gandhi was mistaken when he thought of his nationalism as an indigenous Indian growth. It would have been unthinkable without the cultural contact with the West; it was not a return to pre-British days; it was very definitely a phenomenon arising out of an acquaintance with certain elements of European civilization—with Ruskin, with Tolstoy, with the European voices raised in protest against the bourgeois character of Western nineteenth century civilization, with the rediscovery and reappraisal of India's past by European scholars.[4]

In the same way, German or Russian romantic nationalism, which deepened political and economic competition among the states of the world by introducing an ideological conflict touching upon the ultimate destiny of nations and mankind, was in no way a product of indigenous development, of a unique and exclusive originality, of *Eigenart* and *samobytnost,* as the Germans and Russians called their isolationist character; it was a product of cultural contact and of an erroneous interpretation of the past. Most of the political ideas of the German romanticists came from the West, from Burke, Maistre, and Bonald. The love for the simple common people was derived from Rousseau. The racial theory of Richard Wagner and Houston Stewart Chamberlain, to whom Hitler was so much indebted, was inspired by Count Gobineau. The antiparliamentarian vehemence of the German and Italian nationalists of the right, their predilection for the sword as arbiter, and their anti-economic insistence upon the precedence of political considerations (especially those of foreign policy) over social and economic problems were anticipated by Charles Maurras. Even the famous slogan *Blut und Boden* was foreshadowed in Maurice Barrès' *la terre et les morts.* Barrès, speaking of "acceptance of the necessities of life," and insisting that "the human plant grows vigorously only so long as it remains subject to the conditions which shaped and preserved its species during the centuries," was followed by Hitler, who built his system upon what he called the iron logic of nature, and ended in complete biological determinism.

Nor was there much "originality" in German civilization after the days of Tacitus and Arminius, to which so many German nationalists harked back. From its very inception German civilization was molded by its contact with Western ways of life. This is especially true of the German civilization of the Middle Ages, upon whose national and original character romanticism liked to speculate. Nor was Russian Slavophilism more original. In fact, it owed most of its ideas to the influence of German romanticism. Even its love for the peasant was only an echo of the myth of the noble savage. Its economic leitmotiv, the glorification of the Russian agrarian community, the *mir,* received its directing impetus from a conservative German student of rural conditions, August von Haxthausen, who saw in the *mir,* as did the Slavophiles, an organic development out of the depths of the Russian folk soul. Later on it was demonstrated that such village communities were in no way confined to the Russians or the Slavs, and that the Russian *mir,* far from being in its present form an early indigenous institution or an expression of basic national ideals, had developed in fairly recent times —either as a governmental measure to facilitate tax collecting or as the result of social and economic forces growing out of the increasing pressure of population.

In modern times the forms taken all over the world by national reactions to cultural contact can be reduced to rather uniform patterns. At one extreme stands the negative pattern, represented by the resistance of the Chinese imperial government to the Westernization of China. This resistance took the form of a complete refusal to allow any intercourse between China and the rest of the world. It was an almost totalitarian isolationism; a rejection of the concept of the family of nations and the co-operation of equal states. This complete isolationism led to a number of conflicts in which the Chinese Empire was the loser. That China did not perish entirely in the process may be attributed less to its vast area and the size of its population than to the generally enlightened, though not unselfish, policies of the trader empires, Great Britain and the United States. At the other extreme stands the Turkish Republic under the leadership of Mustafa Kemal. Contemporary Turkey eagerly sought and encouraged intercourse with the West. The result was not only a complete Europeanization of all the external forms of life, but an acceptance of the basic attitudes underlying the achievements of the West. The ideological base of the Turkish government—though not necessarily all its concrete measures and manifestations—implies a full acquiescence in the parliamentary methods and the individual rights of the nineteenth century, which is Europe's legacy from the Glorious Revolution and from 1789. In spite of its transitional dictatorship, modern Turkey belongs fundamentally with the democracies. During the nineteenth century, Westernism and Orientalism fought a protracted duel in Turkey; in the last twenty years Westernism has definitely gained the upper hand, to the exclusion of all isolationist and romantic elements. So far as can be judged at present, Turkey has drawn new strength from her transformation and has entirely changed her status in the family of nations.[5]

Between these two extremes, China and Turkey, lie the more complex phenomena of modern Prussia, Japan, and Stalinist Russia. They provide the most important examples of a voluntary adoption of certain aspects of cultural contact—of an intercourse that has been strictly selective and consciously guided in order to gain new strength for expected armed conflicts. With methodical skill, Prussia after 1806, Japan after 1871, Russia after 1928, adopted (with a high degree of success) the modern forms of industrial life and efficient administration whose seeds were germinated by the French Revolution and by middle class civilization. These countries had become convinced that without thoroughgoing social-economic and technological reforms they would be unable to maintain their position and independence. The speed, energy, and purposefulness with which the task was carried out was remarkable and admirable, especially in Japan and Prussia, where it was done with little or no terrorism and with some regard for constitutional rights. But the reforms were undertaken with no thought of changing the core of spiritual and moral attitudes to bring them in line with the philosophy of the Western nations and of a free industrial middle-class society. Industrialism and reforms were not due to individual enterprise; they were planned and directed by the state; their purpose was to give a surer protection to traditional habits of thought and to social and moral values opposed to the West. Cultural contact brought an outward adjustment in social life, but this was accompanied by a hardening of the core under the new protective armor. The maladjustments ensuing from the discrepancy between outward form and inner life have proved in the last few decades to be a most disturbing factor in international relations and one of the sources of the strife between nations.

Cultural contact in the sense discussed is, of course, a phenomenon as old as history. But only in the last century has this cultural intercourse become world-wide, drawing all peoples into its orbit and reaching down to the masses in an effort to revolutionize their traditional life. The logical outcome of this process would be the development of a world-wide society and a world civilization. But the irrational forces of history, the vested emotional and national interests surviving from the past, new ideologies of world salvation according to historical laws or national lines, the formation of new closed societies, have revolted against this trend. The contemporary great conflicts of nations, accompanied by moral and mental confusion in all countries, have many different causes. Many purely local factors have contributed to their growth. But undoubtedly the conflict can be regarded as the outcome of the historical process of cultural contact on a world-wide scale. Assuming many masks and seizing upon various pretexts, it is the struggle between the two opposed patterns of reaction to the meeting of cultures—the liberal pattern of cooperation in tolerance and of an open society on the one hand, and the irrational pattern which, spellbound by the past, stresses isolationism and peculiarities of race or class above the fundamental likeness of all men as individuals, irrespective of social class or historical nationality, and which rejects individual liberty for the supposed necessities of an inevitable historical course.

III

THE CULT OF FORCE

Dazzled by the bright picture of the progress of rational and liberal humanism in the nineteenth century, the generation at the turn of the century often overlooked or failed to appreciate the portentous consequences which some of the trends, making themselves felt as the nineteenth century drew toward its end, would have in the future. Since then, two of these trends have become dominant issues in large parts of eastern and central Europe: the cult of force and the replacement of reasonable discussion by the appeal of myths. These new trends have least affected Britain and the United States, where the Western attitude of respect for individual liberty and reason, for orderly process and fair play, have shrunk back from the glorification of violence or myth. The United States is in an especially fortunate position. It was born as a nation in the eighteenth century, in the age of rationalism and enlightenment, and it could build its political life on the foundations of English constitutional liberty in a country where the influences of court, aristocracy, and established church were weak. The very fact that the people of America are immigrants coming from many different countries, from diverse racial stocks—and finding in the United States a common promised land of a freedom unknown in the home countries—leads toward an emphasis on a rational future common to all of them and to settlements by compromise and accommodation. There is more of a reasoned humanism and a social Christianity in American intellectual life than in any country on the European continent. In the United States the nineteenth century has proven a stronger mold, not only in economics, but also in the moral and spiritual climate. This was not only due to the vast resources of the country (Russia or Brazil possessed perhaps vaster resources), and not only to her geographic impregnability (which was shared by the two other countries), but to the strength of her liberal tradition, the ripe fruit and expansion of Western civilization. For what the United States succeeded in doing was one of the major accomplishments in history: to imbue many millions of men from various and conflicting backgrounds of civilization with the traditional English concept of liberty under law and thus to broaden it from an English heritage into a universal message and force.[1]

Under these conditions the United States has found itself much less affected by the crisis of the twentieth century than the rest of the world. The crisis is not primarily an economic one. It is a general crisis, or, to use the modern word, a total crisis, embracing the whole of mankind and the whole life of society—its intellectual foundations, its spiritual outlook, its social order, its political forms, and its economic structure. The crisis is total also in another sense. It is the first crisis in history which is not confined to a few countries or to a continent, as were the Renaissance and the French Revolution; it has made itself felt in all its aspects, to varying degrees, all over the earth. This crisis endangers the survival of that civilization which seemed so secure in the nineteenth century in Western lands, a civilization unique in history and one which could only be compared in some respects to the ancient Athenian civilization. Both were secular civilizations with men at their center. In the eighteenth century in western Europe man ceased to look up to heaven and did not regulate his life any more in view of a life beyond. Theology lost the central position which it had reoccupied after the short interlude of the Renaissance in the periods of the Reformation and Counter Reformation. Man did not concentrate his intellectual efforts any more upon defining God and His attributes or upon expounding the Holy Scriptures. Man looked upon the earth as his real abode. He trusted in reason and science as his guides. The new age was, as in ancient Athens, an age of humanism, of confidence in man as the center of all

things, of his right and his power to order this world according
to his wishes and his abilities, to secure for him and his fellow
men the new goods to which he felt himself entitled: life, liberty,
and the pursuit of happiness. Unbounded horizons seemed to
open before man; his reason seemed able to penetrate them.

In some fundamental aspects the nineteenth century went
beyond Attic civilization. Its rationalism divested itself of the
rhetorical element, which seemed inseparable from ancient civilization, and became factual, based upon experience and first-
hand research. The proud, patriotic feeling of the citizen of the
ancient polis, with his rights and responsibilities, again animated
the people, but the representative system allowed for its application far beyond the narrow limits of the city to which it had been
necessarily confined in ancient Greece. Finally—an inheritance
from Judaism and Christianity—the idea of a goal for universal
history introduced a new dynamic force into civilization and in
its secularized form made man the conscious builder of humanity's future.

This civilization believed in man and reason, in the human
and in the reasonable, in what the Greeks had praised as
sophrosyne. Reason was common to all normal men: it was
therefore possible to arrive by rational explanations and by discussion at a reasonable settlement of all disputes. In a world
ordered by reason, the application of force still remained necessary, but it was to be used only as far as it was strictly unavoidable. It was recognized as an evil which had its justification
in the inescapable but diminishing imperfection of man and of
society. Force had to be strictly controlled both in the fre-
quency and in the manner of its application, which were hedged
around with all possible precautions. The development of the
state in the nineteenth century, the state based on the rule of
law, tended to confine force and violence to exceptional cases,
both within the state and in the relation between states. Force
still remained in the background as an *ultima ratio*, but it was
regarded as unfortunate to be obliged to have to take recourse
to it, and it was done only when all other arguments had failed.

As far as men and governments used force, they did it with a bad conscience.

This temper has changed since World War I, especially on the continent of Europe. War seemed to make force legitimate. Men learned to divide their fellow men into friends and enemies. As soon as the war was over, the people in Britain and the United States tried to forget about it; they went out of their way to show consideration to former enemies. Not so on the European continent. There the war had left more lasting wounds; even after it had ended, its temper continued. The war spirit invaded all political and social life. For the totalitarian movements, for communism in Russia, for fascism in Italy, life and history were a relentless struggle which did not allow of any spirit of accommodation. The political theorist of German national socialism, Carl Schmitt, has defined politics as based upon the inescapable antagonism between friend and enemy, as ethics are based upon the antagonism between good and bad and aesthetics upon that between the beautiful and the ugly.[2] Political conflicts are those in which existence itself is at stake and in which war and extermination are always postulated as a guiding and real possibility. This inherent and fundamental friend-enemy relation (in the original German the well sounding alliteration of the words *Freund-Feind-Verhältnis* makes us more easily overlook the fallacies contained in the argument) has to be recognized and accepted, according to totalitarian doctrine, and it is the state and its infallible leadership which decides in its sovereignty who is the enemy, capitalism or Judaism, the international bankers or the warmonger Churchill; and these enemies, whoever they are, and all their friends and helpers have to be liquidated after a relentless and merciless struggle. But politics meant in Athens, and mean in the West, something entirely different: not to acknowledge an inescapable friend-enemy relation, but to avoid such a relation; or if it arose, to try, by good politics, to avoid its aggravation and to smooth it away. There is certainly a primitive instinct in man to regard an adversary or anyone standing in the way of the realization of his desires and aspirations as an enemy, and it seemed to primitive man that the easiest way to deal with the foe was to exterminate him. Civilization and statesmanship consisted until recently in finding the ways and the means to overcome the primitive instinct by law, by compromise, by every effort at a peaceful and friendly settlement.

Professor Schmitt's theory was born in the intellectual climate of the World War. It would, however, be only a philosophical curiosity were it not that it represents a very widespread post-war attitude. Force has come to be regarded as a great master builder. Patience and compromise are laughed at. People do not try to convince their adversaries or patiently solve difficult problems. They "liquidate" their enemies. Force seems to give to the master mind, or to the Party, who know themselves in conformity with the march of history and the progress of man, the supremacy of the world. Right and law protect the weaker; force opens the way for the stronger. With a new cult of force, the cult of the strong man, the infallible leader, and of the strong nation arises. The lesson which Napoleon, as a lone meteor, gave at the beginning of the nineteenth century, has borne fruit in the twentieth century.[3] During the nineteenth century, common sense and moderation dominated an age which many of its artist detractors belittled as "bourgeois" and which certainly did not claim to be "heroic." This hostility remained with Baudelaire and Rimbaud and Richard Wagner in the realm of art; now in the twentieth century, new Napoleons, with their unmeasured aspirations and their identification of indomitable strength with goodness and of heroic success with worth, have entered the field of practical politics. Born to humble civilian life, they have gloried in the leadership of war and, some of them—characteristically those calling themselves socialists—even in the splendor of high military titles. Under their leadership education has become training for combat and for the acceptance of the risks which combat implies.

After the fall of Napoleon, Europe dreamed of peace and harmony, but the events of 1848 changed the temper of the Continent. The *Communist Manifesto* of Karl Marx and Friedrich Engels pointed a new road toward socialism. Socialists before

Marx had stressed moral example and new harmony as the road
to a better world. The *Communist Manifesto,* however, offered
an analysis of history as an incessant struggle. Conflict became
the vehicle of progress, and a call to arms was issued to par-
ticipate in this inescapable and beneficial struggle. The forces
with whom Marx sided in this world-wide war were supported
by the conviction of final and inevitable victory which he gave
them through the apparently scientific basis of his analysis.
While social science thus proclaimed the gospel of force, natural
science added its word in November, 1859, when Charles Darwin
published his epoch-making volume, *On the Origin of Species by
Means of Natural Selection, or the Preservation of Favored Races
in the Struggle for Life.* Soon his biological theories were applied
to society.

Life, not only in nature but also in history, seemed a perpetual struggle. The result of this struggle was, to use Herbert
Spencer's phrase, the survival of the fittest; in the system of Marx
it could be predicted through an infallible understanding of
history who the fittest was. Man and history lost their spiritual
meaning and freedom; they became part of biological nature or
of an inescapable historical process. The powerful no longer
needed any justification for his conquests. Nature afforded the
justification, for it is beyond good and evil, and the fittest sur-
vives, irrespective of goodness. The world belongs to the
stronger; this seemed nature's law, proved by science, the highest
authority of the age. The strong were able to use force without a
bad conscience. The same held true of those who had history on
their side and who fought for the clearly defined progress of mankind. They needed no conscience; what mattered was success.
Darwin published his *Descent of Man* in 1871, the same year
in which Bismarck completed his unification of Germany and
seemed to prove the superiority of disciplined force over humanitarian hesitation. Bismarck achieved the miracle of making
Prussia, a latecomer among the powers, the youngest and weak-
est, the dominant power in Europe. He was not a German
nationalist. He did not hesitate to ally himself with Italy against
Austria, which was then a predominantly German state and a

leading member of the German Confederation. He did not hesitate to incite the Czechs, the Yugoslavs, and the Hungarians against Austria and against the German supremacy in Austria. He was first and foremost a Prussian and he looked for the aggrandizement of Prussia and for her liberation from Austrian hegemony. Prussia had been a great state before Bismarck. Bismarck made her the leading power in Europe.

Prussia originally was a very poor country with very little fertile soil, lacking natural resources, culturally the most backward part of Germany, a land which had been colonized and won over from the Slavs only during the later Middle Ages. The great electors and kings of the house of Hohenzollern succeeded by a remarkable feat in converting this poor country, which was without any natural frontiers, with long borders, and difficult to defend, into a powerful state by the concentration of all the moral, intellectual, and economic resources of the country upon the building up of an army. The army became the center and the lifeblood of the state; the soldierly virtues set the example for the citizen; a highly trained, efficient, and incorruptible bureaucracy guided the people with paternal care in the ways of discipline and in reverence for those higher up, for the uniform of the king, for the ideals of the state. The lonely genius of Frederick II, full of contempt for men, used his excellent army as a tool for his enlightened ambitions.[4] But it is even more useless to claim Frederick II for German nationalism than Bismarck. Nothing was farther from his imagination than a German nationalism. Culturally, he was French and a cosmopolitan; politically, he allied with non-Germans against Germans and Germany; in an entirely non-nationalist spirit, caring little about Germany, he perfected the method and instrument by which Prussia was to become the leader in Germany and by which it was even to grow to European hegemony under Bismarck—the army and its spirit. Although this army was shattered in 1806 at Jena, its spirit survived. Within a few years Scharnhorst, Gneisenau, and Clausewitz had created a new army which, later perfected by Roon, Moltke, and King William I himself, became the powerful instrument which made it possible for Bismarck in three short wars, within seven years, to constitute Prussia the most powerful state in Europe and to put upon the head of his royal master the imperial crown.

The victory of Bismarck not only marked a turning point in German history and the defeat of liberalism in Germany; its importance reached far beyond. Bismarck's success in the sixties of the nineteenth century coincided with the general advance of liberalism throughout Europe. The growing strength of capitalism raised the standard of living of the masses and seemed to assure social peace as it had done in Britain. England was on the eve of the great liberal reform administration of Gladstone; in France, under public pressure, Napoleon III inaugurated the era of the liberal empire; in Italy, the heritage of Cavour and his Western-oriented liberalism seemed to come into its own; Austria was on the road to sweeping constitutional reforms; Russia abolished serfdom, and Alexander II appeared to promise a Westernized regenerated Russia; Spain was preparing for the short and troubled day of her first republic; in the United States, Abraham Lincoln offered the example of leadership in democracy and charity. An immense hope inspired Western mankind, this time not in the enthusiasm of revolutionary fire, but in the slow constructive activity of constitutional progress and social reform. This march of liberalism was stopped in Germany, in one of the most capable and efficient nations of Europe, which under Bismarck's leadership rose as a bulwark against Western ideas. "Such a return of the past," an English historian writes, "was a European calamity on a scale so vast that its meaning could not be realized at the time." [5] German historians began to teach the inevitable victory and superiority of a state organized on principles rejecting Western individualistic liberalism. Struggle for power seemed to be the inherent element in the life of states and in the changes of history. Under these circumstances the individual was no longer the center of society. He seemed no more than a cog in the process of history or in the machine of nature, subject to natural or historical laws, deprived of liberty and of that fundamental dignity which he had attained in Western civilization. The consequences of this dehumanization made themselves felt fully in the totalitarian movements after World War I. Before its coming, the faith in man and reason was still too deeply ingrained to be replaced by any extreme conclusion drawn from the new cult of force and success. Only the solitary genius of Nietzsche saw deeper, recognized the fundamental crisis of all the traditional moral values, and had the dangerous courage to draw the full conclusion which seemed at that time absurd.

Many well meaning people often regard the horrors of war as a possible deterrent. Undoubtedly modern warfare, with its all-dominating mechanization, has dispelled much of the ancient glamour of primitive soldierly heroism. It is characteristic that in some countries during the last wars men who did not do their duties in the hinterland were threatened with the punishment of being sent to the front. Death for the fatherland was apparently—even officially—no longer regarded as sweet and glorious, but as befitting malefactors. Nevertheless, many young men in Europe welcomed war in 1914. It seemed to them, at least at the beginning, a liberation from the daily dull routine of their lives, an escape from mediocrity into something glamorous, from drab offices into the great world, full of excitement and adventure. The great magician of the Italian language, Gabriele D'Annunzio, had glorified in his novels and poems in the last decade before World War I the thrills of aviation, the spirit of record-making sport, of modern gladiators. Under his influence war appeared as a supreme fulfillment, as a unique intensification of life. With some literati, who influenced part of the intellectual youth, the craving for heroism became a compensation for their lack of faith in the traditional values of Western liberal civilization. Benedetto Croce, himself not entirely without some responsibility for this new spirit, characterized as the ideological reflection of "industrialism and Bismarckism, an uneasy condition of mind, a combination of frantic craving after power, restlessness and, withal, lack of enthusiasm and indifference." [6] These literati, a small but vociferous group in all countries, had lost faith in God and faith in man. Would they find a new faith, a new reality which seemed to them worth living for in the excitement of conflict? Would they find certainty in a new dogmatism rejecting the skepticism of Western civilization and following without hesitation the authority of infallible leadership?

The decisive objection to war seems to lie not in its physical horrors, but in its human degradation. War in itself is opposed to the spirit of Western liberalism, not because men are killed and maimed, but because there does not exist any other situation in which the freedom and dignity of man, the autonomous display of his moral judgment, and the equality of men are by necessity suspended as in war. Strict discipline without critical reasoning or questioning, undisputed and practically unlimited and infallible authority, the ready acceptance and application of force and brutality, are the fundaments on which a war is waged, especially a modern war, with its huge masses of men involved. It is for these reasons that all totalitarian societies are organized, even in peacetime, after the model of armies ever ready for struggle.

World War I lasted for over four years; it was fought in the heart of, and all over, Europe; it involved practically the entire populations of the belligerent countries and affected the life of the people even in the few neutral countries. It is easy to understand that the experience of the generation which had spent long and decisive years in the trenches or in the atmosphere of the trenches put a lasting stamp on the succeeding years. Many found, especially in the West, a new faith in man and in liberalism; others turned to cynicism and disillusionment; but in central and eastern Europe, the war itself was followed by a long-lasting unrest, civil war, and revolutions. The experience of the war went on, simultaneously with a breakdown of traditional concepts of morality and often even of the rule of law. Far-reaching economic transformations not only undermined social security, but destroyed the strength, and in some cases the existence, of that middle-class which had been the backbone of nineteenth century civilization. For the new generation, force was no longer a moral issue to be debated: it was the natural outcome of life, the normal element of history. War had seemed unthinkable to the civilized society of the late nineteenth century. World War I came as a surprise and a sudden shock to most. In the years since then, the situation has completely changed; most people think war possible, and some think it imminent or almost inevitable. Few were surprised at the outbreak of World War II, and many people are happy about peace assurances even for a short time. In the nineteenth century men of Western civilization thought themselves secure within a reasonable order. In the twentieth century most people are afraid, and that is logical, for force proclaimed as a principle of history or as the law of nature begets fear. Even the strong, the potential aggressor, feels threatened, at least in his future aspirations, which might be thwarted if he does not act now.

Has the cult of force produced fear, or is the cult of force an escape from fear? The feeling of fear dominates today the leading expressions of philosophy and theology in central Europe. The dialectic theology or theology of crisis, the famous manifesto of which appeared characteristically in the year 1918 in Karl Barth's exegesis of the Epistle to the Romans, and the existential philosophy of a man like Martin Heidegger both start, although they arrive at opposite results, from the fear of man who is unprotected and lonely amid the dangers of life. The revival, or rather discovery, of the theology of Sören Kierkegaard and the interest in the writings of Franz Kafka point in the same direction. Does man need an intoxication to overcome his fear, and does the cult of force, does iron military discipline, does the frenzy of power given to those highest in authority, act as an overcompensation for that weakness which is at the bottom of fear? When subject to fear, man feels strong and secure only if he becomes a member of a great army or of the masses. Thus the ideal of the group community, the rejection of individualism, the exaltation of great superindividual, collective forces and their victorious march have become characteristic of the second quarter of the twentieth century. Thus all education becomes the preparation for coming conflicts. The forces hostile to Western civilization enter the struggle against it equipped with the latest devices and instruments of Western science and technology. But without fundamental faith in the liberty of the individual, all the achievements of Western civilization become meaningless tools of destruction. It is questionable how far force can be creative and productive in rare exceptional circumstances, but there seems no doubt that the cult of force and its application over a long stretch of time can only result in the most unbridled reign of terror, which threatens to undermine the foundation of civilization.

THE DETHRONEMENT OF REASON

THE philosophy of Descartes, who lived in the first half of the seventeenth century, is generally considered as the starting point of modern philosophy, as the first clear and well defined expression of the new intellectual climate which was to become general in the eighteenth and nineteenth centuries. Many preparatory elements of thought were molded by him into a lasting foundation, the rock on which the coming intellectual structure of modern Europe was built. The details of his system are antiquated today. What has remained as a guiding light for Western civilization is the methodical principles from which he started. Like Bacon and Milton in England, he appealed to autonomy against authority. Descartes began by proclaiming doubt as a legitimate attitude of the human mind, the duty and the right of man to scrutinize and analyze for himself every tenet and every opinion until he arrives at a final self-evident truth. Above the gateway to knowledge he inscribed: *De omnibus dubitandum* (We have to doubt everything). He accepted no dogma blindly, no authority. One truth only seemed to him beyond doubt: *cogito, ergo sum* (I think, therefore I am).

Modern man has grown to intellectual maturity through this attempt to think for himself. On its behalf the fight against credulity, against acquiescence in current opinions and traditions, against second- and third-hand thinking, was waged. Descartes's method put upon man the duty to think for himself and not to rest until he had arrived at a clear and distinct perception. *Omne est verum quod clare et distincte percipio* (Everything is true which I perceive clearly and distinctly). Have the courage to think for yourselves; fight the inertia which allows others to think for you; reject authority which claims infallibility; never desist until you have a clear and distinct perception of what you think. A new self-confidence was thus awakened in man, a new dignity given to him. On the strength of his reason, man rose to the position from which he might understand the world and his situation.

This new individualist rationalism had far-reaching consequences which Descartes could not foresee and which he personally would not have accepted. It made man independent, his own lawgiver. Natural law, law founded upon human reason, which is the same in all men, guided man's steps from philosophical rationalism to the political and social rationalism which found its expression in the American and French revolutions. In them, for the first time, men claimed the right to order society on rational principles, starting from the "self-evident truth" that all men are created equal, that they are endowed with certain unalienable rights, and that governments are instituted to secure these rights and derive their powers from the consent of the governed. The application of individualism to political and social life created the most far-reaching revolutions in history. An immense new self-confidence arose in man, a belief in progress which would be the work of man's labor and thought, a faith in the perfectibility of man and of society according to the guidance of reason. Modern civilization was prepared in a long struggle from Descartes to the French Revolution. The occult and dark powers, superstitions and prejudices, seemed routed by reason. The world seemed *entzaubert,* myth and magic taken out of it, the power of the demons and witch doctors broken.[1] Western mankind seemed on its march toward an order based upon the autonomy of the individual.

What we call Europe, not as a geographical but as a spiritual entity, was born in those years through painful labor. The intellectual birth pangs of the decisive period have been admirably analyzed by Paul Hazard in his treatise on *La Crise de la conscience européenne, 1680-1715,* who has given therein the following definition of Europe:

What is Europe? A thought which is never satisfied. Without self-pity, she never ceases her pursuit of two quests, one towards happiness, the other, which is even more indispensable to her and more dear, towards truth. She has scarcely found an estate which corresponds to this double requirement when she becomes aware, when she knows, that as yet she only holds with an insecure grip something temporary and relative: and she returns to the desperate search which is her glory and her torment.[2]

The faith in the individual and reason gave Europe two centuries of unprecedented greatness. Out of the right and duty of man to think for himself grew a new toleration, a feeling of respect for the rights and opinions of one's fellow man, for his freedom of thought, an attitude of live and let live, of acknowledgement of the rights of opposition, an effort to arrive at settlement of disputes by discussion and compromise. This new attitude found its first and lasting expression in the Glorious Revolution of 1689, the truly most glorious and constructive revolution.

Such an attitude was only possible in societies of high political maturity. The political and social philosophy of romanticism, which was especially strong in Germany, began to doubt the right and ability of individual reason to find the truth. Was not the wisdom of collectivity and of history a surer guide? The opposition between individual reason and historical guidance—the latter frequently embodied in the charismatic leader who dominates others by means of their faith in his exceptional qualities in interpreting the march and purpose of history—was well expressed in the famous debate between two leading German jurists at the beginning of the nineteenth century. Anton F. J. Thibaut, then professor of law in Heidelberg, published a pamphlet in 1814 about the necessity of the codification of civil law for Germany, where at that time the most dire confusion ruled, each of the many German states having its own law, mostly antiquated and expressing the spirit of past centuries. He was answered by Friedrich Carl von Savigny, then professor of law at the newly founded University of Berlin, the center of the nationalistic teaching of those days, in a pamphlet entitled "Of the

Vocation of Our Age for Legislation and Jurisprudence," which became a rallying point of political and legal anti-Westernism.[3] Savigny opposed the rational codification of law after the French model, for to him law was an organic growth, an emanation of the *Volksgeist,* and courts of law acted not as the exponents of a common reason, but as representatives of the *Volksgeist,* of the spirit of the people, as true people's courts. It is noteworthy that in the debate between the two scholars, Savigny and romanticism emerged victorious in Germany. Romanticism glorified the popular instinct of the people or the masses, the unconscious working of the *Volksgeist* and its ancient traditions, the roots of which are lost in the past. In the first half of the nineteenth century, romanticism remained a mainly intellectual countercurrent which could serve to remind man of the strength of irrational and collective forces, but the main current belonged to individualism and rationalism.

In the heyday of Hegel's power only one philosopher had dared radically to dethrone reason. Arthur Schopenhauer no longer regarded reason as the great creative force, as man's key for the solution of all mysteries. It was only an instrument of pragmatic importance which the real Master had created for his practical use. Will, the dark and blind urge, was the real essence of the world. This will, which Schopenhauer defined as the will to live without any definite aim or purpose, used intelligence to shed some flickering light in the immense darkness of life and thus to help will reach its goal. Schopenhauer's principal work, *The World as Will and Idea,* which appeared in 1818, remained practically unknown until the beginning of the second half of the last century, and even then, although its fame grew, its pessimism was an isolated phenomenon of philosophical interest which did not influence many. It captivated, however, the imagination of two men of genius, Wagner and Nietzsche.[4] Wagner sent Schopenhauer a copy of his *Nibelungen Ring* in 1854, thanking him for his theory of music; for Schopenhauer had declared music the highest, because the most irrational, form of art, the most naked and unreflected expression of the essence of life, of will. Wagner's work became an exposition of Schopenhauer's philosophy, to which he added the ideas of Gobineau's racial theories which had appeared at that time in the great treatise, "On the Inequality of the Human Races."

Nietzsche transformed Schopenhauer's doctrine of the will to live into a doctrine of the will to power. Schopenhauer was deeply pessimistic, for the struggle of dark irrational forces implied the complete meaninglessness of life. Nietzsche forced himself by heroic effort into optimism. He saw the tragedy of life, its apparently meaningless cruelty, but he proclaimed it the duty of modern man to be heroic in the face of all the hardships and to say a jubilant "yes" to the tragedy of life. His *amor fati* was a great appeal to love of life in defiance of everything. What he looked for was an irrational justification of life as against all reason, "a justification of life, even where it was most terrible, most equivocal, and most false." Nietzsche glorified life and trusted it—irrational, blind life which creates and destroys endlessly without any rational purpose—for Nietzsche believed that not only was the Christian God dead, but also the rational moral values, which he regarded as a secularized Christianity. He outlined his program in sharp words. "The principal innovation . . . instead of moral values nothing but naturalistic values. Naturalization of morality. In the place of sociology a doctrine of the forms of dominion." The will to power is the only meaning of life, a desire to live, to live doggedly, to wish to live forever, again and again, in eternal recurrence.

Nietzsche was unique in his psychological diagnosis of the ills of his time. He illuminated unsuspected depths of the human character and its questionable motivations. He felt European civilization threatened by disintegration, not an economic disintegration, but something which reached infinitely deeper, a moral and intellectual disintegration, destroying all the accepted standards and leaving men in a complete vacuum. Against this nihilism Nietzsche attempted a revaluation of all values. This deep moralist, like a most delicate seismograph, felt the coming earthquake at a time when all the others continued to live as if their foundations were unshakable rock. In the midst of the disintegration, he preached hardness and virility, fighting virtues, not for the battlefield of mechanized arms, but for the more difficult and more dangerous decisions in the intellectual and moral realm. But did not, in the following generation, his heroic and lonely effort, vulgarized and misapplied, increase the nihilism and the chaos and deepen the lack of intellectual orientation and order, from which the twentieth century suffered?

Nietzsche himself had classical rationalism and Christian morality deep in his blood. Perhaps for that reason he felt more strongly than others how near danger was. Only a quarter of a century later the intellectual elite of Europe had become aware of a growing distrust of reason and of the glorification of vitality beyond considerations of good and evil. The trusting rationalism of the eighteenth century had been first undermined by a fast accumulating knowledge of history, by the widening of horizons, through the discoveries in archeology, prehistory, and ethnology. The historical method seemed to lead to a relativization of all positions, but the historical method had to give way at the end of the century to a new method which drew its principles and its inspiration from biology. Modern psychology stressed at the same time irrational or prerational motives as guiding motives in man's life. The subconscious seemed to play a much larger part in life and history than the nineteenth century had supposed. Man seemed subject to biological forces against which his reason was powerless, of which his reason, perhaps, was only an accessory and an instrument. Organic and vitalistic theories gained ground in all social sciences. *Bios*, life, triumphed over *ethos* and *logos*. A new interest in romanticism arose at the beginning of the twentieth century. Long-forgotten authors were reedited and read. The heart and the soul were praised at the expense of reason and intellect. The lonely individual sought refuge in the warmth and security of a homogeneous group. The irrational forces in men and society seemed not only the true directives, but they seemed also the only creative forces able to lift men to enthusiasm and great deeds, to liberate them from the dryness and mediocrity of intellectual life. Out of the unknown dark depths of man, where he seemed in intimate contact with nature, earth, and race, out of his instincts, salvation could come.

Glorification of life and distrust of reason led to a new *Verzauberung* of the world, its derationalization, the reappearance and recrudescence of leaders and slogans, a new triumph of magicians and witch doctors, equipped this time with all the newest devices of technique and mass hypnosis. What had been an esoteric teaching among the intelligentsia before World War I became after the war a fundamental issue with the younger generation. In the growing complexity of the world, after the unprecedented catastrophe of the World War, the bewilderment of the masses led them to a growing impatience with, and distrust of, reasonableness, compromise, and slow progress. This happened just at the time when it would have been most important to mobilize all rational forces and all patient efforts, all critical faculties and all tolerant fairness, for ordering the postwar world so as to avoid even graver catastrophes.

Today, however, in many lands the foundations of civilization, the faith in the dignity of the individual and in the equality of men of all nations and all classes, have been under heavy attack. What remains there, where the attack has been successful, is the tremendous urge of life, a belief in technique, in discipline, in uniform masses in which the individual seems to find a better and safer satisfaction of the urge for security and guidance. The objectivity of truth and the quest for it are abandoned for a vitalistic or dialectic pragmatism. The hope for harmony is belittled; history is proclaimed to be struggle and has to be accepted as such. Man has to bear undaunted its mission and can find his satisfaction only in self-sacrifice for, and in the greatness of, the group with the historical destiny of which he identifies himself.

With the dethronement of individual reason, with the reenchantment of the world through mass slogans and thought control, the development of Western civilization has been threatened by the growth of new collective myths. André Malraux has declared that "myth is not an object of discussion: it lives or it does not live. It does not appeal to our reason, but to our complicity. It takes hold of us through our desires. Myths do not develop through the extent to which they direct the sentiments but to which they justify them." In such an age of myths, individual contemplation and meditation and free discussion are replaced by uncritical enthusiasm and disciplined action. *Cogito, ergo sum* seems replaced by *Agitamus, ergo sumus.* It does not make much difference whether action for its own sake is praised, or whether the consciousness prevails that action follows a path of historical necessity and must lead to triumph. "Sono un camminatore," Mussolini proclaimed: "I am always on the way, I always go on." It would probably seem old-fashioned to object that the most important thing is not to be on the way, but to know and to ponder where the road leads; that it is unimportant that men know how to die and show a spirit of self-sacrifice—they have done it throughout the ages for the strangest causes—but that they die for a good purpose which will enhance the dignity of the individual and his autonomy. But large parts of mankind seem impatient today with the hard discipline of individual thinking, and full of desire to march in masses, to feel the comradeship of masses, to overcome the loneliness and fear in the growing complexity of the human situation. The objectivity of law and of thought is declared a bourgeois prejudice of the antiquated nineteenth century. Right is what helps in a struggle for power. In such a world, with the abstract majesty of law gone, all security has disappeared. Only the concrete situation and its dialectic need decide. With all talk of heroism, the essential form of courage which has distinguished Western man seems to have become extremely rare in large parts of Europe—the courage to think for himself and to face fundamental issues without resort to infallible authority. Science and scholarship itself have been officially proclaimed arms and tools subservient to political goals. The old Republic of Letters has gone; science is believed to be different according to the economic class position or the blood of the scientist. Class and blood, the interests of the group, are proclaimed to be stronger than reason.

The historicism of the great rationalist Hegel, who claimed to find definite laws for history and thus to predict salvation and doom on a rational or scientific basis—thereby replacing prophetic religion—has influenced all those nationalist and class myths that have since become a dominant factor in political thought, especially in central and eastern Europe. For Hegel "the realization of self-conscious reason" found its fulfillment in the collectivity, the state or the nation, and individuals "are conscious within themselves of being these individual independent beings through the fact that they surrender and sacrifice their particular individuality, and that this universal substance is their soul and essence." But the "universal" was really only parochial: a state opposing other states, a class opposing other classes. The individual and the truly universal, which had dominated the thought of Western rationalism and of Kant, became with Hegel "ideal"; the decisive factors in the concrete process of reality, of history, were now the various conflicting collectivities which absorb the individual. The new myths proclaimed history the struggle of collectivities, and ruled that historical reality follows its own inexorable law. Hegel was deeply convinced that history was a process in which even the negative and the evil were to bring about the ultimate good, the utopian end of history. In this process different collectivities at different stages assume positive and progressive roles and overcome opposition. In each stage there is but one collectivity—nation or, according to Marx, class—that is the decisive carrier of the world spirit and of world salvation.

In universal history each nation is in turn dominant for an epoch. Against this absolute right to be this bearer of the present stage of the development of the world-spirit, the spirit of the other nations are absolutely without right, and they, as well as those whose epochs are past, count no longer in world history.[5]

For German nationalists that carrier was Germany; for the Slavophiles, Russia; for the Marxists, it was the proletariat. Marx himself tended to combine, at least emotionally, both myths in his faith in the German proletariat; Stalinists today, at least emotionally, similarly emphasize the Russian proletariat, wherein Bakunin preceded them.

Among Hegel's disciples the most prominent by far was Karl

Marx. None achieved as high fame in explaining history to man as did this indefatigable worker. Marx's system appealed so strongly to less advanced societies and their intellectuals because he emphasized, or rather overemphasized, a number of modern trends which he observed in Western bourgeois life: its transformation by the activization of the people, the emphasis on work and on social and economic relations, the conception of man as a social being, the desire to understand reality rationally, to improve it according to the dictates of reason, and finally the optimistic and secular faith that man's shortcomings can be overcome by better institutions, by reforms, and by hard work. These impressions, gathered in the countries where seventeenth and eighteenth century revolutions had activized the people and where capitalism had mobilized economic progress, seemed destined to stir the people, or rather, the intelligentsia, in the countries in which the modern concept of society had not yet taken root. The faith in science, so predominant in the later nineteenth century, supported Marx's "scientific" socialism. He promised that the utopian realization of the totally new and just order would occur inevitably. In the growing complexity of industrial society in which, as Marx unforgettably described, man feels more and more the object of uncontrollable forces, alienated from reality instead of mastering and integrating it, Marx promised to render to the individual the full wealth of his undivided personality and thus to carry history to its Hegelian end—the realization of liberty beyond the realm of necessity.

In Marx's earlier writings, before he claimed a mechanized course for history, the moral ideas of Western humanism remained his frame of reference. But the construction of history as an inevitable teleological process carried with it in Marx not only a disregard for reality, but a total pessimism about the present world which had to be redeemed in the process, and a total optimism about the future world which was reality redeemed. Thus the forces of evil and salvation were—at least for the Marxian social scientist—unmistakably determined, and history was construed as the battleground of a total and inevitable war fought as bitterly over all political and economic issues as over intellectual and moral ones. Against Karl Kautsky, who regarded the replacing of democracy by dictatorship and the total bellicosity of society as the cardinal sins of bolshevism, Trotsky (then the most brilliant and authoritative spokesman of communism) wrote in 1920: "To sanctify the individual we must destroy the social order which crucifies that individual. This task can only be fulfilled by blood and iron."

Marx, with less sacrificial depth than Nietzsche and with more "scientific optimism," thirsted to seize reality as it "truly" is and force salvation through it. Marx's ideal was that of Western enlightenment, a society of integrated and fully responsible individuals united in liberty and free harmony; but by investing this ideal with the force of a scientific utopia, he distorted reality. To storm "the heavenly city of the eighteenth-century philosophers" against all the obstacles offered by the reality of man and the nature of things, Marx rejected for the time being (until the conquest of the heavenly city) the fundamentals of Western civilization, the respect for the rights of the individual and for objective truth. His teachings that all ideas are conditioned by interest and situation—a means for the devaluation of all opposing opinion—reduce intellectual life to an instrument in the struggle of life and society and destroy all human community. For all human community is founded on confidence, on the possibility of agreement and contract, which presupposes that truth and justice are more than superstructures of the cause of a class or a nation.

The principal myths Hegel bequeathed to the nineteenth century changed character with the changing intellectual climate of the times. One of them consisted in the secularization of the theology of history, which Hegel himself stated in the conclusion of his *Philosophy of History:* "God rules the world. The content of his government, the execution of his plan, is world history." In other passages "God" becomes the "Idea," the "World Spirit"; what remains is a clearly determined process of history fully revealed to the mind of the philosopher Hegel. Twenty years later, when the intellectual climate in Germany was expressed by David Friedrich Strauss and Ludwig Feuerbach, Marx abandoned Hegel's idealistic foundation of history for what he regarded as the deeper reality. Instead of finding the real in the ideal, he wished to find the ideal in the real. What remained unchanged, however, was the character of history as a clearly determined process that was fully revealed to the mind of the social scientist Marx.

In the new age of "science," history was determined by "natural laws which work with iron necessity towards inevitable results." This faith in inevitability was shared by Marxists as well as by Spenglerians. For all their "realism," the Marxists thought in mythical forms and abstractions, but with a new dogmatism. Their deterministic certitude, though claiming to be rational and scientific, became one of the dominant myths of the modern age, supported by the widespread myths of the power of science and the necessity of progress.

Hegel conceived of progress as perpetual movement and perpetual strife. Few myths, perhaps, have done as much harm as this one. While liberal thought held the state to be a mediator above nationality or race, class or caste, twenty years after Hegel the antagonism of nationalities or classes began to be regarded as so fundamental that history was interpreted as a perpetual struggle between them. The state became an instrument of nationality or class in this warfare. Though every state contains oppressive elements, these in no way make out its full or true essence. Yet Engels could declare in his introduction to *The Civil War in France* that "the state is nothing more than a machine for the oppression of one class by another."

The age of individualism and rationalism grouped men according to their individual qualities and their free decisions. It did not regard them as determined by occupation or class, birth or race. The new social myths, on the other hand, demanded group loyalty based upon homogeneity of origin, similarity of conditions of life, and supposed identity of interests. Nationalities and classes were set apart and declared to be fundamentally different and antagonistic: to fulfill their destinies they had to be led by acting and daring minorities conscious of the historical trend and determined to follow its course. Georges Sorel, infusing the class struggle of Marx with the vitalistic *élan* of Bergson, proclaimed the inevitability of the revolution. The imagination of the proletariat, who to Sorel were the true producers and warriors, was fired by myths which were to increase their combativeness and make them reject every attempt at mediation and humanitarian pacifism. In his last years Sorel greeted both Lenin and Mussolini as the successful embodiments of the new myths, as modern heroes "en correspondance avec l'instinct intime des masses," as the charismatic leaders of the twentieth century. When he published in 1919 a new edition of his book "Reflections on Violence," he added a postscript, "For Lenin," in which he greeted Moscow as "the Rome of the proletariat," and which he concluded with the words:

> Cursed be the plutocratic democracies which starve out Russia; I am only a very old man whose existence is at the mercy of the slightest accidents; but could I before descending into the tomb see the proud bourgeois democracies, today cynically triumphant, humiliated! [6]

Sorel believed in the magic power of revolution and desired the end of middle-class society. This faith in the magic blessing of revolution and the doom of the world of middle-class common sense was shared by many intellectuals after World War I; it found few adherents among the masses in those countries where capitalism and middle-class society were most firmly established.

The dethronement of reason has deepened the stresses and cleavages dividing mankind into unbridgeable abysses across which there seems no longer an understanding possible. While Descartes stressed the legitimacy of doubt and the right of the thinking individual, modern totalitarianism has reasserted the same claim to absoluteness as medieval faith. The outlook on life of those who have adopted fascism or communism has nothing in common with the Western tradition of reason. Its liberalism was prepared to admit that alongside one's own path to truth there may be others. This attitude permitted liberty of thought and tolerance and formed the basis for the growth of individualism. What the West had won thus in breadth and freedom, it lost in certainty. The fanaticism of the totalitarians springs from the absoluteness of their faith. The consciousness of the saving truth gives them their assurance: the opponent is always wrong; there can therefore be no compromise. In this secularized orthodoxy, the hardness that shrinks from nothing is a true service to the attainment of the goal. The totalitarian certainty of victory is based on an eschatological confidence free from all moral contexts. The dethronement of reason and the rise of the new totalitarian myth threaten the growth of a unified world and all the progress which the nineteenth century had achieved. This progress did not express itself solely or mainly in the domain of science and technology. In those fields it is well known that there was a greater difference between 1930 and 1830 than between 1830 and 1530. Neither did this progress express itself chiefly in the almost incredible rise of the standard of life, of wealth, of comfort, of health, in the considerable increase of the average length of life, in all classes of society in those countries where modern middle-class civilization has prevailed. The essential progress of the last one hundred and fifty years lies in three other directions—toward the equality of man, toward a more general participation in the fullness and opportunities of life, and toward a refinement and humanization of our mores. In all these three fields Western man is very far from the goal, but has gone further toward it than any preceding period.

Only one hundred and fifty years ago, and even less, slavery and serfdom were generally accepted and were the rule in most countries. Everywhere in the European countries a high barrier of legal inequality separated classes and castes. At the end of the nineteenth century, in practically all civilized countries, the legal equality of all men was established, and in the backward countries the fight for civilization included the fight for the equality of all. This has never been known in history before. Constitutional safeguards protected the rights of the individual against the state—arbitrariness by the powerful or by the police and censorship of beliefs or opinions seemed to belong to a dead past.

In the refinement and humanization of morals and mores, we have perhaps not surpassed the best of the ancient Stoics, their philosophy of *philanthropia* and *humanitas* (Seneca's *homo homini res sacra*), but what with them remained the cultured refinement of a very small elite had grown in the nineteenth century into a vast reform movement to eradicate in the masses, and in all countries as far as possible, the cruelty and the apathy which were commonly and generally accepted as natural one hundred and fifty years ago. We have only to think back to what appears to us today as the inhuman treatment of children, criminals, lunatics, and the poor which existed then, even in the most civilized countries, to measure the road which we have traveled, thanks to Beccaria and other humanitarians who inculcated in men a new consciousness of social responsibility. One hundred and fifty years ago men were not only condemned to death for trifling offenses, but were put to death by the most calculated torture. Lunatic asylums, prisons, and poorhouses were places of unspeakable horror. Corporal punishment was general. Children were seldom protected in their weakness and immaturity. There is no doubt that in all these respects immense progress was achieved in all the countries of modern civilization during the nineteenth century. It was a long struggle and certainly is still very far from the ideal: the nineteenth century movement had its shortcomings, its hypocrisies, its absurdities; but it was a great and serious effort to make life more human and more reasonable. It brought to the countries of modern middle-class civilization such an increase of liberty, welfare, and happiness as no century before had done.

This tremendous progress in such a relatively short time demanded a unique effort on the part of man. The ever increasing pace of invention and production demanded ever new adjustments. No rest was given to man in his efforts. Industrialism, science, democracy, had brought a permanent unrest into life. No sooner was a stage reached than it was surpassed and left behind.

To this difficulty in the tempo of the development, another fundamental difficulty was added, that of its growing extent. As it developed in the nineteenth century, modern civilization did not remain confined to an educated minority or to a definite number of countries. Although it originated with the educated classes in the Atlantic community of northwestern Europe, it carried within itself from the beginning a universal message. Based upon faith in common reason and the dignity of every individual, it appealed to every man and to every people and tried to draw the masses and the most distant countries into its train. The dynamics of its ideas could not be stopped. They penetrated to the masses and to backward peoples: the monopoly could not exist in the face of the immanent dynamic and universal character of rational civilization. The dynamic character of ideas was intensified by the dynamics of capitalistic trade and industrialism, with its permanent increase of production, its demand for new markets and for new raw materials. Thus modern civilization had the task of carrying growing masses in all countries with it, to awaken them from their apathy, to train them for their participation in a richer and fuller life. Those masses had never been integrated before into a living civilization of liberty. They had lived under the dead weight of authoritarian tradition.

It is possible to argue that this tremendous effort of the last century was too much for man and has left Western civilization fatigued and exhausted. Powerful forces seemed arraigned against it. Twentieth century man has become less confident than his nineteenth century ancestor was. He has witnessed the dark powers of history in his own experience. Things which seemed to belong to the past have reappeared: fanatical faith, infallible leaders, slavery and massacres, the uprooting of whole populations, ruthlessness and barbarism. But against all the expectations of the totalitarians, by the middle of the twentieth century, Western civilization has proven its power of resistance against fanatic ideologies. Through this resistance there is a possibility that in the second half of the twentieth century the Western spirit of tolerance and compromise, of self-criticism and fair-minded objectivity, of reasonableness and individualism, may spread again as it did in the nineteenth century. Then, in a new age of reason, an international society will be able to grow with emphasis on common human values and individual personal independence and not on national or class rights and on exclusive schemes of world salvation.

V

THE CRISIS OF THE INDIVIDUAL

THE intellectual trends of one century presage the reality of the following century. It takes a long time for thoughts and discussions to change into actions and social relationships: during that process they are often altered to a degree which would make them unacceptable and even unrecognizable to those with whom they originated in the free and sometimes irresponsible realm of the mind. What eighteenth century aristocrats talked of in a cosmopolitan, truly European atmosphere—the emancipation of the individual from traditions and superstitions, the new humanitarianism, the daring freedom of the human mind, the changed relationship between ruler and governed—was as nearly realized by nineteenth century middle-class society as may ever be done. It was a century full of enterprise and happiness. Europe broadened into the world; new frontiers were conquered; the standard of living rose rapidly; age-old scourges of mankind—pests and famines—were brought for the first time under control; intercourse between countries and civilizations all over the globe became freer than ever before: men, goods, and ideas traveled with few hindrances; peace seemed assured, and long-lasting wars among civilized nations were thought absurd.

The one world which the eighteenth century in its intellectual curiosity visualized seemed assured in the nineteenth century through the magic of universal commerce and free trade. The benevolent merchant offering goods and happiness replaced the warrior hero carrying glory and death. The Victorian poet lau-

reate voiced the general expectation of middle-class society in
1853:

Men, my brothers, men the workers, ever reaping something new;
That which they have done but earnest of the things that they shall
    do:
For I dipt into the future, far as human eye could see,
Saw the Vision of the world, and all the wonder that would be;
Saw the heavens fill with commerce, argosies of magic sails,
Pilots of the purple twilight, dropping down with costly bales;
Heard the heavens fill with shouting, and there rain'd a ghastly dew
From the nations' airy navies grappling in the central blue;
Far along the world-wide whisper of the south-wind rushing warm,
With the standards of the peoples plunging thro' the thunder-storm;
Till the war-drum throbb'd no longer, and the battle-flags were furl'd
In the Parliament of man, the Federation of the world.

For the first time mankind became an open society: the age-
old seclusion of China and Japan was broken; Russia and Turkey—the only two European countries where travelers at the
end of the century still needed passports—entered more and
more into the community of nations; the knowledge of European
science began to penetrate the jungles of Africa and the deserts
of Asia. More important, however, was the spread of the new
humane attitude based upon the growing recognition of the
value and dignity of each individual life: the end of slavery
and serfdom, the unprecedented feeling of social responsibility,
the reform of penal laws. Under the influence of English ideas
of liberty and law, attempts were everywhere made, even in
Russia, Turkey, and China, to limit autocracy, to secure individual rights, to establish the majesty of law. At the beginning
of the twentieth century, the globe seemed well on the way of
coalescing into one world. At Bournemouth on June 12, 1946,
Mr. Ernest Bevin could nostalgically sum up mankind's hopes
by recalling the reality of a few decades ago: "I want to be
able to go down to Victoria Station, get a ticket and go where
the hell I like without a passport or anything else."

The twentieth century has destroyed the hopes of the nineteenth. The apparent turning point was the war of 1914, which

was followed by Lenin's Russian Revolution. Some immediately
recognized the war in its full implication as a crisis of unprecedented magnitude. Sir Edward Grey was not thinking of political
or economic issues when he spoke at the beginning of the war
of the lights going out all over Europe. At the end of the war,
among jubilations of victory and expectations of return to "nor-
malcy," Paul Valéry stated that an extraordinary shudder had
passed through the marrow of Europe. "We modern civilizations
have learned to recognize that we are mortal like the others.
We feel that a civilization is fragile as a life."

With unusual perspicacity, then little heeded, he predicted
that the transition from war to peace would be infinitely more
dangerous and more obscure than the passage from peace to
war; that all nations would be convulsed by it; that in a short
while we might behold the miracle of a strictly animal society,
a perfect and final anthill; and that Europe might lose her
leadership and become what she was in reality, a little cape of
the Asiatic continent. Four years later, in a lecture at Zurich,
Valéry once more spoke of the crisis in the wake of the war.
He described it in words which could be applied as well to
the situation in 1949, after the second war. Today his words
sound familiar; then, in the fall of 1922, they revealed the profound insight of the trained thinker:

The storm has died away, and still we are restless, uneasy, as if
the storm were about to break. Almost all the affairs of men remain
in a terrible uncertainty. We think of what has disappeared, we are
almost destroyed by what has been destroyed; we do not know what
will be born, and we fear the future, not without reason. We hope
vaguely, we dread precisely; our fears are infinitely more precise
than our hopes; we confess that the charm of life is behind us, abundance is behind us, but doubt and disorder are in us and with us.
There is no thinking man, however shrewd or learned he may be,
who can hope to dominate this anxiety, to escape from this impression of darkness, to measure the probable duration of this period
when the vital relations of humanity are disturbed profoundly.

One can say that all the fundamentals of our world have been
affected by the war, or more exactly, by the circumstances of the

war; something deeper has been worn away than the renewable parts of the machine. You know how greatly the general economic situation has been disturbed, and the polity of states, and the very life of the individual; you are familiar with the universal discomfort, hesitation, apprehension. But among all these injured things is the Mind. The Mind has indeed been cruelly wounded; its complaint is heard in the hearts of intellectual men; it passes a mournful judgment on itself. It doubts itself profoundly.[1]

In these words Valéry exposed the fundamental crisis of the twentieth century. The crisis was so grave because of the state in which it found the mind. The intellectual trends of the nineteenth century had presaged the reality of the twentieth. Baudelaire and Richard Wagner, Nietzsche and Dostoevsky denounced their age, its individualism and humanitarianism, the middle-class foundation and its pursuit of happiness. By the middle of the twentieth century, many of their wish projections had become an actuality with a vengeance. But the trends had been gathering momentum for the last one hundred years. It was on June 17, 1852, that Amiel wrote in his *Journal intime*:

Every despotism has a specially keen and hostile instinct for whatever keeps up human dignity and independence. It is curious to see scientific teaching used everywhere as a means to stifle all freedom of investigation in moral questions under a dead weight of facts. Materialism is the auxiliary doctrine of every tyranny, whether of the one or of the masses. To crush what is spiritual, moral, human in man by specializing him; to form mere wheels of the great social machine instead of complete individuals; to make society and not conscience the center of life, to enslave the soul to things, to depersonalize man —this is the dominant drift of the age.

In the eighteenth century the individual asserted himself in opposition to the tyranny of the one; in the twentieth century the individual faces the incomparably harder task of asserting himself in opposition to the tyranny of the masses. The two mass movements of the nineteenth century, nationalism and socialism, originated in the liberal atmosphere inherited from the eighteenth century. They were imbued with a generous benevolence toward everything human, with a desire for a universal embrace, for tearing down all walls of segregation, with a determination to lay the foundations for a truly open society. But a new spirit of militancy gradually shifted the emphasis from the individual to the organization, from open outstretched arms to clenched fists; nationalism centered around barracks, socialism around factories, each one a symbol and model of teamwork and discipline. Yet the mutual hostility of these two mass movements before the war of 1914 safeguarded an area of liberty and individuality. Their fusion in Russia and Germany created the modern totalitarian society with its type of man: worker and soldier at the same time, the total antithesis of nineteenth century man.

Berdyaev has spoken of the "new Middle Ages." In Russia and in Germany—and wherever totalitarianism penetrated—men were fired by a fanatical faith, by an absolute unquestioning certainty which rejected the critical attitude of modern man. Compromise —the foundation of democracy—became now a betrayal of the faith: the certainty of salvation numbed any moral sense regarding the means of the attainment of the end. Primitive beliefs of the power of the blood, of the sacred character of the leader, of the solidarity and primacy of the group, were revived; the individual, his rights and happiness, even his life and dignity, appeared of little value in the midst of the surging elemental forces. Totalitarianism in Russia and Germany—and to a lesser extent in other countries—broke the dikes of civilization which the nineteenth century had believed lasting.

The great freedoms of the mind conquered by Italian, Dutch, French, and English thinkers from the Renaissance to the Enlightenment, first firmly established in seventeenth century England, and taken for granted in the nineteenth century Western world, were scoffed and abandoned outside their original home. In the nineteenth century these freedoms had set out to encompass the globe and to create the one world; now they were again practically confined to the British lands and the northwestern fringe of Europe. Although technological means were improving and more and more people were beginning to talk of "one world," the one world based upon the growing community of concepts and attitudes disintegrated rapidly in the frightful ruins of world wars and the lawless brutality of totalitarianism. New formidable barriers of hatred and misunderstanding have been erected; free intercourse of men, goods, and ideas has ceased; nations have again shut themselves up in a way which the nineteenth century would have considered fantastic.

Sociologically, the nineteenth century, with its ideas of individual rights—which are only attainable in a moral climate of tolerance, compromise, and fair play—found its foundation in a middle-class society with England as its model. Slowly, by the end of the century, such a middle class and its intelligentsia began to grow up even in Russia and in Asia. As a result of the two wars and the totalitarian revolutions, this middle class has been largely destroyed. Its last stronghold, so far unshaken, is the United States, which in the twentieth century inherits in many ways the nineteenth century position of the British Empire. But throughout Europe the war's physical devastations and inflation, taxation, and confiscation have taken their toll of the economic foundations of the middle class. The situation is much worse however: outside Britain, Switzerland, and Sweden the lawlessness of totalitarian rule and of the struggle against it, the lack of information and fear of the secret police, the shattered nerves and the dilapidated homes, have destroyed more than the economic foundations of middle-class life. For a society can think creatively even when its economic power is waning. All over the continent of Europe the landowning gentry and aristocracy were economically a declining class on the eve of the French Revolution and yet daring in mind; eighteenth century Germany and Renaissance Italy were in a state of political disintegration and growing economic weakness; their international policy and influence were negligible; and yet letters and thoughts flourished there more than at any other time. But in 1945 nobody could say whether the European mind, after the horrors of war and totalitarianism, had preserved enough vitality and integrity to reassert itself amid economic decline.

That again enhances the importance of the United States. As a nation, it was born in the eighteenth century out of the heritage of English liberty and out of the universal and rational ideas of the Enlightenment. It thus has formed a continuation of Western civilization under more propitious circumstances. In spite of its political and economic insignificance at that time, it played a great role in the crises at the end of the eighteenth century. It is not impossible that—perhaps it may again be said that in spite of its present political and economic power—the United States may play a similar role in the forthcoming crises of the European mind in the twentieth century.

For the present crisis, the result of the cruel wounds of the European mind, can not be overcome except by a regained vitality which shows itself above all in the independence of individual thinking. Since Socrates, and again since the seventeenth century, it has been the dangerous privilege of the European mind to assume the troublesome burden of thinking, to be driven by a restless inquietude to ever new questioning. It has resisted the self-righteous arrogance of dogmatic simplification. It has tried to view its own situation as objectively and critically as possible. Though the intellectual was as a person and a citizen involved in the melee and took his share of the fighting, the mind made a vigorous effort to rise above the confusion and to guard a sense of proportion. Though it was painfully conscious of its inherent shortcomings, it was anxious not to make them an excuse for abdication. It did not seek emotional release and refuge in easy slogans, attributing all the evils of a complex situation to some single factor, some devil of history or society— the international bankers or capitalism, imperialism or bolshevism, cartels or the Jews, Freemasons or Catholics. It refused to regard collectivities, classes or nations, as endowed with higher faculties and to raise them to a semidivine rank. It did not trust the "virtuous people" over the "wicked government," nor did it believe that participation in a class, group, race or party determined the validity or quality of thought. It realized that all these generalizations tend to absorb the individual, to deform thinking, and to shift the responsibility from the individual to a scapegoat and thus to aggravate the crisis.

For in the twentieth century the individual has been dwarfed by the adoration of force and success and the glorification of bigness. The rapid deterioration in the course of this century has become clear in the fall from Wilson's association of equal nations, small and large alike, backed by the moral conscience and free discussion of mankind, to the 1945 vision of the Big Three and the rule of their united power. In the last ten years a Big Three has appeared twice on the world scene: in 1940, when Germany, Italy, and Japan were set to establish a new world order and to divide the earth into their spheres of influence (two Western powers, of which one overshadowed the other, and an Eastern power)—an uneasy arrangement to couple Nordic Germany and non-Aryan Japan; and in 1945, when America, Britain, and Russia set out for a similar purpose (two Western powers, of which one overshadowed the other, and an Eastern power)—an uneasy arrangement to couple democratic America and totalitarian Russia. In both cases the rule of the world by three "united" giants revealed itself, fortunately, as an illusion. This cult of quantity, of the colossal, considers power as permanent and moral factors as irrelevant. Yet in the year 1940, when the *Luftgeschwader* and the *Panzer Kolonnen* of Germany seemed irresistible in the air and on the ground, Britain, practically unarmed and much inferior in manpower, standing alone and abandoned, broke the overweening power of the Axis, both on the Channel and on the Nile.

With this cult of force and bigness goes the violence of language and volume of noise which shouts down the individual and breaks his independence. Never have verbal attacks been so unrestrained, both in the abuse of the adversary and in the misuse of words and facts. Lenin's Revolution set the pattern, and other totalitarian regimes imitated it successfully; even non-totalitarian nationalist movements in central Europe and in Asia showed themselves masters of the new artless art which with the degradation of the language involves the degradation of the mind. Even the more mature free societies have succumbed to this danger in the milder form of ready acceptance of clichés. Thus in the United States most people assume that a "republic" in itself is better than a "monarchy." That may have been believed in 1791, when there were almost no republics, and perhaps even in 1848; but it is a rather wild assumption today, when so many Latin American republics have for a very long time shown neither civic virtue nor respect for liberties and when the totalitarianism of Russia and Germany grew out of republics and preserved republican institutions. The cliché induces the mind to oppose a hopeful, though nonexistent, ideal situation of the future to the reality of the present, forgetting that the future may invalidate all the bright promises and leave instead more ruin and disintegration. It is especially so with slogans like "national independence" or "revolution," which are often regarded as a good in themselves. The dissolution of the Habsburg monarchy did not raise the standard of tolerance or decency in the Danubian valley; [2] the independence of many nations has been used for the oppression of minorities and the deterioration of human liberties; a revolution may create a void without providing anything better to fill it. In the present crisis loose thinking is more dangerous than ever; wishful dreaming without rational control may hasten catastrophe. The American and British leaders did not respect the dignity of words and facts by speaking of totalitarian Russia as a democratic country and discussing with her "freedom of elections" or "liberty of the press." Whatever momentary advantages this betrayal of the mind may have brought in the confusion of the war has cost dearly. For it helped that softening of thinking, that devaluation of all values which is at the bottom of the crisis.

The cult of force and of violence has produced the worship of the hero. In the totalitarian countries military language has cloaked what were formerly the most civilian of occupations: harvesting of the crops in the fields and teaching of the art of reading, writing poetry and scientific research, become movements of a great army on the march, comprising everything, engaging every individual activity, so much so that in this age of false heroism nothing is left to the independent daring of the individual. In the Soviet Union mothers of ten children become "national heroines." The fanatical fighting spirit of armies and whole populations is regarded as praiseworthy and presented as a justification of the regime, as if Nazi Germany or primitive hordes had lacked such a spirit. The machine has no room for true courage, for what the Germans call—perhaps because they showed it so rarely—*Zivilkourage,* unregimented individual courage. Heroism and the hero are extolled at a time when nothing is more needed than the very civilian virtues which are the foundation of civility and of civilization alike. The present-day hero, inspired by the violent language of fullblast battle cries disguised as social theories or historical messages, has only contempt for two of the four cardinal virtues known to antiquity and to the Christian Middle Ages, *temperentia* and *prudentia,* moderation and measure, *mesotes* and *sophrosyne.* Nor can he lay claim to the two which remain, for fortitude and justice can be shown only by the thinking individual and never by the regimented fighter.

The twentieth century has boasted of its consideration for the welfare of the people, yet it has sacrificed the welfare, life, and happiness of man to idols and molochs with as little a perturbed conscience as primitive ages did. The unjust fate of an individual —an individual unimportant in himself and with no other dignity or demand for respect than the decisive one of being human— could until recently stir whole communities into action. The revolted conscience of intellectuals was alive to individual wrongs, especially to wrongs inflicted by the tyranny of authority or of superstition. In the eighteenth century Voltaire could exact restitution from Louis XV for the execution of Jean Calas in spite of the fury of the masses who sided with the monarch. The storm which swept France as the result of the Dreyfus trial; the overthrow of the Maura cabinet in Spain in 1909 as the result of the execution of the anarchist Ferrer; the wave of protests in the United States against the condemnation of Sacco and Vanzetti are recent outstanding examples which make sad reading at a time when millions are thrown by secret police into prisons, are executed, purged, liquidated, or just disappear without leaving a trace, as if they were not human beings, as if they had never lived—without these events arousing indignation and action even in the free countries. The individual mind has abdicated before the "necessity of history" so that it accepts the most dastardly

degradation of man with a callousness unimaginable in the nineteenth century.

The most dangerous symptom for the future of civilization is
the admiration which even liberal intellectuals hold for liberty's
most determined enemies, for their seeming efficiency and their
success. The astonishing ability of the mind to deceive itself and
escape its responsibilities is revealed in the brilliant array of
excuses and subterfuges. To justify respect for totalitarian
claims, immense demands are put upon free society, which no
society can meet. Its survival is made dependent upon the solution of many problems which by their nature are insoluble, except in a utopia, or allow only a slow and gradual amelioration
by patient and sustained effort. Claims by totalitarian regimes
are accepted uncritically at face value. So it is with the most
popular slogan "unemployment." As if the totalitarian regimes
had solved that problem otherwise than by gigantic preparations
for war or "defense," "guns instead of butter," and, at least in
Russia, with a standard of living which the "unemployed" in a
capitalistic society would reject. But of a time when intelligence
abdicates its independence, nothing is more characteristic than
the appearance of so many saviors with ready remedies for all
the ills of their class, nation, or group, some of them even with
the claim that, at a rather undetermined cost, they may save all
of mankind, or whatever may be left of it after the salvaging
process. That the many accept the panaceas in their thirst for
ready-made faiths and inspiring certainties is understandable;
that the world is again full of magicians and quacks—this time
in scientific garb—is perhaps unavoidable; all this enhances the
responsibility of the individual to maintain his critical independence and to resume the eighteenth century fight for clarity and
human values. It will be an infinitely harder fight. The mind today is more conscious of its limitations, more aware of the elemental strength of the dark forces in man. It will not indulge in
utopian hopes nor in romantic nostalgia. It cannot undo the
present and has to build within the given human reality and
historical situation with creative patience. It will not try to coin

new slogans, but will preserve, amid the ruins, the threatened heritage of civilization, the respect for truth, the rule of law, the sanctity of human life, and the regard for the freedom of the individual and of the mind.

THE CHALLENGE OF TRADITION

Democracy is still upon its trial. The civic genius of our people is its only bulwark, and neither laws nor monuments, neither battleships nor public libraries, nor great newspapers nor booming stocks; neither mechanical invention nor political adroitness, nor churches nor universities nor civil service examinations can save us from degeneration if the inner mystery be lost. That mystery . . . consists in nothing but two common habits, two inveterate habits carried into public life—habits so homely that they lend themselves to no rhetorical expression, yet habits more precious, perhaps, than any that the human race has gained. . . . One of them is the habit of trained and disciplined good temper towards the opposite party when it fairly wins its innings. . . . The other is that of fierce and merciless resentment toward every man or set of men who break the public peace.—WILLIAM JAMES (1897).

The question of Russia in all respects is without doubt the only really world-wide question of our time.—A. S. KHOMYAKOV, in a letter to Samarin, June 23, 1845.

I must have justice or I will destroy myself. And not justice in some remote time or space, but here on earth, and that I could see myself.—DOSTOEVSKY, *The Brothers Karamazov*.

GERMANY: PRUSSIANISM AND ROMANTICISM

TOTALITARIAN dictatorships are phenomena peculiar to the twentieth century through their "democratic" character; they are mass movements. Though they started as seizure of power by minorities, and in the case of Russia by a small minority, they succeeded because they gave form to the shapeless dreams of the national masses and voiced with almost frightening daring and oversimplification their confused and hardly conscious wishes. The mass following of men like Stalin and Hitler cannot be explained by terror alone. A bond of fundamental affinity unites the leaders with their peoples, not any outstanding attractiveness in the leader himself. Hitler was a German mass man. In physical appearance and in creative intelligence he seemed to lack everything that could explain his magic hold over his fellow citizens or distinguish him among them. He was a nothing, as Konrad Heiden called him, "one of those men without qualities, normal and colorless to the point of invisibility," and yet who "could feel the feeling of the masses, and when the nothing spoke with the people, it was as though the voice of the people were speaking." Hitler did not conquer the German masses, he represented them. "He did not dominate the minds of millions, his mind belonged to them. Like a piece of wood floating on the waves, he followed the shifting currents of public opinion. This was his true strength." Hitler's success was based on the fact that he "democratized" or vulgarized for the masses some of the great intellectual and political traditions of Germany.

In that respect national socialism fused and transformed the heritage of two great movements in modern Germany, of Prussianism and romanticism. It was their illegitimate offspring. The two movements were originally not only independent of each other, but in many ways direct opposites. Prussianism was a virile cult of soldiery discipline and rational organization. Romanticism, regarded as a philosophy of life, had many feminine traits of character. It was a revolt against discipline on behalf of instinct and desire; it was not a movement of soldiers, but of intellectual bohemians. Both sprang from similar social foundations, from the weakness of the German middle class. While in Britain, the Netherlands, and in France middle-class merchants and intellectuals were rising to power and molding public opinion, Germany remained an aristocratic country in which the trader and the scribe received scant recognition and remained outside "society." The Prussian nobleman and soldier and the romantic bohemian met in their contempt for the burgher. They transferred their contempt and their opposition from the burgher as a class to the countries where a middle-class civilization had prevailed since the Renaissance. Germany saw itself not only in a political, but even more in a cultural and moral fight against "Rome" and the "West." Ulrich von Hutten had taught Germany to regard the struggle between ancient Rome and the Germanic tribes as the beginning of a permanent opposition between Germanism and Westernism. Arminius, who had defeated the Roman legions in A.D. 9 and thus had blocked, to the misfortune of Germany and of Europe, the civilizing of the Germanic tribes, became not only a successful hero, but the embodiment of German virtues. Rationalistic humanism, the classical love for form and measure, for clarity and self-limitation, the social and active Christianism of Calvinist countries, were not only regarded as alien to Germanism, but as immoral, as proof of superficiality and levity.

Prussianism was virtuous service for a rather doubtful cause. Spengler spoke of the Prussian youth as "Roman in the pride to serve, in the humility to command, demanding not rights from others but duties from oneself, all without exception, without distinction, to fulfill a destiny which they feel within themselves." Prussia was not nationalist in the modern sense of the word. Prussianism did not spring from the people; it sprang from the state. It was created by kings, of whom the greatest, Frederick II, was not interested in German culture; culturally, he felt himself a cosmopolitan and a Frenchman; politically, a Prussian monarchist. To Bismarck, the German *Volksgemeinschaft* did not mean much more. Prussia pursued a policy which was realistic and rationalistic. Its goal was power, but a limited power, controlled by rational and utilitarian considerations. It could therefore be satiated and become static for long periods. It admitted the coexistence of other powers in common tasks. Its great philosopher was Hegel, who constructed a most imposing system of logical interpretation of history and at the same time characterized the people as "that part of the state which does not know its own will." This explains the divided attitude prevailing among national socialists concerning Hegel, whose rational philosophy of the spirit does not take into account the dark instinctive forces of "life and nature."

Romanticism was at first libertarian and individualistic. This individualism, however, had nothing in common with individualism in Great Britain or France. English individualism has its basis in the religious conception of the dignity and equality of all individuals created in the image of God; French individualism, in the rational conception of the equal rights of all men endowed with reason, which is one for the whole of humanity. "Western" individualism is rational and Christian. Romantic individualism in Germany led to an anarchical conception of the "unique" individual and his exceptional rights, to irresponsibility, to the glorification of nature, instinct, the indomitable vitalistic forces, which find their justification in their own strength and exuberance. Individuality in the Western meaning of the word, which also held good for Goethe's conception of individuality, gladly and willingly subjected itself to standards and to laws universally applicable and was ready to limit liberty in free agreement and fair play. Romantic individualism, on the other hand, could not build a free and ordered society. The individual who had escaped from the fetters of a stagnant and oppressive society into extreme individualism, escaped from that untenable position into the security of a mystic whole and its undisputed authority. Romanticism, in discovering the *Volk* as a mystic whole, linked together by a community of feeling and attitudes, distinguishing it sharply from all other groups, transferred the anarchical concept of individualism from the individual to the nation. Its center was the *Volk*, something dynamic, related to the infinite and the absolute, creative in instinctive ways, not subject to any general rational laws. Romanticism is an insatiable longing for an all-inclusive totality.

National socialism—this is the fundamental difference between Bismarck's and Hitler's power politics—had therefore no limited goals. In that it resembled bolshevism, which was similarly different, in its expansionism, from even the most daring czarist Pan-Slavism. Both modern movements could never become satiated; they were always driven by their dynamism, even at the risk of self-destruction. But from their combination with Prussianism and Pan-Slavism they gained a hybrid character which made possible their flexibility, their lack of clarity and definiteness, and their associations with most representative figures of the German and Russian past, although frequently only by the falsification or elimination of some of their essential attitudes and thoughts. At the same time national socialism divested Prussianism and romanticism of their religious, rational, and humanistic links with Western civilization. Although many leaders of national socialism were not Prussians, its prevailing attitude and pattern of behavior was distinctly Prussian. But the underlying philosophy was romantic. It found its expression in the untranslatable word *Weltanschauung*.

Weltanschauung is no rational concept. It is rather an intuitive contemplation of the whole. It claims to be all-inclusive and unfathomably deep. It cannot be understood by rational thinking; it is a product of the deepest instincts, not of the individual but of the collectivity. The Russian poet Tyutchev meant the very same thing when he wrote in a brief poem, that one cannot understand Russia by reason and measure her by a common yardstick, for she has a peculiar nature, and one just has to be-

lieve in Russia. Romantic *Weltanschauung* demanded such a faith
and intuitive understanding for Germany. National socialism
changed, however, the character of the *Weltanschauung* from
a metaphysical to a biological one which seemed more appropri-
ate to a "scientific" age. It did not recognize any freedom of the
spirit; the biological forces decide irresistibly the thought, the
creative faculties, and the fate of man. No similar degradation
of individuality and of the spirit has ever held sway over the
minds of many millions of Europeans.

This *Weltanschauung* was totalitarian and therefore necessarily exclusive and jealous. It was a religion based upon the
certitude of "biological science"; it sanctified "life" and its demands as forces against which no sanctity of law and no objective truth had the right to prevail. This *Weltanschauung* bore in
many ways the stamp of Schopenhauer's primacy of will and
turned it into self-validation of energy, yet in the decisive instant
it broke with the fundamental message of Schopenhauer's ethics.

Although Schopenhauer's philosophy is the basis of all the
present-day vitalistic, dynamic, irrationalistic philosophies and
Weltanschauungen, he was no ancestor of national socialism.
Schopenhauer described the struggles and tragedy of life; he did
not glorify them. He was no admirer of restless energy. He
wished to overcome will, not to be subservient to will and drive
for power. He condemned all vitalism and dynamism, and found
redemption, not for a racial group, but universally, in the victory
of the spirit over the will. While he rejected the application of
his philosophy to his own life, his writings glorified not the conquering "hero," but the ascetic saint, Christian (or, as he called
it, Buddhist) compassion for everything alive, not the triumph
of the strong. His philosophy did not serve life but truth. Two
months before Hegel delivered, in 1818, his famous inaugural
lecture at the University of Berlin, Schopenhauer ended the
preface to the first edition of his chief work with the following
words: "But life is short and truth works far and lives long: let
us speak the truth." In this point the two great antagonists would
have entirely agreed and would have differed fundamentally
from national socialism. National socialism had its roots un-

doubtedly in the intellectual traditions of Germany, but its *Weltanschauung* is not—in spite of its claims—the eternal and only expression of the German mind. Yet national socialism shared with Prussianism and romanticism their antagonism to the West and intensified it to the highest degree.

In that sense Hitlerism was Germany's latest answer to the challenge of Western ideas and the impact of Western forces, as Stalinism is in the case of Russia. For more than a century, many German and Russian thinkers and dreamers, deeply conscious of, and endlessly meditating about, their difference from the West, have proclaimed its inferiority and predicted its decline. The twentieth century seemed to fulfill their prophecies of the doom of the West. Western civilization has been put to an unprecedented strain by three centuries of rapid progress in the liberty of man, the pursuit of happiness, and the unbinding of the masses. The strain of this process has finally weakened the moral faith and social cohesion in Western society and has raised doubts and fears everywhere, though in a very different degree, according to the intellectual climate and the social structure of each country. National socialism and communism, which promised a new certitude to frightened men, a sense of fulfillment to distracted lives and perplexed minds, have aggravated the crisis by their very reaction to it. But they took for granted that Western civilization was as much undermined in the West as it was in Germany and Russia; thus they became convinced of the imminent triumph over the hated West. With them the opposition to the West no longer came from the ruling classes, but from the masses who for the first time represented their nation and national traditions. National socialism in Germany represented the effective blending and vulgarization of Prussianism and romanticism for consumption in an age of masses and industrial technique. All the inner and deep contradictions of the two trends were smoothed over by the emphasis upon German racial mission and superiority. German world conquest and totalitarian world revolution became to the national socialists two sides of the same process; their fusion gave *élan* and power to both—a certitude and a world-encompassing goal which Prussianism and romanticism never possessed. All their restraints were thrown overboard; the national-socialist youth, filled with a fanatical faith, believed that it was living in a unique time of decision, when almost everything could become reality, if willed with wholehearted determination. In this determination they again reflected the transformed heritage of two great Germans of the nineteenth century.

The brilliant period of the German mind which lasted from 1760 to 1830, and which gave to the world Kant and Hegel, Mozart and Beethoven, Lessing and Humboldt, Goethe and Schiller, was followed by seventy years of comparative exhaustion. The Germans' steep ascent to power seemed to dull their creative abilities. Above this general mediocrity three men achieved greatness, men differing in personality and outlook, yet each expressing and shaping the German character and tradition—Richard Wagner, Karl Marx, and Friedrich Nietzsche. All three rejected the bourgeois nineteenth century and wished to overcome it: one, through a new stage art; the second, through a new social order; the third, through a new human personality. Marx lived the life of a scholar; Nietzsche withdrew into the lofty loneliness of a philosopher; Wagner was the typical romantic artist. Of these three men, Wagner and Nietzsche became friends; though they soon parted, their brief meeting was of significance. In their ideas and in their personal life, they stood in many ways at opposite poles; yet a strange amalgam and vulgarization of their two influences shaped the mind of the German youth in the twentieth century and accelerated the dangerous drift toward national socialism. Wagner was a pure romanticist who combined with the veneration of hoary myths a predilection for grandiose spectacles which demanded the full employ of the most up-to-date technology; in Nietzsche there was, in spite of his individualism and his dislike for the state, a secret admiration for the Prussian aristocratic warrior which his disciple Spengler systematized.

Everything in the bourgeois world of the nineteenth century appeared rotten to Wagner—politics, capitalism, the French and the English and, above all, Jewry and its influence, which to him personified finance and gold. He became the first noted German proponent of the racial theory which his son-in-law, Houston Stewart Chamberlain, later systematized in *The Foundations of the Nineteenth Century*. Wagner raised the German myths of gods and heroes of a dim prehistoric past to the dignity of an inspiring example for modern man; he saw the future of Germany in a regeneration of racial consciousness and purity. With the youthful and enthusiastic King Louis II of Bavaria, Wagner hoped to realize his vision of a Germany reborn through that religion of art of which he was a prophet. Nuremberg, "German in its blood and bones," the home of the Meistersinger, would become the political center of the country, with near-by Bayreuth the residence of the master and savior. Not only Germany, but the whole world would be saved by this new German culture; for as soon as the Germans, regenerated by racial purity— and also by vegetarianism and the fight against vivisection— accepted Wagner's leadership, their innate superiority over all other peoples would work out mankind's salvation.

In his egocentricism Wagner identified himself and his ideas with Germany and Germanism. He thought himself the German genius and the bearer of Germany's world mission. Out for power and lust, he always tried, as Ernest Newman put it, "to get what he wanted by representing it as something not desired by himself but something vital to the larger design of Providence for the cosmos." He easily persuaded himself that he was the most ill used man in the world; and he explained any frustration by the wickedness of the world, but never thought it might be due to his own fault. "The possibility that people might dislike him because of notorious defects in his own character would not occur to him; his own view of all such matters was that a world incurably evil had entered into a conspiracy of hatred against the one truly righteous man in it." He was a romantic artist whose passion overstepped the boundaries of art and wished to transform the world; it appeared to him as a dramatic stage where the wand of the divine genius could by the sheer power of his will—though not without support from modern technique

—mold and transfigure a reality. This impatience with the imperfections of reality and the apocalyptic dream of a radically new world Wagner shared with Marx and Nietzsche. All three assigned to themselves decisive roles in bringing about the birth of a new mankind, but only Wagner identified it with the German *Volksgemeinschaft*, the mystical concept of a folk community.

Four years after Richard Wagner's death, a German sociologist, Ferdinand Tönnies, published a book, *Gemeinschaft und Gesellschaft* (Community and Society), which became fundamental for German social science. It contrasted two ideal types of societal organization. "Community" saw totality and wholeness in the group, of which the individual was only part. It was formed by unconscious factors, by the deep dark forces of instinct. It was irrational in its origins and in its ties, deeply embedded in the forces of nature, growing organically. It was characteristic of primitive and, to a lesser extent, feudal, times. "Society," on the other hand, was characteristic of modern bourgeois civilization. It saw wholeness and totality in the individual, who was prior to the group, which is viewed as a sociological concept, owing its origin to rational motives and clear insight into individual interests. Though Tönnies showed some nostalgic longing for "community," he understood that "society" was the mark of high civilization and of a higher morality, that it demanded a respect for truth and law and their universality, a sense of reciprocity and of contractual fidelity, unknown in the more primitive forms. But German social science soon contrasted the "organic depth" of "community," regarded as peculiarly German (though the Russian Slavophiles claimed it as peculiarly Russian), with the "mechanic superficiality" of "society," regarded as characteristic of Western bourgeois society. This contrast was often expressed as that between *Kultur* and civilization. By a daring step one could then doubt the value of civilization and of civilized life at all, and oppose to it the primeval forces of nature.

This revaluation of all values was the work of Friedrich Nietzsche, undoubtedly one of the leading and most fascinating figures of the latter nineteenth century. A solitary prophet, with a critical mind of unprecedented sharpness and a burning vision of unprecedented daring, he was typically German in his disregard of social and political reality and in his total absorption in pure and irresponsible thought. This lonely philosopher in a vacuum exhibited an audacity of exploration which makes his work one of the most memorable feasts of the spirit; he pushed his thoughts to the limit where the abyss yawns in which he finally went down himself—a tightrope walker over the dark worlds of the subhuman and the titanic, in which the human is irretrievably lost. He represented an extreme case of the complete break between the world of thought and the world of reality which characterized so much of German intellectual life; he had no feeling of responsibility for the consequences of his thought once it was brought down from his lofty and unreachable mountain peaks to the lowlands of common humanity, which he despised.

Relentlessly he unmasked all the shames and compromises of civilization, all the weaknesses and pettiness of man. Ethics which had dominated Western life from the time of Socrates and of the Hebrew prophets—ethics which found a fundamentally similar expression in Buddhism, in the Stoa, and in Christianity —he rejected contemptuously as a Jewish-Christian invention for the protection of the weak and the dispossession of the strong. He wished to destroy all the accepted ethical values because they seemed to him, like the whole of Western civilization, decadent and no longer valid, no longer able to sustain man to the fullness of life. For the new man for whom he longed, he wrote new tables of law, the laws of life and nature which would support man to develop all his abilities to master life and to direct history in the world-wide decisions which Nietzsche felt impending. Nietzsche had no love for the Germans; he despised racial theories and he felt himself a European. While Wagner was fundamentally an actor, Nietzsche was a moralist. But his sermons and appeals—for that was his philosophy and poetry in its late stage—found nowhere as willing an audience as in the German youth who delighted in the contempt for Western bourgeois civilization and in the ecstasies of the birth of a new man able to live reality in all its stark truth. Oswald Spengler predicted the coming age of Caesarism, the triumph of the power of the blood of well bred men over bourgeois gold and reasonableness. He lived long enough to witness what he considered the disfigured realization of his philosophy and to turn away in disgust from the realities of national socialism. For Nietzsche and he had longed for the lonely aristocratic individual; instead of that, national socialism brought mass emotionalism; Nietzsche and Spengler had rejoiced in intellectual daring and, though they had abused and slandered it, in the cold clarity of reason; national socialism clamped upon the Germans the rule of the simplifying slogan and of the confused half-truth.[1]

Though the true representatives of Prussianism and romanticism, and Nietzsche and Spengler themselves, might turn in disgust from the national-socialist transformation of the heritage—the resistance to the national-socialist regime in Germany came more from Prussians than from the masses—they bore much of the responsibility for the fact that in the thirties of the twentieth century the government of the German nation could abandon the framework of common civilized values and start a relentless campaign to destroy it. Vague and partly distorted notions of Prussianism and romanticism, of Wagnerian music and Nietzschean prophecy, had imbued the German youth with a death-defying will to fulfill the German mission, whether triumphant upon the ruins of the world or prostrated upon the pyre of its own happiness. The government was helped in its task by the sense of subordination and the lack of personal independence so characteristic of the Germans. Goethe in his conversations with Eckermann on March 12, 1828, praised the liberty of Englishmen, "das Glück der persönlichen Freiheit," which endows them with uprightness, while in Germany every little boy grows up under the strict eye of the police. Whenever he tries to feel himself at liberty, "sogleich ist die Polizei da, es zu verbieten." It may be that this lack of personal liberty in social and political life induced the daring exploits of intellectual liberty and irresponsibility in which many German thinkers indulged, and that the absence of the "Glück der persönlichen Freiheit" found its compensation in far-flung dreams of disciplined power and conquest.[2]

Only a very few years after Friedrich List drew up—amid a people still apparently composed of dreamy poets and quiet thinkers—the first clearly coordinated politico-economic power program for national aggrandizement and German *Weltgeltung*, Ferdinand Kürnberger published in 1855 his novel, *Der Amerikamüde*, a cultural picture of the United States. In this thoughtful but angry book, one of the enthusiasts for the coming unity and freedom of Germany envisaged the future of the United States, of the German element in it, and of himself as one who will work for this future:

What the German farmers in Pennsylvania were able to do unconsciously, to preserve German life through a whole century so strongly that even today whole communities of theirs do not understand one English word, should I be less able to do, with my enthusiastic consciousness of German kind and culture? I am not afraid of it. No, I shall last, a German in Yankeedom, and the fall which I foresee for this racial mixture can worry me as little as we are worried by the fate of a goat which has nursed Jupiter to strength. May it then happen, as these pages dare to prophesy, we shall not perish in the civil wars of the Union. Germany will send her fleet, and will know how to protect her German province, Pennsylvania. What do I say: Pennsylvania? The whole of North America will become German, for our immigration leans upon a powerful mother country, as Yankee England leaned upon old England. But what do I say: the whole of North America? The whole world will become German, for Germany's rise will mean England's decline, as Holland declined before England, and all English colonies will then fall to the Germans; the guards of culture on the whole earth will be changed and their posts will be occupied by German troops. Germany awakens, and no people on earth can keep its old rank, for all live thanks to the German sleep and perish with German awakening.[3]

Extravagant dreams such as this were not shared by the overwhelming majority of more sober-thinking Germans. But the underlying sentiments were expressed, in a more disciplined way, by some other German thinkers, leaders, and dreamers.

With the miraculous successes of the Prussian army and of Bismarck's policy, their number grew. Germany perfected step by step her instrumentalities for power politics on a worldwide scale. In the First World War she came within reach of her goal. Though numerically and in resources much inferior to her enemies, she far surpassed them by the range of her preparations and by her intelligent and thorough coordination of the different branches of life for the purpose of the war.

When Germany lost the war, many Germans believed that it was due to the insufficient integration of the masses into the German national purpose, to the insufficient mobilization of all the resources of the people and the land. Hitler did not raise any new goals before the German nation; he made what had been the conscious aim of a small minority into a dream shared by the people; he prepared the whole German nation, all its classes and especially its masses, for a total mobilization which would no longer allow internal dissensions, doubts, class and party antagonism to weaken the German war effort. The school of thought that he represented was convinced that Germany had not been defeated by the arms of the enemy from without, but by the strength of liberalism, socialism, pacificism, by all that which is known as Western thought, Christianity, or bourgeois humanitarianism, from within. For that purpose he preached the new concept of a closed Germany, complete self-sufficiency, and elimination of everything alien, the destruction of all common bonds with whoever did not share the true faith. Hitler wished to prepare the Germans for their world-encompassing task through absolute hostility to everything without and an absolute cohesion within. "If the German nation," Hitler wrote, "had achieved in its historical development that herd-like unity ... then the German Reich would be today master of the globe." Under his leadership Germany would realize the exemplary solution of the world crisis. For "Germany's position is a central one. She is the focus of all political, economic, intellectual problems. If the world wants salvation, and so far as it deserves salvation, Germany will be able to express whatever this revolutionized world can hope to salvage." Thus the German plan of mastery of the globe merged with the world revolution. In its consciousness of a world crisis—which it much exaggerated, especially in its validity for the West—national socialism was, at least for some time, able to exploit to its own profit the weaknesses in the moral and social texture of its adversaries. It confused them by calling them to account and demanding their perfection. It tried to put them on the defensive, following therein with similar din the methods and tactics of communism. But when the Western nations liberated themselves from a false feeling of guilt, it soon became clear that Prussianism and romanticism—even streamlined and vulgarized—were no sufficient foundation for a victorious challenge to Western civilization. The defeat of national socialism should not only undo the work of Bismarck—the unification of Germany around Berlin as its center —but start the reintegration of Germany into Western civilization.

VII

RUSSIA: THE PERMANENT MISSION

In 1815 Friedrich Gentz noted:

Napoleon's downfall was a pure and unqualified advantage for
Russia; for the rest of Europe, and especially for the states bordering
on Russia, it was largely balanced by the increased strength that she
secured for herself at the expense of the general equilibrium. For
this great power there is virtually no further real danger; if she
attacks her neighbors her greatest risk is merely that she may fail in
her purpose and have to postpone her venture to a more favorable
time. The difficulty of penetrating Russia's interior is now so generally recognized that only lunacy and despair could prompt an
attempt to conquer this great empire. While the other states of
Europe exhausted themselves in the struggle against Napoleon, Russia,
who allied herself with him, understood well how to extract the most
solid benefits from the ephemeral union. It would be easy for her to
fall upon her neighbors, for she has so many greedy and ambitious
reasons for trying it, and, if the expression be allowed, such substan-
tially centrifugal habits, that war, which others regard as a necessary
evil, will always be to the Russians a matter of choice, of emotion,
and of speculation.

Then, as recently, the immensity of the Russian empire, the
exceptional hardship of the Russian winter, and the endurance
and stamina of the Russian people defeated world conquerors.
Napoleon was by far a more formidable opponent than Hitler:
a great military genius who had proved his worth over sixteen
years and who led forces of unsurpassed size. No supplies or
guns poured into Russia in 1812: out of her own strength she
drove the proud enemy from the land. When, with her new
allies, Russia's soldiers entered Paris, she stood at the pinnacle

of prestige, backed by her immense army and her role as "Europe's savior." Europe trembled before the potentialities of the new situation. But her fears proved unfounded: the Russian autocrats of the period were not men of steel; nineteenth century Russian statesmen walked the conservative path; Russian society looked to Europe as the "land of holy wonders"; the Russian masses had not yet gained consciousness of their elemental strength.

Even 1815 was not the first time that Russia moved far into Europe. At the beginning of the eighteenth century, Peter I tried hard to convert Montenegro into a Russian foothold on the Adriatic Sea; from 1711 to 1918 Russian armies occupied Rumania ten times; they stood on the Rhine in 1735 and in 1747; in 1760 they looted Berlin, and Empress Elizabeth intended to annex eastern Prussia; in 1797 Czar Paul accepted the grand mastership of the island of Malta, and in 1798 General Suvarov, created prince of Italy by his grateful emperor, drove French armies out of Milan and Turin.

By 1815 the empire embraced all the lands and peoples from the Vistula to Alaska. Most Russians agreed with the historian Nikolai Mikhailovich Karamzin that "looking on the immensity of that monarchy which is unique in the world, our mind feels overwhelmed. Never did Rome equal it in greatness." The glorious victory over Napoleon, and the growing contact with Europe, sharpened with pointed pertinence the question of the nature and destiny of Russia—a vast realm, secluded and unknown as none in Europe, and yet, since the sixteenth century, convinced of its universal mission for the true progress of mankind; a people of fast growing numbers, primitive and backward and yet with dynamic power expanding in an almost uninterrupted flow for centuries into all directions and colonizing ever new lands.

What was to be the relation of this realm and people to Europe after the common struggle against Napoleon had brought them unexpectedly together? Only a few Russians (among them the Czar) regarded the war as a common European enterprise and felt any responsibility toward Europe. To the overwhelming majority of the Russians, Napoleon had stood for Europe: their defeat of Napoleon had been the defeat of the godless West. They were convinced that Europe as a whole hated and despised Russia and was united against her. Russia and Europe faced each other as two different worlds, with hardly any traditions or ideas in common.

Modern Russia, like modern Europe, rose in the sixteenth century—for Europe, the seedtime of individualism and of the rise of the urban classes, of rational science and of the growth of political liberty; for Russia, the very opposite.

Medieval Russia, centering between the Baltic and Black seas, around the trading cities of Kiev and Novgorod, looked toward Byzantium, whence it received its church; and toward Scandinavia, from where its dynasty came. When Kiev succumbed to the Mongol invasion, modern Russia was created by the will and the ruthless cunning of great princes around Moscow. The new capital grew up, like the German cities founded east of the Elbe, far from the old cultural centers to the West, on recently colonized land where traditional urban liberties were unknown. Its people were no longer the Slavs of the Dnieper, but a new race in which Slav, Finnish, and Mongol blood freely intermingled. From Moscow no roads led to the West; the rivers pointed to the steppes and deserts of Asia; the political, cultural, and economic ties were with the great empire of the Tatars to whom it was tributary.

Though the church in Moscow kept the communion of faith with Byzantium, the ties grew weaker. The church in Moscow became purely Russian. Its Slavonic liturgy cut it off from Byzantium as well as from ancient civilization; not only Virgil and Cicero, but Plato and Aristotle were virtually without influence in Russia until contact with the West brought them there in the eighteenth century. This national church, conscious of its universal mission, dominated the whole life.

Moscow felt itself a community of the true faith. Its struggle against the Tatars was neither racial nor cultural. The Greeks fought the Persians in defense of political liberty and higher

civilization; the Muscovites accepted the civilization and the
political order of the Tatars. The Greeks boasted of their racial
superiority; the Russians were free of such a feeling. The bap-
tized Tatar, irrespective of race, was fully accepted as an equal
in the common brotherhood of the true faith. This character of
the struggle has remained: the Poles in the seventeenth century,
Napoleon two hundred years later, the capitalists today, have
been not just political enemies, but enemies of "the faith," whatever its dogmas. The greatest hatred has always been reserved
for deviations in the interpretation of the dogma (whether of
Christ or of Marx) which would endanger the unity of faith that
assures salvation.

The Orthodox faith came from Byzantium, but the Russians
became convinced that Moscow alone preserved it in undefiled
purity. Had not the Byzantines, desperately pressed by the
Turks, bowed before the Latin infidels? Had they not, at
the Council of Florence, accepted the union with Rome and the
primacy of the Pope? Moscow rejected the union and remained
uncompromisingly hostile to the West. To the Russians the fall
of Constantinople, the capital of the universal empire and the
universal church for eleven centuries, seemed to be God's punishment for the apostasy of the Byzantine church. Moscow alone
was now the guardian of the faith. God had clearly rejected the
Rome of Augustus and the new Rome of Constantine as un-
worthy of the task to order the world and to guide it to the true
faith. "A new and third Rome has sprung up in the North, illuminating the whole universe like a sun," wrote the monk Philo-
theus. "The third Rome will stand to the end of history, for it
is the last Rome. Moscow has no successor; a fourth Rome is
inconceivable." Russia became the holy land, Moscow the successor to the imperial mission of Rome. When in the middle of
the sixteenth century the last strongholds of the Tatar empire,
Kazan on the lower Volga and Astrakhan on the Caspian Sea,
were conquered by the Russians, and the way lay open to the
penetration of Asia, Moscow added the Mongolian heritage to
its imperial mission.   The new Caesar, or Czar, assumed the
legacy of the Byzantine emperors and of the Tatar khans "to

unite in an organic whole the diverse nations of the East and
of the West."

This sacred guardianship of the true faith deepened primitive
attitudes of suspicion and seclusion. They were directed even
against the Greek Orthodox. Moscow's primacy over Byzantium
was jealously maintained. When the reform movement of the
seventeenth century tried to introduce some Greek customs into
the Russian church, the Russian masses reacted with forceful
spontaneity. The so-called Old Believers "were ready to testify
till death their belief that the Russian church had received from
Christ a special responsibility to preserve the true apostolic traditions, lost by the West, compromised by the Greeks." For them
"the Russian standard of faith and worship possessed a final and
universal authority."

Naturally, the resistance was even greater when half a century
later Czar Peter attempted the Westernization and secularization
of Holy Russia and led her into "Babylonian captivity." Moscow
was deposed from her seat of pride; St. Petersburg became the
capital of a new empire which seemingly cut all ties with the
past. With his ruthless and masterful energy, which respected
no rights, Peter seemingly destroyed the foundations of national
life; in reality he performed, at tremendous cost, a national task:
he gave the nation an indispensable new armor for the fulfillment of its traditional mission. Human values and individual
dignity did not concern him. For his support he looked to a
newly created elite, devoted to him and his work.

But the nation was not prepared for the sudden shift. Peter's
violent methods were unable to arouse, even in the elite, a com-
prehension of the fundamentals of Western civilization—the respect for the right of the individual and for the objectivity of
truth.

The decades following the victory over Napoleon made Russia conscious of her might and power as never before. Yet she
had ceased to represent one nation with one faith. Two nations
faced each other—the educated classes, a tiny minority, who
spoke and wrote French with greater ease than Russian and who

seized avidly upon everything that came from Europe; and the peasants and tradesmen, who looked upon European ways, in government as well as in literature, as a work of the devil. The court in St. Petersburg, separated from both, distrusted the educated classes and disregarded the masses. It accepted Western or, better, German methods to strengthen its apparatus, which grew in size but hardly in efficiency; it rejected the Western mind and the Western freedoms. The court had the power, the people had the momentum; between them, the intelligentsia, with all its wealth of ideas and ideals, with all its abundance of zeal and devotion, was impotent. Russian literature, from Pushkin's Eugene Onegin to Chekhov's Ivanov, presented the hopeless hero, the superfluous man, the frustrated generation.

Into this poorly prepared soil the most various and daring European ideas suddenly poured: revolution and romanticism, mysticism and materialism, Hegelianism and socialism—all the conflicting and turbulent currents of the first half of the nineteenth century. Detached from their social background and intellectual tradition, they appeared even more bewildering and extremist. They challenged the Russian intelligentsia into ever new perspectives for Russia's relation to Europe. Should Russia follow Europe? Or was Europe, in its confusion and crisis, in need of Russia's guidance? The answers differed. Some rejected Peter's reform and wished to return to the old order of Moscow; others accepted the contact with Europe and smarted under Russia's backwardness; some looked forward to surpassing Europe's revolutionary socialism; others believed that Russia alone could conserve true Christianity.

But almost everyone had faith in Russia's mission, and most came to despair of Europe. The two greatest writers of the Russian earth, two men so different in outlook as Dostoevsky and Tolstoy, rejected with equal vehemence and total finality Western civilization, which they considered inadequate to answer the ultimate questions. Kant's criticism and English thought found hardly any followers in Russia: their cautious approach, their sense of responsibility and of limits, did not appeal to a Russian extremism which was as violent in the affirmation of faith as in its denunciation.

Yet the first close contact between Russia and Europe, though obstructed by the autocracy and distrusted by the people, made Russia, for the first time, know the freedom of the spirit and the greatness of literature; while Pushkin and Lermontov, Gogol and Turgenev, Dostoevsky and Tolstoy, revealed to Europe a new world of fascinating depth and attractiveness. Less known than this galaxy of creative giants, though not necessarily less worthy of Europe's attention, are six more Russian thinkers and essayists of the nineteenth century.

Peter Yakovlevich Chaadayev (1794-1856) and Alexey Stepanovich Khomyakov (1804-1860), Vissarion Grigoryevich Belinsky (1811-1848) and Alexander Ivanovich Herzen (1812-1870), Mikhail Bakunin (1814-1876) and Konstantin Nikolayevich Leontyev (1831-1891), were men of sincerity and high purpose. They all were—though not in the technical sense of the word— philosophers of history. Their thoughts centered incessantly on the destinies of Russia and of humanity, which, to them, were one. In all their differences they were united by faith in Russia and distrust of European middle-class civilization, whose underlying social realities and mental attitudes remained incomprehensible to them. Their conversations and controversies, their friendships and conflicts, this whole intense intellectual life with its endless talk and weighty articles—books and deeds were equally rare—illumined the face of Russia as she struggled to gain consciousness of herself through contact with the alien world of Europe.

This period closed with the end of the nineteenth century. Even as the last "superfluous men"—the pale heirs of Petchorin and Oblomov and Rudin—were dying with a whimper in Chekhov's plays, a new type was growing up. Capitalism and the spirit of enterprise began to penetrate the country; an understanding of reality and responsibility was awakening; the struggle for liberty under law and the education for legal concepts and rights were undertaken in earnest. The free flight of imagination, with its fascinating fancies of a legendary past and a utopian future, was disciplined. Great progress was made. But the efforts of the educated classes were crushed between the unbelievable stupidity of the corrupt government and the dark, backward inertia of the masses. The integration of Russia into Europe, which could have endowed the Western mind with a new searching vitality, was cut short in 1917—the very year when it seemed accomplished.

Lenin's total rejection and contemptuous hatred of "bourgeois" European civilization struck a responsive chord in the hearts and traditions of the Russian masses. His burning faith and his utopian assurance were not alien to them. True, the dogma came from outside Russia; but, like Byzantine Orthodoxy, Marxism was soon nationalized and became a Russian church.

Marxism itself combined liberal ideals of English origin (the "withering" of the state) with an anti-Western method of revolutionary sociology through which alone the "ideal" could be realized and this utterly corrupt world saved. While Marxism never exercised great influence in Britain or the United States, it gained a dominant position in Germany and in Russia. There its basic elements dissociated: the German social democrats stressed more and more the Western elements and divested them of their utopian absoluteness; the Russian communists perfected the method and endowed it with the passionate assurance of an apocalyptic struggle.

In the dogmatic utopianism of Marxism, the Russian masses found an affinity with their own faith. Marxism attracted because it promised salvation according to the tenets of science and through the means of technology. It called the people from the communal passivity of the old faith to the collective activity of proud construction. And Russia became again a closed and secluded society, anxiously guarded from contact with the infidel world. At the very moment when it seemed to appeal to the whole world as never before, it withdrew into itself with an unprecedented ruthlessness. From the maritime periphery where Peter had placed it, it returned to its hallowed center in the Kremlin. Moscow was raised from the secondary place to which the secularized empire of St. Petersburg had relegated her. Russia, once again the holy land, was to lead mankind to salvation.

But the contact with Europe, the brief interlude between the old certainty and the new certainty, though it ended so soon, had been, for Russia and for Europe, a time of great fertility. To study its intense questioning about Europe and Russia may help a deeper understanding of both.

Chaadayev was the first to interpret Russia's past and present in the light of a philosophy of universal history, though he never got beyond the introduction, formulated in several "philosophical" letters.

Like most Russian intellectuals of his generation, he had served as an officer of the guard and participated in the campaigns against Napoleon. His strong sense of independence made him resign his commission; he spent the rest of his life as a lonely and gloomy wit on the fringes of Moscow society. Suddenly the stillness of his life was broken, in 1836, when his *Lettre philosophique écrite à une dame* (written in 1829) was published in a Moscow periodical.

Its impression on the Russia of that time has so been described by Herzen:

It was a shot that rang out in the dark night; it forced all to awake. What, one may wonder, is the significance of two or three pages published in a monthly review? And yet, such is the strength of utterance, such is the power of the spoken word in a land of silence, unaccustomed to free speech, that Chaadayev's letter shook all thinking Russia.

In the midst of exuberant national pride, a courageous voice described what was—the desert of the Russian past, the deadness of the Russian life. The periodical was immediately suppressed; the censor who had passed the article was dismissed, the editor exiled, the author declared insane by order of the Czar. Chaadayev's few remaining articles and letters, all written in French, could be published only after his death.

Yet, Chaadayev was no revolutionary, did not call for the

overthrow of the government, or demand liberal reforms. He merely questioned the general conviction of the primacy and superiority of Russia and of the Orthodox church. He explained Russia's backwardness by her separation from the universal church of Rome. Russia had received Christianity from "decadent and corrupt" Byzantium and had vegetated—unaffected by the civilizing influences of antiquity, of the Middle Ages, and of modern times.

We have lived, as it were, outside of history, and have remained untouched by the universal education of the human race. . . . The historical experience does not exist for us; generations and centuries have passed without use for us. Considering us, one could say that the general laws of mankind do not apply to us. Isolated from the world, we have given or taught nothing to the world; we have added no thoughts to the sum of human ideas; we have in no way collaborated in the progress of reason and we have disfigured everything that penetrated to us from this progress. From the very first beginning of our social existence we have done nothing for the common weal; not one useful thought grew on the barren soil of our land; no great truth came from our midst; we made no effort to think for ourselves, and from the thought of others we have taken over only the deceiving surface and the superfluous frills.

Chaadayev was struck by the discrepancy between the great power position of Russia and the political and cultural immaturity of her people. The face of the Russian masses he found strangely expressionless, mirroring an inner emptiness. The ideas of civil rights and duties, of individual dignity and freedom, ideas inherent in the air which Occidental peoples breathed, were alien to Russia. "The history of other nations is a story of their emancipation. Russian history is the development of serfdom and of autocracy." How could Russia, a nation without any contributions to civilization, claim a mission? Russia must first break her isolation, learn from Europe, vitalize her faith by contact with the Western church, join the common stream of European unity, for which the Catholic Middle Ages seemed to him to set a model.

Naturally, Chaadayev fully approved Peter's reforms. "Peter

the Great found only a clean slate. With his powerful hand he
wrote on it the words: Europe and the West. Since then we
have belonged to Europe and the West." Chaadayev never abandoned his conviction that Russia must join the West. He never
doubted Europe's leadership. He never idealized Russia's weaknesses, nor did he overestimate her strength. At the beginning
of the Crimean War, he advised the Russians to sue for peace
as soon as possible—he did not share the general belief in his
country's victory.

But then he changed his evaluation of Russia's role and possibilities. The very fact of her isolation and backwardness might
allow her, in learning from Europe, to avoid the mistakes of
Europe and, in inheriting the whole experience of the West,
to improve upon it. Because she was virgin soil, without a past
and without spiritual traditions, Russia enjoyed the freedom of
judging and choosing without prejudice. She might become, he
wrote on January 15, 1845, "the true divine people of modern
times." She would answer all the questions which disrupt Europe
and solve the riddle of history—not through time-consuming and
painstaking research, but through a powerful *élan* which in a
sudden burst would carry her to a height never reached before.
"The day will come when she will occupy in the moral life of
Europe the same place which she has now achieved in its
political life. She has lived so long in isolation because all that
is great matures in solitude and silence."

In this faith Chaadayev was at one with the Slavophiles; in
every other respect he and they disagreed completely. The Slavophiles idealized the Russian past and saw the only hope of salvation in a return to it. They found Europe infinitely inferior
to Russia in its past development, in full decay in its present
state. They condemned Peter the Great for having exposed the
Russian people to the influence of an alien world. They rejected
his reforms as artificial and the St. Petersburg government as
soulless and separated from the people, which to them was the
only true source of national strength. They called upon the Russian educated classes to return to their people and its faith.

However, with all their hostility to European thought, they

were deeply influenced by it. When they opposed the true
organic community of early Russian society to the party strife
and commercialism of modern European civilization, they were
following in the wake of German romanticism. Herder was the
first to draw, under Rousseau's influence, a picture of a primitive,
peaceful Slav "democracy," an idyll of rural freedom and harmonious living, and to prophesy (though vaguely and briefly)
a great future for Slavdom. Of the dawn of this Slav day in
history, the Slavophiles were deeply convinced. They turned
European romantic thought against Europe: Europe's romantic
dreams seemed to them capable of realization in Russia alone.

Fichte regarded the Germans as the *Urvolk* and pointed with
pride to the supposed originality of the German language. To
the Slavophiles, Russia appeared as the *Urvolk* endowed with an
incomparable language. Russia must emphasize her own kind
and identity and develop an independent civilization on a strictly
national basis. Only by becoming herself could Russia become
creative. She must accomplish this task for the sake of mankind.
Ivan Vasilyevich Kireyevsky wrote in 1829 that the Occident had
finished its role and that Russia must take over the torch and
become the capital of civilization. "When all these goods will
be ours, we shall divide them with Europe and will repay it our
debt one hundred times."

The Slavophiles opposed the court and government of St.
Petersburg because they were not Russian and national enough.
And in their opposition to the government the early Slavophiles
were, in their own way, "democrats." They were not uncritical
of the Russia of their day. Khomyakov, a famous conversation-
alist and a sincere humanitarian, fought valiantly for free spiritual development and for the emancipation of the serfs with an
allotment of land. The Slavophiles held a deep faith in the dark
masses; some of them even dressed like peasants and, as the
Teutschtümler did in neighboring Germany, appeared in society
in fantastic costumes which to them resuscitated the cherished
customs of ancient Russia. With the lag of a century, Slavophile
Russian intellectuals idealized nature, the peasant, and rural life
as the physiocrats and Rousseau had done so long before. (In

a similar way, and with the same lag, twentieth century Russia
was to idealize progress through technology and the industrial
worker, as Europe had done in the nineteenth century.)

Europe was the creation of Roman and Teuton conquests, of
Catholic rationalism and Protestant individualism. All these elements led to internal strife, to the disintegration of community,
to the decay of faith by doubt. But Russia, the Slavophiles
believed, was an organic growth permeated by the feeling of
unity and spiritual integrity, therefore not threatened by any
fundamental division.

With this unity of faith, Russia did not need the legal and
formalistic safeguards of European democracy: she possessed a
true democracy. Decisions by majority were, according to Khomyakov, only the "expression of a clumsy material superiority";
the Russian traditional ideal was decision by unanimity, the
"expression of a high moral unity." "Not private, wavering, and
arbitrary conceptions which by nature tend to dissension, were
the foundation of opinion [in the Russian tradition] but the
ancient customs—the same for all the Russians, and the divine
law—the same for all the Orthodox."

The ideal of a true community seemed to the Slavophiles
realized in the Russian commune, the agrarian *mir* and the industrial *artel*—communities based on the Russian faith of
brotherhood. Legal guarantees were needed in states founded
upon   conquest and threatened by the conflict of classes and
races; they were superfluous in a Russia with harmony of classes
and friendship of races. By her own nature Russia could not build
a society like the West, torn by dissensions and disfigured by
shortcomings. Russia must become the most perfect society—or
she cannot exist at all. Though the few critical minds among the
early Slavophiles were painfully aware how far from perfect
Russia actually was, they were ready to take the undisputed
"fundamental" perfection of Russia for an actuality. They compared the idea of Russia, as they constructed it, with Europe's
reality, and arrived, naturally enough, at self-complimentary
conclusions.

The Slavophiles regarded European power politics as the

heritage of greedy and conquest-bound Rome. But for Russia power was not a goal or a proud right, as for other nations; it was a burden and a duty, a means to a high end. For Russia had no desire to rule, but to serve. Hers was a terrifying responsibility for the spiritual and social destiny of mankind. Russian tradition, in the opinion of the Slavophiles, was not narrowly nationalistic; it was, as Dostoevsky later claimed in his famous speech on Pushkin, panhuman.

Dostoevsky's oration is like an echo of Khomyakov's words: "When the Russians find themselves, they will gain such a clear understanding of the whole world that even the Germans can't comprehend it." The Slavophiles found the Russian spirit embodied in the Russian faith. They did not wish, as did the government of St. Petersburg, to make religion subservient to the interests of the Russian state; they wished to promote the triumph of the true faith with the help of Russia, its foremost servant. They found the spirit of the Orthodox faith expressed in the verse of the liturgy: "Let us love one another so that we confess with one common thought the Father, the Son, and the Holy Spirit." In this spirit of unity the Russian church alone realized the identity of liberty and unity and, thereby, true society. The Russian church alone. For Catholicism sacrificed liberty to unity and led to despotism; Protestantism sacrificed unity to liberty and led to anarchism.

The Slavophiles regarded themselves as conservatives. But the revolutionary implications of their doctrine were suspected by a Russian diplomat, Prince Ivan Sergeyevich Gagarin, the cousin of Yury Fedorovich Samarin, Khomyakov's foremost disciple. Gagarin joined the Catholic church, became a Jesuit priest, and attacked Slavophilism in his pamphlet "La Russie, sera-t-elle catholique?" (1856). To him, it appeared as *la formule russe nationale de l'idée révolutionnaire,* because of its identification of national passions and political interests with religion. He wrote of the Slavophiles:

In their domestic policy they wish to establish the most complete religious, political, and national uniformity. In their foreign policy, they wish to fuse all Orthodox Christians of whatever nationality, and all Slavs of whatever religion, in a great Slav and Orthodox empire. These strange Christians are above all preoccupied with the hegemony which their church could exercise in the world. I doubt that the revolutionaries of the Occident had ever proposed anything better suited to act upon the masses.

For Khomyakov, Russian leadership was mainly spiritual: Russia was chosen because she was poor and humble, simple as a child, self-sacrificing as a lover. Soon this lofty message of salvation and service was used to justify expansion and conquest, called protection of the common faith and liberation of the kindred.

In 1838 Mikhail Petrovich Pogodin, professor of Russian history at the University of Moscow, foresaw (in his *History* written for the later Czar Alexander II) a Russia which would soon count one hundred million inhabitants. With the other Slavs, who in spite of their current political separation were by race and language one with Russia, the immense empire would represent one-ninth of mankind.

Is not the political fate of Europe, and therefore of the world, in our hands? Emperor Nicholas, quietly sitting in Tsarskoye Selo, is nearer the realization of Charles V and Napoleon's dream of a universal empire than the two ever were even at the zenith of their fame. But another and more desirable honor awaits Russia. The time of European nations is past, their strength runs out. They can produce nothing higher in religion, law, science, or art, nor have they carried mankind to its moral goal. Now the future belongs to the Slavs who will serve mankind. Russia, as the representative of the Slav race, will fuse ancient and modern civilization, reconcile heart and head, establish everywhere law and peace, and prove that mankind's goal is not only liberty, art, and science, or industry and wealth, but something higher—the true enlightenment in the spirit of Christianity, the guidance by God's word which is assurance of all happiness.

In 1840, when Pogodin returned from an official mission to Austria, he predicted the rise of a Slavonic empire from the Pacific to the Adriatic, a realm without equal in history, which would command the rest of the world. During the Crimean War, when Russia seemed isolated and the whole of Europe (with the exception of Prussia) united against her, he reiterated his program. Russia's only reliable allies, he insisted, were the Austrian and Balkan Slavs. Russia must unite them into a Danubian federation with Constantinople as the capital, not out of ambition or territorial greed, but because such a development was inevitable. Greece and Hungary, Rumania and Asiatic Turkey, though not Slavic, would join for geographical reasons; the federation would allow them self-government while granting them protection and strength. Such a plan presupposed a conciliation of the two leading Slav nations, Russia and Poland. Pogodin demanded a united Poland federated with Russia. Poland would regain her Prussian and Austrian lands but would have to renounce her eastern provinces with their Russian majority. Thus both nations would profit: Poland could securely exist only in a Slav federation under Russian protection; Russia could securely develop behind a continuous wall of friendly Slavic states. (This, one will remember, was written in 1840.)

The Polish question was the major obstacle to the Pan-Slavic projects of the nineteenth century; it was also a focal point in Russia's relations with Europe. Most Russians saw the Poles as the spearhead of Western aggression, as renegades to Slavdom and the true faith. Tyutchev, who held out hope for the Catholic Czechs because of their Hussitism, called the Poles Judas "honored by the kiss" of Slavdom's enemies.

Among the Poles there were always some who, for reasons of *Realpolitik*, looked for association with Russia. In the middle of the century, Count Alexander Wielopolski followed Stanislaw Staszic's advice to the Poles: "Unite with the Russians and educate yourselves." Half a century later, Roman Dmowski, the leader of the rightist nationalists, focused his book *Niemcy, Rossya i kwestija polska* (The Germans, Russia and the Polish Question, [1908]) on the danger from Germany. He was even ready to trade Poland's eastern borderlands for a firmer grip on the Vistula and the Baltic, which Poland should regain from the Germans. But most Poles contrasted the Russian tradition of autocracy with the Polish concept of liberty. There was a Slav

civilization, they believed, and a Slav mission outside Russia—
not aggressive and semi-Asiatic but peaceful and European. Of
all the Slavs, the Poles had suffered most and had served European civilization best. Were they not to lead the small Slav nations who were threatened by Russia's expansion just as much
as the other European peoples?

Some European liberals, among them Mazzini, proposed a
federation of the smaller Slav nations as a barrier against both
German and Russian expansion. Austrian Slavs hoped to convert
the monarchy into a predominantly Slav state, the center of a
free and European Slav civilization. The Slovene scholar Bar-
tholomäus Kopitar and the Czech historian Palacký favored the
plan, and the Slav Congress in 1848 was called at Prague to promote it; but the pro-Magyar policy of the Habsburgs destroyed
it in 1867. The same year a Slavic Congress was held in Moscow;
now the Czechs led the pilgrimage to Moscow, but the Poles
were absent.

But to some Russians the faith seemed of greater importance
than "the call of the blood," Constantinople more essential than
Cracow or Prague. Three months before the outbreak of the
Revolution of 1917, the Russian prime minister promised Russia
would realize in World War I "the immemorial and sacred dream
of the Russian people," the possession of Constantinople. Four
times in the nineteenth century Russian armies had approached
Constantinople without attaining the goal. When they entered
Bulgaria in 1811, Napoleon planned his campaign of 1812 not
only to "solve" the Polish question, but also to "protect" Constantinople, "the key to world rule."

Germany's unification seemed to the Russian Pan-Slavists to
hasten the inevitable struggle between Europe and Russia, centering on Constantinople. Liberal and radical Germans were
frankly opposed to Russia. During the Crimean War, Marx
sharply criticized the British for their reluctant halfheartedness
in fighting the Russians. Ferdinand Lassalle approved Karl Rod-
bertus-Jagetzow's hopes of seeing Germany inherit Turkey and
German soldiers guard the Bosporus.

Nikolai Yakovlevich Danilevsky, in his *Russia and Europe*

(1871), anticipated Spengler's interpretation of history and his apocalyptic visions. He predicted a federation under Russian leadership as the outcome of a great and long war between Europe and Russia. The compound would consist of Russia (including Galicia, northern Bukovina and Carpatho-Ukraine), Yugoslavia (including Istria and Trieste), Rumania, Czechoslovakia, Hungary, Bulgaria, Greece, Constantinople, and parts of Asiatic Turkey. Like most Russian nationalists (differing therein from the Germans), he cloaked his call for conquest in the language of peace and love—according to him, two typically Slav qualities. Dostoevsky and Fyodor Ivanovich Tyutchev (1803-1875) enthusiastically supported this concept with the fullness of their hearts and the might of their words.

Tyutchev, whom Turgenev and Tolstoy recognized as the greatest living poet of the day, spent twenty years abroad as a Russian diplomat. His two wives were foreigners. Though he wrote some of the most beautiful of Russian poems, he spoke French and wrote his political articles in that language. (Samarin thought that this very remoteness from Russian, "combined with his deep knowledge of French and German, made him discover in the Russian language resources and finesses of expression none before him had realized.") In 1849 he visualized the apocalyptic struggle between Europe and Russia.

The Occident is dying, everything crumbles, everything collapses in the general conflagration, the Europe of Charlemagne as well as the Europe of the treaties of 1815, the Roman papacy, and all the thrones of the Occident, Catholicism, and Protestantism, faith long since lost and reason reduced to absurdity. Above this vast shipwreck, appears, like an Ark of the Covenant, the Russian Empire, more vast than ever.

When Russia had organized eastern Europe, she would "rebuild the true empire of the East of which the first—that of Byzantium —was only a faint and imperfect shadow."

Constantinople, the city of the czars, as the Russians call it, was the goal of Tyutchev's hopes; with its possession the chosen people of Russia could establish world order. Like Dante,

Tyutchev dreamed of a universal monarchy; it could not center in the pagan capital, but only in Constantinople, where the seat of empire was transferred when it was Christianized. Russia would restore the definitive Christian Empire while the Occident, through the Papacy, Reformation, and Revolution, was ever declining. "The Russian people," Tyutchev wrote, "is Christian not only through the Orthodoxy of its faith, but by something more intimate. It is Christian by that faculty of renunciation and sacrifice which is the foundation of its moral nature." His poems evoked this Russia:

> These poor villages,
> this sterile nature
> homeland of patience,
> land of the Russian people!
> The proud glance of the foreigner
> can neither see nor observe
> that which pierces through and shines hidden
> in its humble nakedness.
> The king of heaven under the guise of a serf
> has traversed and blessed thee,
> Thee my native land,
> bowed down by the weight of the cross.

With daring faith Tyutchev outlined the future. After the conquest of Constantinople, the new empire would take under its protection the old imperial lands of Italy and Germany and reunite the churches: the Orthodox emperor in Constantinople would protect Rome. Moscow, Rome, and Constantinople would be the three capitals of an empire embracing the lands from the Nile to the Neva, from the Elbe to China, from the Volga to the Euphrates, from the Ganges to the Danube. And this Russian Empire would last forever. Tyutchev wrote to Chaadayev:

But it will be a Russia very different from what she is at present. She will have become herself, and yet, she will be associated with so many other elements which will complement and transform her that her very name will be changed. It will no longer be an empire, it will be a world.

To that end, however, the Russian government must become more national and build closer ties with the people. Tyutchev, himself a government censor at the time, stressed the necessity for the government to create a live public opinion. Prohibitive censorship was insufficient; a conscious directing of the minds was necessary. Only with the help of awakened popular forces would the government accomplish its task. The more national the Russian autocracy grew, the more autocratic would become the nation. This Russian absolutism based upon faith would differ from Western absolutism; it would be a moral force, while Western absolutism was the negation of morality.

Similar apocalyptic visions haunted Leontyev who, like Tyutchev, spent his formative years as a diplomat abroad (in the Near East). He shared Tyutchev's faith in Russia's mission and his hatred for the European bourgeois. But he was no Slavophile, nor a Christian like Khomyakov or Dostoevsky. This solitary Leontyev felt, like Baudelaire, the overwhelming power of worldly beauty and the terrors of the flesh's damnation. Like Rimbaud, he wished to escape from the boredom and vulgarity of bourgeois Europe to exotic ecstasies. Like Nietzsche, he adored aristocratic values and hated the herd morale. He lived in dread of the inevitable age of the masses which would destroy civilization through equalitarianism and humanitarianism. He had no faith in the common man or in the Russian people. Neither nations nor racial missions counted for him. He believed in a universal idea, and in nations only so far as they were disciplined and served by the ideal Byzantinism. To him, Russia was not a creation of Slav originality; she owed her strength and her value to Byzantium.

Unlike the Slavophiles, Leontyev loved ancient Europe, the chivalry of the Middle Ages, the aristocracy of the Renaissance. He hated the middle class and democracy. Like Wagner and Nietzsche, he fought the nineteenth century and its liberalism. He expected a catastrophe in the twentieth century which would produce a new society,

no longer established on liberal foundations but, on the contrary, on a principle of great limitations and constraints of all kinds. It is possible that a new kind of slavery will emerge. It will probably adopt the cruelest form of domination the community could impose upon the individual and the state upon the community.

Leontyev accepted socialism because he believed that it would turn antiliberal, introduce new and higher forms of authority, discipline, and terror. Leontyev welcomed violence as long as it promoted the growth of the idea and its power.

He loved to think that liberalism had no future in Russia.

If the monarchical authority lost its absolute significance in Russia, if the people learned that they were no longer ruled by the monarch but by the representatives elected according to a voting system that is meaningless in their eyes, they would doubtless realize that they no longer had a reason to obey.

Russia seemed a poor soil for liberty.

It is no minor affair to teach our people the spirit of law; such instruction might well take a century. Unfortunately, the great events will not wait so long. Our people love and understand authority better than law. They consider a military chief more accessible and even more sympathetic than an article or a legal code. A constitution which would weaken authority in Russia would not have the time to inculcate the devotion the English have for legislation. Anyway, our people are right. Only a strong monarchical authority, limited solely by its conscience and sanctified by faith, can solve the contemporary problem which seems to us insoluble—the conciliation of capital and labor. We must draw ahead of Europe on the question of labor and we must set the example. What the West regards as a genius of destruction, must become with us a creative work. Our people need affirmative faith and material security more than they need rights and true science.

Leontyev knew that Russia had not yet found her form nor spoken her word. He wrote that the true Russian thought would at the same time be progressive and conservative, dynamic and reactionary. It would advance far in certain directions, but only with the help of a strong authority ever ready to use force.

In 1890 he wrote to Anatole Alexandrov:

Sometimes I see a Russian czar at the head of the Russian movement [of revolutionary socialism] organizing it as Emperor Constantine organized Christianity. But what does such organization mean? Nothing else than constraint, an enlightened despotism, the legitimatization of a chronic violence, applied in adroit and wise doses, a violence which exercises itself upon the personal will of the citizens. It is hardly probable that one could organize this new and rather complex slavery and make it last without a mystic faith. If after Russia's annexation of Constantinople an extraordinary concentration of the Orthodox ecclesiastic bureaucracy should coincide with the development of the mystic faith, and with the inevitable workers' movement, one could guarantee for a long time the political and economic bases of the state.

Here he was, in 1890, a Russian autocrat who would organize world socialism from Constantinople, with the blessing of the Orthodox church, in the name of economic and political stability, with the means of traditional despotism.

Leontyev had no use for the western Slavs, who (the Czechs, particularly) seemed lost beyond hope to middle-class democracy. Nor did he wish to "liberate" the Balkan Slavs; he praised the Turkish "yoke" for protecting them from Europeanization. He loved the Turks and Islam.

The greatest of the Russian Westernizers was Belinsky. But even he paid tribute to that enchantment with "historical necessity" which has cast its spell over much German and Russian thought.

In 1837 he and Bakunin discovered Hegel's "rationality of actuality."

In the course of the summer we read Hegel together and a new world opened before us—might is right and right is might! No, I cannot describe to you with what emotion I heard these words—it was a liberation. I understood the idea of the fall of the empires, the legitimacy of conquests; I understood that there is no wild material force, no rule of the bayonet and of the sword, no arbitrariness, no contingency—and my worry for the fate of mankind was ended and the significance of my fatherland appeared to me in a new shape. The word "reality" became for me synonymous with the word God.

Man can live: everything in him, every moment of his life is great, true, and sane.

At that time he wrote in a review of an article celebrating the Battle of Borodino:

The word "czar" embodies miraculously the consciousness of the Russian people; it is filled for them with poetry and secret meaning. It is no accident but most rational necessity which reveals itself in the history of the Russian people. Its course is opposed to that of Europe. With us, government always marched ahead of the people and was always their guiding star on the road to high destiny.

Yet a year later Belinsky regretted the article: his thought had turned from German historicism to French individualism.

Belinsky died young, exhausted by overwork, poverty, and disease. He left volumes of articles and critical essays, a unique enterprise of national education. More than anyone else, he invigorated the Russian mind and brought it to maturity. He loved freedom of thought and hated all constraints which limited it. He was convinced that Russia's malady was rooted in

the lack of personal independence. As a consequence, the government did not respect the individual and the individual did not oppose the government. To the cynicism of the authority corresponded the forbearance of the people. Russia's future will be a great danger to Europe and full of misfortune to herself if there is no emancipation of individual rights. One century more of despotism will destroy all the good qualities of the Russian people.

In his years of maturity, Belinsky never subordinated ethical considerations to the "demands" of history. No end could justify means which sacrificed the individual or the present. He, almost alone in Russia, insisted on the constructive importance of the middle class for the intellectual and political development of Russia. For Russia needed, not faith nor mysticism, but respect for laws and individual rights. He could have echoed the words which the Decembrist Nikita Mikhailovich Muravyev wrote in criticism of Karamzin's history:

Woe to the land where all are unanimous. Can one expect there cultural progress? There the intellectual forces are dormant; there no value is placed on truth, which, like glory, must be acquired by effort and constant labor. Who dares to establish order by violence? Violent means are illegal as well as pernicious; for higher policy and higher morality are one and the same.

A few months before his death, in a famous letter to Gogol, Belinsky stressed that the Russian people must wake up to the sentiment of human dignity, lost for so many centuries in the mud; it needs rights and laws in accord with justice and common sense.

Belinsky's revolutionary friends, Bakunin and Herzen, who survived him by about twenty-five years, paid a much heavier tribute to Russian messianism. Mikhail Bakunin left Russia in 1842. Two years later, he published in Germany (under a French pseudonym) an article, "The Reaction in Germany," full of apocalyptic presentiments.

Everyone whose vital organs are not paralyzed looks with trembling expectation to the approaching future which will utter the word of salvation. Even in Russia, in that immense and snow-covered empire of which we know so little and which is perhaps destined to a great future, dark storm clouds are gathering. The air is sultry, it is heavy with storms. . . . The love of destruction is also a creative lust.

In 1847 Herzen followed Bakunin to Europe. He went with a mystical faith in the forthcoming revolution and in the West as its messenger. But the events of 1848 disenchanted him: Europe did not live up to his revolutionary expectations. "Despotism or socialism—there is no other alternative," he wrote in 1854, anticipating the famous dilemma, "fascism or communism." "Europe has shown a surprising incapacity for social revolution. We believe that Russia is not so incapable, and in this we are at one with the Slavophiles." Despairing of Europe and despising liberalism—"Russia will never be the *juste milieu*"—Herzen succumbed to the lure of Russian messianism. And so did Bakunin. The conflict between him and Marx which destroyed the International Working Men's Association sprang partly from the clash between Pan-Slavic messianism and German contempt for the Slavs. At the Slavic Congress in Prague in 1848, Bakunin, the only Russian there, demanded a great Slavic federation under the leadership of Russia, while the other Slavs looked to the West and to liberalism for guidance.

Imprisoned after the congress and extradited to Russia, Bakunin, the revolutionary anarchist, wrote in prison in 1851 a confession to the czar. A repentent sinner, he implored the czar to become a truly national leader, the head of the Pan-Slavic movement.

In spite of my democratic convictions, I have worshipped you profoundly in the last years, as it were against my will. Not I alone but many others, Poles and Europeans in general, have understood, like myself, that you are the only one among the ruling heads of the time who has preserved his faith in his imperial calling.

In Bakunin's opinion a convinced autocrat compared favorably with the feeble liberals of Europe. "There, wherever you turn, you see decadence, unbelief and the moral corruption which stems from unbelief." Bakunin hoped Emperor Nicholas would accept his concepts of a popular dictatorship.

Russia needs a strong dictatorial power which concerns itself with the elevation and enlightenment of the masses, a power which is free in tendency and spirit but without parliamentary form, a power which prints books of a free content without introducing the freedom of the press, a power which is surrounded, advised, supported, by the free cooperation of like-minded men, but which is not limited by anybody or anything.

Bakunin was sent to Siberia, in 1857, where he met General Nikolai Muravyev-Amursky, one of the great Russian empire builders who had taken from China the left bank of the Amur and the region of the Ussuri River. In a long letter to Herzen, written from Irkutsk on November 17, 1860, Bakunin described his enthusiasm for Muravyev. "He is unconditionally one of us and Russia may expect her salvation from him." The imperial governor general and the anarchist exile shared a contempt for parliamentary constitutions and for liberal intellectuals. Muravyev hoped that "the peasants' ax will set St. Petersburg right and will make possible there that national dictatorship which alone can save Russia. This dictatorship is also necessary to establish Russia's power in Europe and to turn that power to the liberation of the Slavs from Austria and Turkey." Bakunin and Muravyev wished to transform the Germanized court of St. Petersburg into a national dictatorship supported by the masses. They would have gladly followed a Romanov if he would change from a St. Petersburg emperor into a national czar.

Herzen never followed Bakunin's wild ecstasies. For twenty years, almost until his last days, his mind was a battlefield where Russia and Europe, hope and despair, realistic criticism and messianic intoxication were struggling. It seemed to him that Europe was unable to realize the ideal; that the bourgeoisie was the final form of European civilization; that European life was settling down after many storms into stillness. So Herzen looked outside Europe—and found two countries vigorously expanding and full of vitality: America and Russia. Russian peasants, like American settlers, cleared immense uninhabited spaces and turned them to agricultural life. But

America presents no new element; it is a further development of Protestant Europe, set free from its historic past, and put under different conditions of life. The grand idea developed [there] is purely Anglo-Saxon, the idea of self-government, that is, of a strong people with a weak government, the home rule of every tract of land without centralization, without bureaucracy, held together by an inner moral unity.

Russia, to the contrary, was not a continuation of Western Europe, but a quite special world, free from obligations to Europe's past. True, Russia's present was dark. But, hoped Herzen:

In the natural simplicity of our peasant life, in our uncertain and unsettled economic and judicial conceptions, in our vague sense of property, in our lack of a strong middle class, and in our extraordinary capacity for assimilating foreign ideas, we have an advantage over nations that are fully organized and exhausted.

Herzen, sharing the illusion of the Slavophiles, transformed actual weaknesses hopefully into potential national assets, and told the Europeans:

We share your doubts, but your faith does not inspire us. We do not understand your attachment to the heritage of your forefathers. We are too downtrodden, too unhappy, to be satisfied with half-freedom. You are restrained by scruples, you are held back by mental reservations. We have neither reservations nor scruples. We only lack strength.

They now have that strength. The new Pan-Slavism of 1948 is not guided by the western and liberal ideas of 1848 as the Pan-Slav Congress of Prague then was. The centenary did see Bakunin's wild dream of 1848 fulfilled in its essentials. Much more than the cause of Russia and Orthodoxy in the nineteenth century, or of Spain and Catholicism in the sixteenth century, the causes of Russia and communism have become indistinguishably one. World-revolutionary communism has fused with Russian messianic nationalism. One strengthens the other in the acceptance of autocracy, in the distrust of the West, in the faith that Russia alone is the bearer of the true religion and the only good social order, in the certainty that a hostile world will finally be saved from conflicts and chaos by Russia's faith and harmony.

THE CHALLENGE OF OLD MYTHS AND
NEW TRENDS

In this obscure, tormented, and already vacillating world, salvation can come only from the truth of Rome, and from Rome will it come.—MUSSOLINI, *Scritti e Discorsi,* viii, 140.

Fascism wants to remake, not the forms of human life, but its content: man, character, faith.—*Enciclopedia Italiana,* XIV, p. 848.

The victory of the proletarian revolution is a victory of the new morality—the morality of the communist society. Our morality is subordinated to the interests of the class struggle of the proletariat. From the point of view of the communist morality, ethical or moral can be only what forms a means to annihilate the old world, the world of exploitation, and what strengthens the new socialist constitution.—*Kratki Filosofski Slovar,* ed. by P. Rosenbaum and P. Yudin, 2nd ed. (Moscow: Politizdat of the Central Committee of the All-Soviet Communist Party, 1940), p. 177.

VIII

IMPERIALISM

IMPERIALISM, like nationalism or religion, presents many facets: will to power and magic superstition, lofty ideals and economic exploitation. For many centuries the main motivating force behind empire has been an idea—perhaps the most influential single idea for two thousand years—the ordering of human society through unified dominion and common civilization. In the twentieth century, the age of world wars, the idea of world dominion and world mission has served again as an inspiration, first for the builders of the Soviet Union, and then, in imitation and counteraction, for the artisans of the millenium of the German Reich. In each case the victory of one idea was intended to mold humanity into a firmly knit uniformity assuring peace and stability. The Holy Roman Empire of the German nation and the Russian heritage of the Byzantine and Mongolian empires faced each other. They drew their inspiration and their power of attraction from men's hopes and aspirations for a world order. They revived ancient and powerful trends of human thought, though in perverted form: in the past the imperial idea has always rested on Stoic and Christian foundations, before which all men, irrespective of class or race, were equal.

Among the peoples of antiquity, the Athenians were distinguished by their sense of political liberty and their hatred of authoritarian despotism, their delight in rational thought, and their recognition of universal ethical standards.[1] While their classical thinkers still regarded the differences between Greeks and barbarians as fundamental and reserved the possibility of rational thought and liberty to the Greeks alone, Aristotle's pupil,

119

Alexander, disregarding the admonitions of his teacher, set out to unite all men in a new community of civilization. Plutarch has pointed out that Alexander was the first to vitalize and realize the Stoic doctrine that we should consider all men to be of one community and of one order common to all.

For Alexander did not follow Aristotle's advice to have regard for the Greeks as friends and kindred, but to conduct himself towards other peoples as though they were plants or animals; for to do so would have been to cumber his leadership with numerous battles and banishments and festering seditions. But as he believed that he came as a mediator for the whole world, he brought together in one body all men everywhere, uniting and mixing in one great loving cup, as it were, men's lives, characters, marriages, the very habits of life. He bade them all consider as their fatherland the whole inhabited earth, as akin to them all good men; clothing and food, marriage and manner of life they were to regard as common to all, being blended into one by ties of blood and children.[2]

Out of the Stoic philosophy grew the Roman imperial idea. The Stoic philosophy enriched the Latin language with the new word *humanitas,* an individual norm by which man might cultivate the human in him, and a universal norm, the consciousness of the human quality common to all human beings. The "one world" seemed nearer realization than ever since: the whole earth seemed destined to become one city, with a common civilization which all shared and to which all contributed, and with a common rational law superseding all previous tribal differentiations of customs and rights. Cicero summed up the underlying idea:

Those who say that we should consider our fellow countrymen but not foreigners, violate the common humanity: should that perish, then kindness, generosity, goodness and justice could be utterly destroyed. Those who destroy these things must be regarded as offenders against the immortal gods. For they overthrow the human society which God himself has established. The strongest bond of this society is the conviction that it is more contrary to nature to rob one's fellow men out of self-interest than to suffer any conceivable loss, whether of property or person or even of one's very soul, so long as such losses do not involve violation of justice. For justice is the one supreme mistress and queen of all other virtues.

Pliny, in his panegyric of Emperor Trajan, summed up the function of the empire:

> To enjoy the protection of the Roman empire is a blessing indeed for all the provinces, especially under our present emperor. For he has organized a system whereby the wealth of the world can be distributed to any part of the earth, as occasional need may demand. He regards the distant tribe across the sea as part of the people of the Rome, equally to be protected and nurtured. He knits East and West together by an interchange of goods, so that all peoples may know the assets and deficiencies of each and understand how much better it is to serve a single ruler than to be the slaves of discord masquerading as freedom. For where each people selfishly keeps to itself its own goods, each bears the burden of its own disasters. But where all share and share alike, no one suffers from private misfortunes, while every one's good fortune is enjoyed by all.

At the same time, imperial Rome, in a tolerant and understanding way, brought to her provinces, along with the security of law, the right to diversity.

In the then prevailing state of technology, a universal empire assuring peace and justice to all was impossible of achievement; great distances could not be overcome, and the adaptation of democracy to large masses and vast territory by a representative and federal system was not envisaged. Outside the empire and within, barbarian masses remained culturally unintegrated. But in spite of all its imperfections, the empire remained for many centuries the great political inspiration of mankind, the promise to which men looked back longingly and which they strove to rebuild to escape self-annihilation by eternal combat. Even in its full decay, after the sack of Rome by the Goths, a Gaul, Claudius Rutilius Namatianus, sang its praise in unforgettable words:

> Thou hast made a common fatherland for different nations;
> Useful it was for the unjust, to be caught under thy domination.
> While thou offerest to the vanquished the community of thine own law,
> Thou hast turned into one state what had been previously the globe.[3]

The Roman Empire was destroyed by Germanic tribes who established their rule over most of the known earth. The Germans began to regard themselves as the heirs of Rome. Only in the East did the legitimate Roman Empire continue. However, in the West the governors could not replace the empire in its mission because they lacked the only acceptable foundation of civilization, a universal moral law. To use the words of a modern German historian: "The German way was not the need for salvation, which was unknown to them. Nor was it the quest for a moral law; that they carried within them as will to courageous self-assertion and protection of tribal honor." [4] The Visigoth Ataulf, Alaric's successor,

at first ardently desired to blot out the Roman name and to make all the Roman territory in fact as well as in name a Gothic empire, so that, to use the popular expression, *Gothia* should take the place of *Romania*. Having discovered from long experience that the Goths, because of their unbridled barbarism, were utterly incapable of obeying laws, and yet believing that the state ought not to be deprived of laws without which a state is not a state, he chose to seek for himself at least the glory of restoring and increasing the renown of the Roman name, wishing to be looked upon by posterity as the restorer of the Roman Empire, since he could not be its transformer.[5]

Thereafter, all efforts at civilizing the Germans were undertaken by princes who claimed to be heirs of Roman imperialism and of its civilizing mission. After a long period of "darkness," when civilization continued only in the East, Charlemagne, as a conscious renovator of universal civilization, renewed the Roman Empire in the West and subdued the Germanic Saxons to Roman civilization.[6] When after his death the empire was divided and the seeds sown for the growth of a parochial instead of a universal loyalty, Florus Lugdunensis lamented in his *Querela de divisione imperii* [7] the end of unity which left *pro regno fragmina regni*, an order fragmentary not only in the political, but also in the spiritual sense.

This fragmentary order was never accepted by the thought of the Middle Ages, which continued to regard the empire as the only legitimate order and found its supreme voice in Dante's faith in the oneness of the *civilitas humani generis*. Shortly afterward, however, the world center shifted from the ancient heart of the empire to its furthest outskirts, Spain and England. There a new imperialism grew up, directed no longer primarily to the past hallowed by history, but to the future and the unknown, fixed with a new spirit of adventure on lands far beyond the dreams of any Roman emperor. Charles V, the Habsburg prince who became king of Spain, was the last emperor in the traditional sense,[8] as his grandfather, Maximilian of Germany, had been the last knight. But the traditional concept of empire became untenable. With the widening *orbis terrarum* distance seemed to erect insuperable barriers; with the revelation of great civilizations outside Christendom, the old concept of the *res publica christiana* was no longer self-evident. A new concept of imperialism emerged, empires knowing themselves definitely as parochial organizations, as only parts of the whole; and with this concept came the new phenomenon of conflicting imperialisms and empires, not as claimants for one and the same office, but as legitimate competitors within a system of balance of power. Tommaso Campanella, in his *De monarchia hispanica*, at the end of the sixteenth century still regarded Spain as a basis for an *imperium mundi* in Dante's tradition. In opposition to Machiavelli, he pleaded for the reunion of mankind in a universal spiritual and political unity. He visualized a Spanish monarchy as a great civilizing force, like Alexander the Great, mixing and assimilating all races, treating the Indians as brethren and training some of them in Spain as peasants and artisans. But before long he realized the utopian character of his hope and abandoned his confidence that Spain could embody it.

The old imperialism was irrevocably dead at the dawn of modern times; in the seventeenth century England rose as the foremost representative of the new imperialism. Though far removed from the old seats of power and civilization, she was favored in the new age by geographic and economic conditions, by the character of her people, and by the fortuitous blending of the two new forces of the age, the enthusiasm of the Reformation and the enterprise of the new commercialism. Though in the sobriety of the dawning Enlightenment, English imperialism abandoned all claims to world empire, it retained, largely through the Puritan revolution, the Stoic and Christian basis of the old imperialism. English imperialism accepted the new age of contending states. Empire could now be shared with other nations; its foundations, based on universal Christian and rational principles, were not regarded as peculiar to England— they were general human principles, destined ultimately, through a process of education, for the subject races too. The thought of England's representative thinkers in the decisive seventeenth century, of Milton and Locke, centered in the idea of liberty, individual liberty for Englishmen primarily, but human liberty, ultimately. Many Englishmen thought of seventeenth century England, the birthplace of the modern English and American traditions, as the center of a *Weltpolitik* of individual and universal liberty.[9]

Locke started his first *Treatise of Government* with the sentence which may be regarded as its very essence: "Slavery is so vile and miserable an estate of man, and so directly opposite to the generous temper and courage of our nation, that it is hardly to be conceived that an 'Englishman,' much less a 'gentleman,' should plead for it." More than one hundred years later, in the great debate in the British House of Commons on the abolition of the slave trade, on April 2, 1792, Pitt carried Milton's and Locke's ideas to their logical conclusion:

If we listen to the voice of reason and duty, some of us may live to see a reverse of that picture, from which we now turn our eyes with pain and regret. We may live to behold the natives of Africa engaged in the calm occupations of industry, in the pursuits of a just and legitimate commerce. We may behold the beams of science and philosophy breaking in upon their land. Then we may hope that even Africa shall enjoy at length those blessings which have descended so plentifully upon us in a much earlier period of the world.

The new concept of an imperialism based upon liberal ideas spread from England over the earth. This imperial expansion was not based primarily on glorified state power, but on individual initiative; though the political element was not lacking, its motivation was more economic than political. As has been contemptuously said by the theorists of totalitarian, anticapitalist imperialism, the imperialism of the eighteenth and nineteenth centuries was an imperialism of money. Money was the rational and universal means of exchange in a world of free and unlimited trade intercourse. Edward Young, in his *Imperium Pelagi,* has given to this universal harmony of commercial interchange a cosmic expression:

> Kings, merchants are in league and love;
> Earth's odours pay soft airs above,
> That o'er the teeming field prolific range.
> Planets are merchants; take, return,
> Lustre and heat; by traffic burn:
> The whole creation is one vast exchange.

This imperialism felt the restraint not only of a rational business civilization, but also of its Christian and liberal foundations. Often no more than lip service was paid them, and sometimes not even that; but the tradition was strong enough to impose moderation and to make it possible again and again for many voices to be raised and heard in ardent protest against the inhumanities and exploitation involved in nineteenth century imperialism. The self-restraint seems incredible to modern totalitarians who regard only power and not the moral and traditional limitations of power. Though Canada lay open to the vastly superior forces of her southern neighbor, her unprotected frontier sometimes tempted, yet never invited actual conquest. The German historian Treitschke failed to grasp this attitude. "Canada," he wrote, "gives the people of the United States so little uneasiness that their thoughts are much more turned towards annexing the country themselves, an enterprise to which I for one heartily wish them success." [10] Though the rich Dutch East Indies were potentially an easy prey for the British fleet, the Netherlanders but rarely felt any apprehension on this point; the Boer War, much protested in Great Britain, was followed by a complete reversal in public feeling and the election of a

Liberal government which promptly gave full self-government to the defeated Boers. Even in Germany public indignation forced the repeal of General von Trotha's order of October 2, 1904, to shoot every Herero and to fire indiscriminately on women and children; and in the summer of 1905 von Trotha was superseded by von Lindequist and his more conciliatory policy. The liberal imperialism of the nineteenth century was not only controlled by the recognized plurality of empires and by the restraining force of the acknowledged validity of universal ethical standards, above class or race, but its inner logic led to its own withering away. The process of decolonization, of increasing concessions to the independence of colonial peoples, had begun on the part of Britain, the leader in liberty, well before the outbreak of the First World War; it was resumed at its end with almost un-British thoroughness and alacrity, and it set a pattern followed by other nations, the transformation of empire of inequality into a federation of equals, assuring peace and liberty, a great aspiration, though like every historical effort, perpetually threatened by the frailty of human nature and the complexity of all political life.

While thus in the West a new form of imperialism arose in modern times, the medieval idea of world empire continued to exercise its influence in Germany and to grow stronger in Moscow, which began to regard herself in the sixteenth and seventeenth centuries as the third Rome, the heir to Byzantium and to the Roman Empire. When Constantinople, the legitimate center of world empire and the seat of the true faith of Christian Orthodoxy, fell into the hands of the infidels, the devout Russian people assumed the task of the defense and spread of the true religion against the heresies of the West. The princes of Moscow took unto themselves the title of Czar and with it the mission of continuing the work of Alexander the Great and of the Roman Empire, "to unite in one organic whole the diverse nations of the East and of the West." When the Patriarch of Moscow was installed in 1589, the charter affirmed that "because the old Rome has collapsed through the heresy of Apollinarius, and the second Rome, which is Constantinople, is now in the possession of the godless Turks, thy great kingdom, O pious Czar, is the third Rome. It surpasses with its devotion everyone else and all other Christian kingdoms are now merged in thy kingdom. Thou art the only Christian sovereign in the whole world, the master of all the Christians."

In Russia, different therein from the medieval West, the secular and the spiritual empire fused. The czar was supreme worldly ruler and at the same time supreme leader of the faith. Before his omnipotence no liberty under law nor freedom of thought was imaginable. The last traces of individual rights and social stratification were abolished under Ivan the Terrible. To unite the people into a closely knit bundle of strength and to use it as an instrument of expansion and glory, in the service of Russia's mission, autocracy seemed the most effective regime. The exacting tyranny of the state was patiently borne by the Russian people, because as its end beckoned the promise of a perfect order according to the true faith.

In Germany it was not the princely power, hallowed by the church and leaning upon the army, but poets and dreamers who kept the vision of world empire and consciousness of world mission alive. While the Renaissance never even touched Russia, which remained entirely outside its influences, and while it produced new political and social forms in the West, it helped in Germany to preserve and to deepen the medieval *Reich* concept. The German humanists constructed a glorious past for the people, not only independent of, but superior to, Roman Christianity. The antiquity of the Germanic tribes and their victorious migration throughout the ancient world were discovered. The claim to dominion was supported not only historically, but also ethically. The equation of German and good, of alien and evil, led to an exuberance that, in the midst of an ill defined political reality of historically limitless horizons, fused national strength and world empire. In the words of a twentieth century German historian, "The German people, the noblest of the world, chosen by God for the Imperial dignity, the Empire radiant with supernatural splendor, destined for the redemption of mankind from strife and sin, and therefore the necessity of

Germanizing the whole world, including the Romance peoples, under the supremacy of the German Emperor—these are the extravagant and exuberant fantasies which on the threshold of modern times cling to the idea of the Reich." [11]

The last great artistic expression, half melancholy and half satirical, of this dream of the future lordship of the world, is found in the fourth chapter of the third book of Grimmelshausen's *Simplicissimus,* the masterpiece of German seventeenth century prose. There a fool who thinks himself Jupiter speaks of the "German hero" who will come and "conquer the whole world, and make an end of all the godless." He will ask his enemies to submit, and if they refuse, he will execute those whom Hitler and other totalitarians call "warmongers," because they oppose plans of "historical necessity" and prevent the people's submission. The foreign princes he will divide into three classes: the wicked ones he will punish; those who are ready to live as commoners under German overlordship he will allow to do so; those, however, who are too proud for that, he will send to Asia. A perpetual peace will then reign between all nations and, as Grimmelshausen goes on, "the German people's standard of living shall be more plentiful and comfortable than is now the life and household of a king." The German hero will not only reorder the world but also reform all religions into one, by calling together all the theologians and, if they refuse to listen to him, forcing them by means of hunger and the gallows to abandon their "stiff-necked false doctrines. When Unity is achieved he will proclaim a great festival and declare to the whole world his purified religion; and whosoever opposes it, him he will torment with pitch and sulphur." A fantastic picture indeed, yet by the middle of the twentieth century the vision of the "fool" of three centuries ago—forceful unification of the earth by the dynamic expansion of a totalitarian doctrine which will be proclaimed as the new world religion—seems less fantastic.

But the Enlightenment of the eighteenth century seemed to dispel these visions and dreams. Peter the Great tried to force "the third Rome" into the communion of secular Europe, an attempt for which the Slavophiles could never forgive him. The rationalism and humanism of the West penetrated to Germany in a broad stream and brought about an unprecedented flowering of the German mind in philosophy, literature, and music, and for a time established a German world leadership among the Western nations in a common recognition of the universal standards of Stoic and Christian civilization. When at the end of the nineteenth century, through Bismarck's unification, Germany became a strong and centralized power, Germany—like Russia and Japan during the same period—adopted the external forms of liberal imperialism. Slowly but surely, all three seemed on the road to a progressive liberalization of their constitutional life and social structure. Of the three, Germany offered by far the most advanced and Westernized aspect.

But even then, observers penetrating beneath the surface discerned the peculiar character of German imperialism. While in the Western nations, individual initiative played a great role in the development of imperialism, in Germany, in Russia, and partly in Japan the economic structure was tied much more closely to the state and its power politics. A scholarly analyst of German nationalism, Paul Joachimsen, has pointed out that "the special difficulty of German imperialism consisted in the fact that the German economy . . . entirely dependent upon the state, had become an instrument of governmental power. Thus economic expansion implied also expansion of state power in an entirely different sense than, for instance, in England." Similarly that shrewd American observer of the Second German Empire, Thorstein Veblen, stated the case of Germany in terms equally applicable to Japan, both representing what he called "dynastic" states: "What makes this German imperial establishment redoubtable, beyond comparison, is the very simple but also very grave combination of circumstances whereby the German people have acquired the use of the modern industrial arts in the highest state of efficiency," while at the same time they retained many notions and loyalties in contradiction to the West, where modern industry and science had been developed. With such a people, Veblen believed, negotiations were extremely

difficult, because any peace arrangement would to them necessarily "be an armistice terminable at will and serving as a season
of preparation to meet a deferred opportunity. For the peace-
able nations it would, in effect, be a respite and a season of
preparation for eventual submission to the Imperial rule." [13]

Thus in the twentieth century a new totalitarian imperialism
abandoned the pluralism of empires in a world of equal nations
and of diversity, and returned to the medieval conception of a
world empire based upon unity of faith. Now, at last, this vision
seemed realizable as a result of the progress in military art and
in the technique of the manipulation of the mass mind. But this
new imperialism repudiated the ethical and humanitarian foundations of empire which, since Alexander, have imposed a
restraint upon the relations between man and man, even between victors and vanquished—a restraint often not effective,
yet never fully and consciously rejected. In this respect the new
imperialism, though corresponding to the longing for world
order of antiquity and the Middle Ages, yet represented its
actual perversion.

At the beginning of the nineteenth century, Napoleon attempted to renew the empire of Charlemagne in Europe and
even that of Alexander in the world. "He believed himself capable of conquering the world, as if nothing was unattainable
for him, and no limits existed to his career on earth." [14] Napoleon
did not achieve his ambition, but the very age of nationalism
and contending imperialisms which followed created the basis
for an outwardly more unified world than has ever existed; not
only by technical discoveries, but by drawing through the effects
of liberal imperialism even the most distant peoples into the
orbit of commercial intercourse and of rational civilization, and
by establishing to an unprecedented degree an open society
all over the globe that did not impose regimented unity and
recognized the fertility of diversity.

The influence of Western imperialism aroused the peoples in
Asia, and later on in Africa, out of their lethargy. It promoted
the rise of a native intelligentsia; it spread the desire for far-
reaching reforms; it introduced for the first time the concept of

equality before law and the dignity of the individual. It caused the rise of nationalism among the native peoples; though it was authoritarian and often oppressive, it accepted the restraints imposed by Western civilization and transmitted them. Within the framework of the liberal nineteenth century society, the dispossession or transplantation of whole populations was unthinkable: for that purpose no nineteenth century imperialism was ruthless enough. Only the totalitarianism of the twentieth century reintroduced these practices of antiquity. National socialism and communist regimes expelled and shifted whole peoples, even in the heart of Europe, for real or alleged disloyalty and in the interests of the new order.

For these regimes were fundamentally different from liberal imperialism, which was based upon the recognition of an international community. Communism and national socialism established a closed society to a degree unknown before. They regarded themselves as the guardians of the only true interpretation of history, and while the national socialists claimed the "iron law of nature," the communists claimed the scientific and inescapable "dialectics of history" as the justification for their fanatical faith in the triumph of their cause. Both divided the whole of mankind into two irreconcilable camps, their own and that of the adversary who represented absolute evil; both believed that history demanded a merciless struggle between the two camps, and they had no doubt of the outcome. In this struggle there was no sympathy with human suffering, no recognition of human dignity in every individual, as far as the enemies of the cause were concerned. For them, pitiless hatred and cold-blooded liquidation seemed justified by the necessities of history. Both promised a universal new order, in which there would no longer be any revolutions or wars; but of the two, communism, rooted through Marx in the messianic expectations of the prophetic tradition and the promise of liberty of German idealistic philosophy, carried a wider appeal. Though identifying itself more and more with the Russian idea of the chosen people, with the tradition of Moscow and the third Rome, with the Slavophile hostility to Western civilization, communism invited men of all nationalities and races to share in the new faith, and held up to them a vision in which ultimately all would be equal, provided they bowed to the infallible leadership of Moscow which they were offered.

But it is more than doubtful whether world order in the twentieth century can be achieved by the imposition of unity and authority, both secular and spiritual, whether such a rule over body and soul could be acceptable, especially to Western mankind, after the experiences of the Renaissance and Reformation, of the Enlightenment and of the nineteenth century.

IX

RACIALISM

THE political and social questions involved in the differences of color and race have gained in intensity and importance in the nineteenth and twentieth centuries. Closer geographical contact, the spread of more uniform patterns of civilization and aspirations all over the earth, and especially the proclamation and propagation of the "racial" interpretation of history have emphasized a growing trend. In the political and social controversies much confusion is due to the indiscriminate interchange of three different meanings in which the word "race" is used today. The tension produced by color and race theories is responsible for some of the most fateful misinterpretations and maladjustments which threaten to create bitter conflicts and to demoralize human relations by arrogance and prejudice.

The word "race" is primarily a biological term and denotes groups of men differentiated by anatomical characteristics. None of them shows any fundamental or far-reaching differences among the races: in all essential features mankind is one and clearly differentiated from all other species of the animal world. It is only in minor secondary attributes, like shape of skull, form of nose, texture of head hair, quantity of body hair, and color of skin that there is any measurable or appreciable difference among the various racial groups. The biblical story of the common origins of the human race has not been contradicted by any modern scientific discovery.

Old and primitive superstitions have linked race and class with blood. In reality no such link exists. Medical science, in its early attempts at blood transfusion, has discovered four different types of blood; but these types are found among all races. Certain of these blood types do not mix without agglutination of the red cells. Modern medical practice has eliminated this danger by the removal of the red and white blood cells; the remaining plasma in its dried form is entirely independent from all types of blood and equally usable for all men.

Whatever the anatomical differences of various races, there is no scientific proof for any correspondence between color of skin or texture of hair and mental ability. The idea that differences of color imply differences of mental ability is comparatively recent. All civilizations originated with "colored" races, the yellow men in the Chinese river valleys, the brown men of India, Mesopotamia, and Egypt, and the swarthy men of the Mediterranean basin. Among them all the great religions of mankind were founded; their depth of religious feeling and of metaphysical thought was never surpassed in Nordic lands. Throughout the Middle Ages, Europeans and Orientals met as equals; Greek civilization was transmitted to the rising universities of the West by Arabian scholars.

Marco Polo, traveling to the Far East, was awed by the splendor of the Oriental realms. Islamic civilization, including Caucasians, Negroes in Africa, and brown men in the East Indies, has always been entirely free from any color feeling. It began to show itself only after the center of Western civilization shifted from the Mediterranean to the North Atlantic.

With the sixteenth century began a rapid progress of Western European civilization in the conquest of nature, in scientific research, and in the application of rational and humanitarian principles to the art of government. In the eighteenth and nineteenth centuries far greater progress was achieved in the North Atlantic region in these fields than in all preceding ages and civilizations. The spirit of individual liberty under law made great strides in economic prosperity and intellectual discovery possible. Equipped with the liberal methods of scientific inquiry and responsible government, the European communities, especially those bordering the North Atlantic and the North Sea, soon faced the other lands and peoples with such a superiority that by the middle of the nineteenth century the whole globe was controlled by Western man. Ancient and powerful empires, like the Chinese, Mogul, Persian and Ottoman empires, had to bow before the rising influence of the white men, a superiority based not only on scientific rationalism and technical inventiveness, but above all on a new spirit of civic responsibility, of individual initiative and of enlightened humanism.

In the middle of the nineteenth century Count Joseph Arthur de Gobineau, in his book *Essay on the Inequality of the Human Races,* proclaimed the true Nordic Germans, whom he identified with the French aristocracy, the supremely creative race. According to him the human races were unequal in creative ability; it was impossible for them to reach the same level of cultural life; he ascribed the decay of the Nordic race, which he, as a violent opponent of democratic trends, believed to be taking place in the nineteenth century, to race mixture. This theory found very few followers in France or England, but it was taken up and popularized by German scholars, propagandists, and artists like Richard Wagner, who developed a race theory based upon the premises that there is a definite hierarchy of races and that the German people (sometimes identified with the Nordic and sometimes with an "Aryan" race) represent the highest and most creative race; and that the ability of a race depended upon the "purity of its blood" and that therefore intermarriage was detrimental to civilization. This theory, widely held in Germany even before the rise to power of national socialism, became in 1933 the official fundamental doctrine of German science and of the German state. Its propaganda outside Germany served as an instrument of German aspirations. This accentuation of racial prejudice was one of the aggravating factors in the era of violent political and intellectual clashes following the rise of national socialism. It was German influence which made the racial myth an integral part of fascist movements, to which it had originally been alien.

In reality it is impossible to define any modern nation by somatic characteristics. The whole "mythical" and unscientific character of the racial theory was recognized by the leading German authorities themselves. For how many people in Germany corresponded to the "Nordic" character of blond, tall, blue-eyed, and straight-nosed humanity? Among all nations racial intermixture has gone on everywhere over a long period. Sexual attraction is common between people of different races, and even taboos and legislation have been unable to check it. Negroes and whites in the Caribbean and in the United States, Spaniards and Indians in Central and South America, Boers and Hottentots in South Africa have successfully intermingled. There exists no objective proof to show that offspring of even widely different races decrease in efficiency, intelligence, or vitality.

This insufficiency of somatic characteristics led the "racialists" to use the word "race" increasingly in the ethnical sense meaning "nation" or "people." Thereby the confusion and the propagandistic value of racial theories has been many times increased. While the Nordics represent a biological race, tall, blond-haired, and blue-eyed, the Germans or the English are not biological races but mixtures of several races; they are nations held together, not by common somatic characteristics or uniform descent, but by a common civilization and loyalty. Nor are there any Polish and Russian "races"; both are sometimes regarded as members of the same Slavonic "race," but in reality they represent nations with different civilizations and loyalties. Even Slavs are not a "race," but a linguistic group, peoples of Caucasian, Tatar, Finnish, and many other racial strains, yet speaking closely related languages.

Race can be as little identified with modern nations as with linguistic groups. The term "Aryan" does not denote any racial community, but a linguistic group, people speaking Aryan or Indo-European languages, a group including Nordics and colored people, white men and brown men. Languages and civilizations have migrated and have been imposed or accepted irrespective of any boundaries of race or color; in the seventh century Arabic became the language of all the various peoples in Syria and North Africa, while Latin was accepted by the

Iberians in Spain, the Celts in Gaul, and the complex racial mixture living in Rumania.

With the failure of somatic or any other objective characteristics, the racialists fall back upon the "racial spirit" or *Volksgeist*. Unfortunately the Nordic racial spirit is not "instinctively" shown by all men of Nordic "blood"; it even had to be forced upon Germans, and the truly Nordic Norwegians show very little of it and are predominantly dominated by the "un-Nordic," "unheroic" spirit of Western or "Jewish" liberalism. The German racialists regard what corresponds in their opinion to the presupposed mythical racial soul as *arteigen*, what is alien to the racial character as *artfremd*.

Yet the general division of mankind into several primary races, largely distinguished by color, is a fact which gained political and social importance with the growth of the "superiority" of the white race in the nineteenth century. This "superiority" did not remain unchallenged. Western civilization, fundamentally rational and liberal, regarded itself from the beginning as universal in scope and its message of liberty destined for all. With the spread of European control throughout Asia, Africa, America, and the Pacific, the Western methods of political and economic organization and the underlying civilization of rational humanism and belief in progress began to influence the non-Western populations and to arouse them from the tradition-bound ways of life. The Western skill in administration, the integrity of the judicial system, and the blessings of ordered liberty were understood and partly assimilated by tiny but growing numbers of non-Western intellectuals. With the spread of Western education, the populations of India, China, and other countries began to accept the Western methods and standards as their own and to resent the superiority of the white man, especially its often tactless and arrogant assertion.

It was, above all, the contact with the liberal civilization of England, the mother country of modern liberty and of the spirit of tolerance, as it began to develop in the seventeenth century, which infused a new spirit into the colored races, as it had influenced the growth of liberty in France and in the European

countries. England offered the best example of a political organization which succeeded in adapting itself to a changing public
sentiment with unparalleled flexibility and without doctrinaire
theorizing; at the same time it derived its vigor from ideas
which seemed to promote the evolution and the liberties of all
mankind. English rule brought the most powerful ferment to
the colored races, especially to India, from where it began to
radiate to the Far East on the one hand and to Mohammedan
Asia on the other. English policy and methods stirred the desire
for extended liberty and self-government, unknown formerly in
the Orient. In bringing to the Orientals English civilization and
ideas, England roused in them the desire for their political
freedom which is the inherent right of civilized man in the
Western concept.

As chairman of the Committee of Public Instruction in India,
Thomas Macaulay presented in 1835 a memorandum pleading
for the introduction of a system of education based upon the
knowledge of natural science and of the growth of the tradition
of liberty from ancient Greece to nineteenth century England.
He wrote:

It may be that the public mind of India may so expand under our
system that it may outgrow that system, and our subjects having
been brought up under good government may develop a capacity
for better government, that having been instructed in European
learning, they may crave for European institutions. I know not
whether such a day will ever come, but if it does come it will be
the proudest day in the annals of England.

This belief in the idea of liberty and in progress through education was later also applied in the United States to its colored
peoples, whether Negroes within the continental limits or
dependent peoples in the Pacific and Caribbean areas. Under
the influence of Western ideas, the educated classes among colored peoples began, at the end of the nineteenth century, to
demand complete equality; they became the leaders in the
"revolt of the East," the rising tide of the colored peoples,
which in the twentieth century made itself felt in varying

degrees, yet without exception, among Indians and Negroes in
the Americas, in Africa, and, above all, in Asia.

With great justice the Montagu-Chelmsford *Report on Indian
Constitutional Reforms* (1918) characterized India's intelligentsia in a way applicable to the modern intelligentsia of all colored peoples:

> Our obligations to them are plain, for they are intellectually our
> children. They have imbibed the ideas which we ourselves have set
> before them, and we ought to reckon it to their credit. The present
> intellectual and moral stirring in India is no reproach but rather a
> tribute to our work. . . . We owe him [the educated Indian] sympathy
> because he has conceived and pursued the idea of managing his own
> affairs, an aim which no Englishman can fail to respect.

The multiracial character of the empire was at the same time
stressed: It

> can not be based on ties of race. It must depend on a common
> realization of the ends for which the empire exists, the maintenance of
> peace and order over wide spaces of territory, the maintenance of free-
> dom and the development of the culture of each national unity of
> which the empire is composed.

The intellectual and moral stir among the colored peoples
and their desire for managing their own affairs and for complete
equality was greatly accelerated by the victory of Ethiopia over
Italy in 1896 and, above all, of Japan over Russia eight years
later, the first two defeats of white powers by colored peoples
in modern times. Japan, which succeeded within a few decades,
by unsurpassed national energy and discipline, in modernizing
its governmental and economic structure and being recognized
as an equal by the white powers, set an example for the colored
races everywhere. Unprecedented revolutionary movements
shook the ancient theocratic empires of Persia (1906), Turkey
(1908), and China (1912) and converted them outwardly into
constitutional monarchies or republics after the nineteenth century Western model. These revolutions aimed not only at internal reform, but also at securing independence from foreign
interference. Equality and self-government became the goals of

all peoples under white control. In the Americas the Indians began to stir after four centuries of lethargy and oppression, and the revolution in Mexico in 1917 succeeded in their interests. The colored and oppressed peoples of the Russian Empire saw in the Revolution of 1917 an opportunity for equality and self-government, and their aspirations were, at least partly, fulfilled by the Soviet government which, though refusing to them independence or true autonomy, granted equality to all races of the multiracial empire. Nor did the Allied slogans of self-determination during World War I prove less effective. Constitutional reforms were everywhere introduced, the facilities for education and economic development increased, and a new feeling of confidence and rights began to animate the masses of the colored peoples. The example of complete emancipation of dependent peoples was first set by Britain, which gave independence to Egypt (1922, completed 1936) and to the Arabs of Iraq (1932), and followed by the United States in 1934, when Congress promised to grant independence to the Philippine Islands after a transitional period of twelve years.

A widespread popular error assumes that racial conflicts and color prejudice are confined to the relations between white and colored populations. But racial arrogance and conquest and exploitation of weaker races have been practiced by all races, white and colored alike. Colored races, whether Asiatic Mongols or African Bantus or American Aztecs, have been great conquerors throughout the ages, many of them down to present times, and they have on the whole treated their subject races with much greater cruelty than the white man ever has in modern times. In fact, in many colored areas like India and Africa, the white man's administration has brought peace and has, by establishing the principle of equality before the law, considerably lessened existing racial tensions and exploitations.

The most extreme system of color bar and racial prejudice has prevailed in the caste system of Hindu India, which has been sanctified by religious tradition. As the name for caste, *varna* or color, reveals, the hereditary and strictly separated castes were originally determined by color. The lowest of these castes, the so-called "untouchables," pariahs or panchamas, represents in all probability the aboriginal, deeply dark-skinned races who have retreated before the more light-skinned "Aryan" invaders from the northwest to the south. According to the Indian census of 1941, their number amounted to 48,813,180 among a total population of 254,931,000 Hindus. Their position among the Hindus has been infinitely worse than that of the Negroes in the Union of South Africa or in the southern United States. It amounted to a Jim Crowism of fantastic proportions. Only lately has the position of the untouchables improved; in the twentieth century one of them, Bhimrao Ramji Ambedkar, became through the help of a native prince a doctor of science of Columbia University and was appointed a member of the viceroy's executive council in charge of the All-India Department of Labor. Finally, in 1948, the Constituent Assembly of the Union of India legally abolished untouchability.

Nor are the colored races free of a highly elated racial superiority complex equaling, by the open assumption of divine sanction, even the most extreme cases of white racial superiority feeling. Japanese imperialism has been based on a racial theory similar to that of Germany. As the Germans regarded themselves as a race set apart from other white-skinned peoples (Poles or Czechs), and destined to govern them irrespective of color, so the Japanese established an official religion of state, Shintoism, which proclaimed Japanese racial superiority over all others, whatever their race or color. The Japanese regarded their country as "the Land of the Gods, whence we perceive the reason why our national structure is supreme among all the nations of the world." Japan was founded, according to the formerly official Japanese doctrine, by the sun-goddess, Amaterasu Omikami, from whom the imperial house descended. Japan and the Japanese emperor were therefore singled out above all other nations for world domination, the divine Japanese imperial throne, "coeval with heaven and earth," being destined, in the official word, to "bring the whole world under one roof," the sacred policy of Hakko Ichi-u.

Racial conflicts and prejudices in the colored world are in

no way confined to the Japanese Empire. Even light-skinned Negroes feel a "color prejudice" against the black Negroes with pronounced Negro features. The Chinese Empire has extended its dominion over numerous non-Chinese tribes in southwestern China, over Mongolia, Tibet, and Sinkiang, and in the recent past over countries like Annam, Siam, and Burma, which all wish to maintain or to regain their independence. Racial conflicts among colored races are not only provoked by attempts at domination, by conflicting expansionist ambitions, or by the subordination of (often very large) minorities to majorities, but also by immigration and economic competition. The immigration of Hindus to Burma has been as much resented as Chinese immigration to the Dutch East Indies, to Burma, Thailand, and other Oriental countries. The British colony of the Straits Settlements in Malaya had on June 30, 1940, a population of 17,322 Europeans, 149,074 Indians, 904,512 Chinese, and only 309,226 Malays. Even in the native Malay States the Chinese immigrants have outnumbered the Malays; there, as in many other Oriental countries, the Chinese immigrants dominate most of the economic life of the land.

Nor are bitter "race conflicts" within the same color group confined to Asiatics or Africans: they are as frequent among the whites, many of whom speak the same or kindred languages and are closely related in descent. The relations between English and Irish, Poles and Russians, Czechs and Germans, Hungarians and Rumanians, Castilians and Catalans, Croats and Serbs, Greeks and Turks, have evoked the same protests against "oppression," the same bitterness and affirmation of incompatibility of national temperaments as ever colored races voiced against white control.

The position of colored races is often much better in colonies dependent upon imperial governments than in independent countries where the white element predominates politically. The Negroes in British West Africa or in the French colonies of Guadeloupe and Martinique enjoy a much wider participation in political liberty, in economic and social advancement and educational facilities than the Negroes in the southern United

States or in the Union of South Africa. In the latter the Boer has been an especially hard master for the colored population; his "colour feeling has something almost religious about it. He considers it his duty to hate black blood in all its manifestations." In the parts of South Africa under direct British imperial control, the position of the natives is much better. Cecil Rhodes regarded every educated man, irrespective of color or race, as a citizen with a right to vote, but the complete independence granted the Union of South Africa by Britain led to a general deterioration of the position of the natives throughout its territory. The South African territories under imperial control, Basutoland, Bechuanaland, and Swaziland, protect the status of the natives and their interests far better, and the natives have therefore violently protested all demands for the transfer of the territories from the British Empire to the Union of South Africa. On the whole it may be said that the imperial government acts, often together with Christian missionaries, as the protector of native rights and well-being against the white settlers and against native oppressors.

That color feeling and resultant color bars are nothing "natural" or "inherent" has been shown in a number of countries where harmonious relations among races in spite of differences in color have been established. Such is the case in New Zealand with regard to the Maori, and in Brazil, where the white population mingles with Negroes, Indians, and mulattoes, without any feeling of color bar. Brazil follows therein the example of Portugal, where a strong African element, largely composed of imported Negro slaves, has been completely assimilated and absorbed. At present miscegenation is going on in the Soviet Union on a large scale. There, as in Czarist Russia, little race feeling exists. In pre-Soviet Russia all peoples were accepted, provided they professed the "true faith." Pushkin was a direct descendant of a Negro who held a high position at the court of Peter I and married a lady of the aristocracy. That even in countries with a severe color bar no "instinctive" rejection of contact exists can be seen in the southern United States, where Negroes occupy the position of trusted and intimate house servants.

From the end of the nineteenth century, there has been much irresponsible and unrealistic talk of a great coming conflict of races, a final struggle between the white and the colored man for the control of the globe. Japan's victorious war in 1894 and the Chinese Boxer revolt induced the German Emperor William II to predict "Asia's struggle against all Europe" and to warn of the "Yellow Peril." A generation later Oswald Spengler, one of Germany's representative thinkers, regarded the great coming decision as a war of the colored peoples, among whom he counted the Russians, for the control of the globe against the white race. He summoned the white race, as Emperor William had done, to a crusade, under German leadership, against the specter of a fusion of class war and racial war. At the same time colored people began to talk of a united colored front, or of Asia for the Asiatics (without always explaining which Asiatics should dominate other Asiatics) and Africa for the Africans. None of these slogans, fears, and hopes had any foundation in reality. Neither the white nor the colored races did or could act as a united force with identical interests. In World War I as in World War II, Japanese and Chinese interests and their political ideals were as opposed as German militarism and British liberalism. In Korea the Japanese were more hated, in the Malay Peninsula the Chinese more feared than any white people. Though the Germans often envisaged a racial war for the conquest of the globe, nevertheless they ultimately fought their racial kin, the British and French, the Norwegians and Dutch, and allied themselves with racially much more distant peoples, like the Italians, Magyars, Finns, and the Japanese. The division of mankind and the lines of conflict have been drawn throughout the modern period, not according to color, but according to national allegiance and political ideas. Nation fought nation, idea opposed idea, irrespective of color or race. And many nations, especially the empires of Russia, Britain, the United States, and France, included men of many races in a common loyalty.

Though color and race are in no way a decisive factor in contemporary group conflicts, color plays a special role because it renders the conflicting groups easily recognizable, facilitates segregation, places each member irrevocably into his own group, and renders the border line much less flexible than in any other order of division. These differences of color make it easier to impose political, economic, social, and cultural restrictions on weaker groups and to keep them underprivileged. These restrictions show a great variety, ranging from minor discriminations in employment and social intercourse to most serious handicaps, even to complete human degradation, as formerly with the untouchables under Hindu rule, or to total annihilation, as with the Jews in Germany.

The most acute color problems are not found in the relations within empires or within the international world, but in some multiracial countries. There the policy pursued can be either one of segregation, rarely on the basis of equality, but mostly on that of privilege or even of legal discrimination, or one of amalgamation. As environment and opportunity shape human character more than heredity, amalgamation is opposed rather from irrational motives than from any rational consideration. Racial segregation often serves as an artificial protection for the status of the poorer classes of the dominant race, as a weapon for the maintenance of privilege. Racial stereotypes are used to rationalize political and economic relations.

The events leading to World War II, the extreme use made by the Germans of racial prejudice, the growing acuteness of the dangers of race conflict and of the involved human degradation again put the demand for equal opportunity and equal rights of all races into the forefront of public interest. The majesty of justice and law, the substance of democracy and liberty, are threatened everywhere by the passions and fears evoked by race prejudice. Christian conscience as well as rational humanitarianism demand the recognition of human dignity and individual rights in every human being, irrespective of class, political beliefs, or race. The solution of the problems arising from these differences forms one of the great tasks set before the generation liquidating World War II, in which both Germany and Japan have put racial differences into the center of their propaganda, while communism has stressed class conflicts, both to the detriment of man and to the confusion of reason.

X

FASCISM

Fascism is one of the two great authoritarian mass movements which started in the twentieth century in conscious opposition to the middle-class capitalistic civilization of the nineteenth century. It came first to power in Italy under the leadership of Benito Mussolini. Similar movements arose after World War I in other countries, among which German national socialism was the most prominent. By 1940 fascism could be regarded as a form of societal organization and as an attitude of mind which had its adherents in practically all countries of the earth. The original Italian name of *fascismo* is derived from the Latin *fasces*, "bundles," denoting in ancient Rome a bundle of rods with an ax, borne before Roman magistrates as a symbol of authority.

The origins of the fascist movement in Italy are to be found in both the wave of disillusionment and the exacerbated nationalism that swept Italy after 1918. Even before the war of 1914-1918, Enrico Corradini had preached a doctrine of extreme and belligerent nationalism which had fanned enthusiasm for the Libyan War of 1911 and for imperial expansion, and the poet Gabriele D'Annunzio had exalted in verse and prose not only the mission of a victorious Italy, but also the love of danger, adventure, and war. In the military coup by which he and a legion of black-shirted followers gained possession of Fiume in September, 1919, and during the sixteen months in which he ruled the city as Duce, D'Annunzio introduced a constitution foreshadowing the "corporative state" and all the rites, salutes, allocutions, and mass shouts which later became characteristic of the fascist movement. Mussolini himself, before 1914, had been a leading member and editor of the Italian social democratic party, where he had always represented the extreme left wing, tending toward revolutionary syndicalism, with emphasis upon direct action and enthusiastic will. Contrary to the attitude of his party, Mussolini supported Italy's entrance into the war in the fall of 1914; on November 15 he founded his own newspaper, *Il Popolo d'Italia,* in Milan, which called itself an organ of combatants and producers and carried the revolutionary motto of the French socialist Louis Auguste Blanqui, "Who has steel has bread," and Napoleon's dictum, "The revolution is an idea which has found bayonets." Mussolini's first famous editorial bore the characteristic title, "Audacity."

In the social unrest and moral confusion which followed the war of 1914-1918, Mussolini founded the Fascio di Combattimento on March 23, 1919, in Milan. The new group had no definite program; at first Mussolini was still a revolutionary syndicalist who advocated the expropriation of the land, the mines, and all means of transportation. The movement was then outspokenly anticapitalist and antimonarchist. It was not until the beginning of 1921 that he allied his group openly with the propertied classes, with the landowners and the industrialists. But whatever his sociological affiliations, he was moved throughout by a fierce nationalism and by a love of violence and adventure. When he ran for a parliamentary seat in Milan in the elections of November 16, 1919, he received less than 5,000 votes out of 346,000. But the deep social unrest prevailing in Italy in 1920 gave Mussolini a chance, and though the danger of any bolshevist success had faded by the end of the year, he and his squads of violent young men appeared to the frightened upper classes as a guarantee of security. Thus, with the connivance of the army, Mussolini's followers set for themselves the task of "restoring order" and breaking up socialist movements and organizations. With a boastful ruthlessness, with a proud sacrifice of all ethical scruples, the local *squadristi,* under the leadership of men like Grandi, Balbo, Farinacci, and others, undertook the conquest of power in the name of youth, in opposition to what they called "the tottering parliamentarism" of the "senile" and undecided bourgeoisie. The lack of resistance on the part of the government, the army, and the police emboldened the fascists, who had formed themselves into the national fascist party in November 1921.

In the following year Mussolini abandoned his original socialist, antimonarchist, and anti-Catholic program. He had no definite doctrine to offer. "Our program is simple: we wish to govern Italy. They ask us for programs, but there are already too many. It is not programs that are wanting for the salvation of Italy, but men and will power." On October 28, 1922, the famous march on Rome was staged. Though the fascists and the nationalists were outnumbered in the Italian parliament by ten to one, and though with some show of resolute action the fascists could easily have been stopped, the king refused to sign the proclamation of a state of siege which his government had prepared, and on October 29 invited Mussolini to form a new government. Though the new prime minister at first accepted a coalition cabinet and seemed willing to collaborate and compromise and even preserve the forms of a liberal state, within a very few years all the substance and influence of parliamentarism were gone, all other parties outlawed, all civil liberties and constitutional guarantees suppressed, and a full dictatorship established. The process was accelerated by the reaction of the country and of the civilized world to the murder of the socialist deputy Matteotti, in June, 1924, on the eve of his exposure of the graft and corruption of the fascist party. Highest fascist officials were alleged to have been implicated in the murder. To save his regime from the outraged feelings of the country, Mussolini established a totalitarian order in which the state was identified with the fascist party, which in turn was identified with its leader. Though he professed to fight bolshevism, he successfully adopted its methods, without, however, being able to carry them in the different climate of Italy as far as they were carried in Russia and later on in Germany. The various *squadristi* organizations had been reformed on February 10, 1923, as the Milizia Volontaria per la Sicurezza Nazionale.

Fascism in its beginnings was not a doctrine and had no clearly elaborated program. It was a technique for gaining and retaining power by violence, and with an astonishing flexibility it subordinated all questions of program to this one aim. But it was dominated from the beginning by a definite attitude of mind that exalted the fighting spirit, military discipline, ruthlessness, and action and rejected contemptuously all ethical motives as weakening the resoluteness of will. Fascism is power politics and *Realpolitik* in their most naked form; all theoretical considerations are subservient to what is regarded as the "inexorable dynamics" of the factual situation. Ultimately everything depends upon the ever changing decisions of the leader, decisions which cannot be discussed, but are blindly obeyed and immediately executed. Thus fascism could present itself in a given situation as a bulwark of the social order against social revolution, against Marxism and the proletariat, and could, in a different situation, become the propagandist and spearhead of a proletarian world revolution against conservatism and wealth, against the bourgeoisie and capitalism.

With its stress upon the irrational, upon instincts and activism, fascism insists upon the "iron logic of nature" which will always make the strong prevail over the weak, the more resolute over the irresolute, and thus aims at educating the nation to develop its strength, courage, and resolve and by these means to ensure its victory. All fascist activity is devoted to this preparation for what it regards as the inevitable and beneficial struggles which form the life of nations. Fascism, therefore, repudiates, above all, the idea of peace and harmony. "War alone brings up to their highest tension all human energies and puts the stamp of nobility upon the peoples who have the courage to meet it. Fascism carries this antipacifist spirit over even into the lives of individuals. It is education for combat." These words by Mussolini are amplified by his famous statement: "War is to the man what maternity is to the woman. I do not believe in perpetual peace; not only do I not believe in it, but I find it depressing and a negation of all the fundamental virtues of man." Therefore, to continue in Mussolini's words, "the whole nation must be militarized. . . . I consider the Italian nation in a permanent state of war." The creed of fascism is heroism, praise of audacity and danger, devotion and sacrifice for the nation and its necessary wars.

Fascism regards itself as a rejection, a complete and uncompromising denial of the principles of liberalism and democracy as elaborated and realized in the Anglo-Saxon and partly in the French revolutions of the seventeenth and eighteenth centuries. It is above all totally alien to the spirit of the British Revolution of 1688, with its insistence upon the democratic process of discussion, compromise, and tolerance and its emphasis upon the rights and dignity of the individual. It is a return to an authoritarian order based upon the subordination of the individual and the authoritarian control of thought. The liberty of the individual is denied in favor of the state; the actual inequality of man is proclaimed as immutable and beneficial. The "bourgeois" achievements which liberalism had secured from the time of the English revolutions of the seventeenth century on are not only abandoned, but derided and combated. From the beginning fascism has acted as the implacable enemy of democracy and of the rights of man. Society is to be built strictly upon a hierarchical order: the leaders are not to be elected, nor are they to be responsible to the people; on the contrary, the people are responsible to the leaders, whose appointment depends only upon those above them. Military discipline and blind obedience are to permeate all civilian life. One of the famous slogans of fascism was "Credere, obbedire, combattere" (To have faith, to obey, to fight), and another was "Mussolini ha sempre ragione" (Mussolini is always right).

The first eighteen years of the fascist regime, from 1922 to 1940, were devoted to the military preparation of the Italian nation for a coming struggle for what was regarded as the mission of the Italian people, the rebirth of the Roman Empire. The cult of the Roman Empire and of its expansion was stimulated in every possible way. Boastfulness about the inevitability of a fascist success animated all speeches of Mussolini. Thus, in a speech delivered on October 27, 1930, from the balcony of the

Palazzo Venezia in Rome, on the occasion of the eighth anniversary of the March on Rome, he stated: "By the year 1950, Italy will be the only country of young people in Europe, while the rest of Europe will be wrinkled and decrepit. People from all the frontiers will come to see the phenomenon of the blooming Spring of the Italian people. . . . Today I affirm that the idea, doctrine and spirit of Fascism are universal. It is Italian in its particular institutions, but it is universal in spirit. . . . It is therefore possible to see a Fascist Europe which will model its institutions on Fascist doctrine and practice, a Europe which will solve in the Fascist way the problems of the modern State, a State very different from the States which existed before 1789, or which were formed afterward. Today, even as yesterday, the prestige of nations is determined absolutely by their military glories and armed power. Fascism is an army on the march."

In a speech before the senate on March 30, 1938, Mussolini painted a glowing picture of Italian armed strength and military preparedness. Italy, he declared, could raise an army of 9,000,-000 men, of whom some 5,000,000 were first-line fighters, ready to hurl themselves under his personal direction against any enemy. According to him, this army was amply supplied with the most modern instruments of destruction, which would enable it to break through the stoutest defenses in conformity with the fascist maxim that a war must be decided within a few months. The powerful navy was mainly composed of recently launched vessels, which were to be used with boldness and decision. The air force was equal to any and would rain death and destruction on enemy territory. The quick success of Italian arms in any struggle would be guaranteed by ample reserves of supplies and by the fact that Mussolini himself would assume command of the operations.

When Italy, greedy for conquest, entered the war in 1940 to deal the death blow to the British Empire and its concept of liberty, the sordid reality, the inefficiency, and corruption of fascism, were quickly revealed. The Italian armies and navy were everywhere ignominiously defeated, and Mussolini's regime was overthrown by the king in Italy in July, 1943. It was saved by the Germans for a temporary existence as a fascist republic in northern Italy, but the Anglo-American advance put an end to it in the spring of 1945. Mussolini died an ignoble death at the hands of the Italian people.

In many ways fascism can be regarded as an exaggerated and even absolutized nationalism which entirely obliterates both individualism and humanity. The nation becomes the supreme arbiter, its service the one supreme duty. Only actions, thoughts, and sentiments which help to increase the power of the nation can be called good. This absolute devotion to the nation—not to a nation which is governed by ethical rules of divine or of rational origin, but to one which is an end in itself and is entirely identified with the fascist party and its leader—becomes the guiding principle of all education in fascism. This education is not confined to the schools alone nor to the youth organizations of the fascist party; like bolshevism in Russia, it determines everything printed in the press and in periodicals, heard over the radio, presented on the screen or stage, so that it ultimately colors every thought and every sentiment of the people. This kind of indoctrination is especially effective because no other information or critical attitude or independent inquiry is ever allowed to reach the people. Fascism leads to a complete destruction of all free cultural and intellectual intercourse with other nations.

But fascism is not a national attitude in the sense that it is confined to certain nations. Though it is true that fascism finds a much better soil for its growth in the cultural and social traditions of some nations, it represents a general attitude which can be found everywhere. Its rise has been facilitated by the growing complexity of life in the age of masses and machines and by a feeling of disillusionment and cynicism in the postwar generation after 1914. Democracy, which has grown up in the last three hundred years, represents, with its emphasis upon individual responsibility and individual decisions, the most difficult societal system and requires a definite human maturity. Fascism and totalitarianism in general can in many ways be regarded as an escape from this difficulty into the irresponsibility of following a leader who deprives the masses of their liberty and maturity but promises them social security and economic progress. This totalitarianism, however, was in such complete opposition to the trends of the eighteenth and nineteenth centuries that its emergence found democracy completely unprepared for the heavy and decisive blows which its implacable enemy intended to deal it, through propaganda, infiltration, and, ultimately, war. Thus it happened that fascism, which in the 1920's seemed confined to Italy, became in the 1930's a worldwide movement that not only put democracy on the defensive, but in mortal danger.

Mussolini could rightly say in 1934: "Since 1929 fascism has become not merely an Italian phenomenon, but a world phenomenon." On October 25, 1932, he had assured his audience at Milan of the coming world leadership of fascist Italy. "Today, with a fully tranquil conscience, I say to you, that the twentieth century will be the century of fascism, the century of Italian power, the century during which Italy will become for the third time the leader of mankind." In that Mussolini was at least partly wrong, because the following years proved very quickly that even in the case of a world-wide victory for fascism the leadership would not fall to Italy, but to Germany, which in 1933 joined the ranks of the fascist powers and very quickly dwarfed Italy in importance.

Fascist principles had become accepted by 1936, to a varying degree, by the governments of Austria, Hungary, Poland, Rumania, Bulgaria, Greece, and Japan. In most of these countries fascist parties were formed which imitated not only the doctrinal concepts of the Italian and German movements, but also many of their external symbols, though every country expressed its peculiar national tradition. Thus, while the Italian fascists donned black shirts and the Germans brown, the fascists in Hungary donned green shirts and chose the cross and arrow, instead of the swastika, as their symbol. In some of these countries the local brand of fascism was a product of popular movements, and not created by the government. This was the case in Rumania, where a young lawyer, Corneliu Zelea-Codreanu, founded in 1927 a Legion of the Archangel Michael for the

Christian and racial renovation of Rumania, which later developed into the terrorist organization of the Iron Guard, and when disbanded by the government, constituted itself as a party, "Totul pentru tara" (Everything for the fatherland). Though this party had fought enthusiastically for a pro-German orientation of Rumanian policy, it was nevertheless sacrificed by the Germans to the needs of the hour and succumbed in bloody and tormented internal strife. Different was the case in Greece, where fascism was initiated not through a popular movement, but by the government of General Joannes Metaxas, who on August 4, 1936, inaugurated the "Third Hellenic Civilization," with its symbol, the Spartan salute. In Spain the falangists revived at the same time the dream of the great Spanish Empire of the golden century, which had attempted to impress its Catholic civilization upon the whole world and which had ruled in the Americas and in the South Seas. The fascist movements did not remain confined to Europe. The most outstanding Asiatic example was in Japan, where a number of suprapatriotic terrorist organizations of young officers and students tried to stamp out the influences of Western liberalism and to bring Japan back to the ancient virtues of the old order. In Latin America the integralist movement in Brazil was perhaps the most prominent example, but certain fascist tendencies, in part the product of an intensive German and Italian propaganda campaign, were noticeable in many Latin American countries. The fascist parties in the countries with a strong democratic tradition were relatively weak. Only the strength and success of Germany lent them some temporary significance.

The strength of fascism in the international scene was much increased by the close cooperation of the leading fascist powers. From 1936 on, Germany and Italy entered into a number of political, cultural, economic, and military agreements, and in 1937 this "axis" was extended to include Japan. After 1938, the German form of fascism, known as national socialism, became so predominant that it impressed its peculiar character upon all other (and even upon the older) forms of fascism. This is especially true of the acceptance of anti-Semitism by Italian and even Japanese fascism. Japan has no Jews and practically has never had any Jewish problem. The number of Jews in Italy was insignificant; they had been completely assimilated into the national life, had participated prominently in all Italian national movements and wars, and many of them had from the beginning belonged to the fascist party, had been for years in Signor Mussolini's inner circle. Official fascist sources had repeatedly declared anti-Semitism an absurdity, but in 1938 Italian fascism suddenly accepted the German racial theory.

In May, 1939, Italy and Germany concluded an outright defensive and offensive military alliance. The Soviet-German agreement of August, 1939, forced a reorientation in fascist propaganda. Until then fascism had always insisted that its official archenemy was communism, and national socialism especially had reserved its most violent diatribes for "Jewish communism," of which Moscow was regarded as the seat and center. Now the propaganda against communism ceased entirely; national socialism laid a new emphasis on its own proletarian revolutionary character which explained and made possible its understanding with communism. The attacks on "Jewish communism" were replaced by even more vitriolic attacks on "Jewish capitalism" and democracy, which were sometimes called plutocracy, the heart of which seemed to be first London and then Washington. The main enemy, against whom, however, much fascist propaganda had always been directed, now officially became the "international bankers," "Wall Street," or big business, who were accused of a conspiracy to foment wars for their own profit and for the enslavement of all peoples. Fascism appeared as the defender of the true interests of the common man against the power of gold. In reality, with the fascists as with the bolshevists, the real enemy was Anglo-American, or Western, liberalism.

On September 27, 1940, Germany, Italy, and Japan concluded in Berlin a formal fascist alliance with the intention of imposing what the fascists call "the new order" upon Europe, Asia, and Africa. The fascists tried to prepare for the easy conquest of the democracies by undermining their understanding of the situation and by breaking down or softening their will to timely action. The most refined technique of propaganda was coupled with a strategy of terror to produce the desired disintegration of the democracies. Since the time when General Mola declared that the conquest of Madrid, which was then still in the hands of the Spanish republican government and which was being attacked by four columns moving toward the city, would be helped by a "fifth column" of Franco sympathizers within the city, the expression has been frequently used to designate the conscious and more often unconscious abettors of totalitarian penetration into the democracies.

Though the fascist powers succeeded in conquering a large number of countries, they could in no way quench the spirit of national resistance. Small groups, succumbing to anti-British and anti-Semitic propaganda, everywhere cooperated with the Germans. Thus, in France, the defeat of June, 1940, gave a reactionary group under Marshal Pétain, Pierre Laval, and Admiral Darlan the chance of seizing power. Democracy in France was officially abolished, the achievements of the French Revolution abandoned and vilified, the famous words "liberty, equality, fraternity" discarded in exchange for a mixture of the old French prerevolutionary order and an imitation of the German-Italian fascist models. In Norway a Major Vidkun Quisling established with German help a pro-German, anti-British government. Only in Poland were the Germans unable to find any "Quislings" or collaborators. The heroic uprising in Warsaw in August, 1944, under General "Bor" marked the climax of the spirit of resistance, which made itself felt in all countries overrun by the fascist alliance. Fascism, which started in the early 1920's as a movement of purely Italian national significance, had entered at the beginning of the 1940's the struggle for world domination, to make the twentieth century a fascist century. But its plans miscarried. World War II, begun by the great fascist powers, ended in complete defeat for them. Small fascist groups survived everywhere; the regimes in Spain and Argentina preserved some characteristics of fascism; but fascism as a world movement and as a world power had come to an end.

XI

NATIONAL SOCIALISM

NATIONAL socialism in Germany started as the Nationalsozialistische Deutsche Arbeiter-Partei (NSDAP) of Adolf Hitler in Germany in 1919. Its name from the first revealed its emphasis upon nationalism, socialism, Germanism, and the working class. Like Mussolini's fascism, it combined an appeal to nationalism with a revolutionary call to the masses. From the beginning fascism and national socialism, which may be regarded as the German form of fascism, had many traits in common. Both proclaimed themselves the implacable enemies of liberalism and the rights of the individual and of tolerance and the spirit of free discussion; both stressed the subordination of the individual to the state, the inequality of men and races, the right of the strong to rule the weak, and the necessity of the principle of blind and unswerving obedience to leaders appointed from above. Both praised the military virtues, despised and rejected compromise, humanitarianism, and charity, glorified hatred and conquest, and aimed at the transformation of the whole nation into an armed camp and an instrument in perpetual readiness for warfare.

But national socialism had peculiarly German roots. They can be traced to the Prussian tradition as it developed under the inspiration of great soldier kings, like Frederick William I and Frederick II, and men of blood and iron, like Bismarck. This tradition has always regarded the militant spirit and the discipline of the Prussian army as the model for all individual and civic life. To it was added the tradition of political romanticism, with its sharp hostility to rationalism, to the principles underlying the

French Revolution, to the "superficiality" of the West, and with its emphasis on instinct, on the past, even on the remote past, and its proclamation of the rights of the exceptional over all universal laws and rules. Thus the exceptional became a law unto itself. These two traditions were later enforced by nineteenth century adoration of "science" and of the "laws of nature," which, with their "iron logic" worked out beyond all concepts of good and evil and by a biological theory of life, led to the acceptance of racialism. Racialism itself was first proclaimed by the Frenchman Gobineau, in his *Essay on the Inequality of the Human Races,* and then propounded by Richard Wagner, who combined it with a heroic ideal of the Nordic superman, and by his son-in-law Houston Stewart Chamberlain, whose *Foundations of the Nineteenth Century* profoundly influenced early Hitlerism. To romanticism, national socialism owes the vague and fluid conceptions of folk as the basis of cultural and political organization, and of *Weltanschauung,* or "total world outlook," as opposed in the name of *Kultur* to the more legal concepts of civilization in the West.

In addition to these currents in the German tradition, it ought to be pointed out that Hitler's development was influenced during his youth by specific Austrian movements. National socialism owes much to Dr. Karl Lueger, who organized the Catholic lower middle classes of Vienna in an anticapitalistic and anti-Semitic movement called the Christian social party, but who remained loyal to Habsburg conservatism; and to Georg von Schönerer, who combined racial anti-Semitism with a violent anti-Catholicism and pan-Germanic expansionism and a bitter hostility to the Habsburgs.[1] Schönerer's disciple Karl Hermann Wolf founded among the Sudeten Germans in Bohemia a German workers' party which was later to assume the name of Deutsche National-Sozialistische Arbeiterpartei, a few years before Hitler founded his almost identically named NSDAP in Munich. Much of Hitler's ferocious nationalism and his contempt for the Slavs can be explained by the experiences of his youth amid the bitter nationality struggles of the multiracial Habsburg Empire.

When Hitler started his agitation in Munich immediately after the war of 1914-1918, he found the intellectual soil well prepared by the writings of the German romanticists, and of the German publicists of the War of Liberation. The last years before the war of 1914-1918 were characterized by a renewed interest in romanticism and in the War of Liberation of 1813. In those years a German youth movement, longing for a true community, a *Gemeinschaft*, a rebirth of the nation, and with a vague mystical enthusiasm for leadership and comradeship, expressed opposition to rationalism and "bourgeois" liberalism. It had come largely under the influence of Friedrich Nietzsche and the German poet Stefan George. Oswald Spengler, the author of *Decline of the West, Prussianism and Socialism,* and *Years of Decision,* and Moeller van den Bruck, the author of *Der preussische Stil* and *Das Dritte Reich,* can be regarded as the immediate forerunners of national socialism in the intellectual field.[2] But the intellectual preparation would in no way have been sufficient for the growth of national socialism in Germany if the defeat in the war of 1914-1918, with its ensuing disillusionment and pauperization, especially in the lower classes, had not paved the way for Hitler's propaganda. The peace treaty of Versailles gave Hitler a starting point, but the violence of his charges was not in reality directed against the peace treaty but against the fact that Germany had been defeated and that her plans had been frustrated. From the beginning Hitler's propaganda appealed to those who regarded the peace only as a temporary setback in Germany's expansionist program. He added to the pan-Germanic aspirations for world hegemony the almost mystical fanaticism of a faith in the mission of the German race and the fervor of a social revolutionary gospel. In the years of political and economic depression which followed Germany's defeat, Hitler's appeal to the German masses as the bearers of the most exalted racial ideals in the world was eagerly accepted to counteract their inferiority complex.

Though Hitler, even more than Mussolini, accepted many elements of the technique of the bolshevik revolution and, above all, its militant and complete rejection of Western civilization and liberty, like Mussolini he found a powerful ally in the wide-spread fear of bolshevism, which he exploited, first in Germany and then on a world-wide scale, posing as a bulwark against bolshevism. On the other hand, he gained the adherence of the masses by promises of an anticapitalistic order. The banner of the NSDAP was the red flag of the revolution, but altered to the German imperial colors by the addition of a white circle and a black swastika in the center. Thus Hitler combined the appeal of a violent anticapitalistic social revolution and that of a militant and mystical nationalism; the extraordinary flexibility of his dynamic doctrine enabled him to stress different elements at different times and to adapt his attitude momentarily to changing circumstances, with complete disregard for previous statements. His most important individual contribution to the theory and practice of national socialism was his deep understanding of mass psychology and mass propaganda in the contemporary world and his genius for using the most refined and elaborate technique. Herein he even surpassed his unacknowledged teacher Lenin. He openly proclaimed the need for utter simplification: the repetition of clichés and slogans replaced the effort of thought on the part of the individual in the face of complex realities. His chapter on propaganda in *Mein Kampf* can be regarded as of the most fundamental importance. He stressed the fact that all propaganda must keep its intellectual level down to the capacity of the least intelligent of those at whom it is directed, and that its content of truth does not matter compared with the only valid criterion, success. "The slighter its scientific ballast, and the more exclusively it considers the emotions of the masses, the more complete the success."

Hitler understood that, especially with as wide an aim as world domination, it is of the utmost importance to be able to supply one common denominator for all potential adversaries who may themselves change according to the circumstances.

The art of truly great popular leaders in all ages has consisted chiefly in not distracting the attention of the people, but concentrating always on a single adversary. The more unified the object of the people's will to fight, the greater will be the magnetic attraction of the movement and the more tremendous its impact. It is part of a great leader's genius to make even widely separated adversaries appear as if they belonged to but one category, because among weakly and undecided characters the recognition of various enemies all too easily marks the beginning of doubt of one's own rightness.

While the other great totalitarian movement ascribed all the ills of the world to "capitalism," and could always identify any opponent of the movement as a "lackey of capitalism," Hitler found this common denominator in the Jews and in Judaism. This enabled him to discover the "Jew" behind all his changing adversaries, sometimes behind communism or Moscow, at other times behind Great Britain and the United States—in short, behind everybody and everything which at a given moment seemed to oppose his wishes or to arouse his wrath.

National socialism proclaimed the Germanic race as the new *corpus mysticum* on which the salvation of the world depends, as the embodiment of all creative genius, as the *Reich* which must become the world-controlling *Reich*. This *Reich* necessarily had to have a *Gegenreich*, a counter-race, which on a similar world-wide basis would represent the antithesis of salvation and creative genius. Thus the Jewish race became the counter-race. National socialism saw its duty not only in the destruction of this counter-race, but in the preparation of the German race for its real task of establishing the new world order. The Third Reich, ruled by what Hitler called "the highest human species given by the grace of the Almighty to this earth," "will have, by suitable education of the youth, in the future a generation mature for the ultimate and greatest decision on this globe. The nation which will first take this road will be victorious," and become "one day the master of the globe." [3]

Working from these principles, Adolf Hitler was able to carry his party from its small beginnings in a beer cellar in Munich to a dominant position in world politics within twenty years. It took fourteen years for the NSDAP to conquer power in Germany. It had been born at a time when it was only one of many semirevolutionary terrorist organizations springing up as *Freikorps* throughout Germany, composed of former officers and soldiers, students and other elements dissatisfied with the bourgeois democratic and peaceful order which seemed to dawn for Germany in 1919. That it survived and absorbed all others was due to Hitler's leadership. On November 9, 1923, Hitler, supported by General Ludendorff, attempted his first Putsch in Munich, but it miscarried. The ensuing years of political and economic consolidation in Germany did not allow Hitler to make any considerable progress, but the economic crisis at the beginning of the 1930's and the lack of energetic measures on the part of the government against the indefatigable propaganda to undermine democracy brought the first great success of the NSDAP in the Reichstag elections of September 14, 1930. An intrigue, started by Franz von Papen, prevailed upon the aged president of the German republic, Marshal Hindenburg, to name Hitler chancellor on January 30, 1933. Like all totalitarians, he first accepted the collaboration of a coalition. Soon, however, plots of the opposition were "discovered" (the famous Reichstag fire)—and these "plots" always provide the pretext for totalitarians to eliminate all pretense of true collaboration with other parties. The new Reichstag meeting on March 21, 1933, in the garrison church in Potsdam, the historic receptacle of Prussian military spirit, "enabled" the government to assume dictatorial powers. From that moment on, the relentless process of *Gleichschaltung* began, and within a very few months the German Reich had become a totalitarian state which was entirely identical with the NSDAP in every concern of public or private life, and that meant with the will of its leader. The death of Hindenburg on August 2, 1934, removed the last conservative obstacle. Hitler became *Reichsfuehrer* and chancellor, the presidency was abolished, and all troops and officials were immediately forced to take the oath of fidelity to Hitler himself. The third Reich was now ready to create the "new order" which, according to Hitler, was to last for one thousand years.

But it was not to be a new order of a "new" or "true" democracy for Germany alone. Its dynamism was bound to expand and to spread. Like all totalitarian movements, it could not recognize any limits of its own volition, only limits set by opposed superior force. The first years were spent in concentration upon forging that instrument which would enable national socialism to establish its military and industrial superiority and thus to fulfill its ambitions. During those years, Hitler insisted again and again upon his peaceful intentions. He needed peace to build up Germany. "Capitalistic" unemployment was completely abolished by a gigantic armament program. The welfare of the working masses was promoted in every way. With mounting success, the aims grew in quick progression. The first aim was to unite all Germans within the Reich on the basis of "self-determination," which was proclaimed as the right of the German, but denied to other peoples. The next step concerned the creation of a *Grosswirtschaftsraum,* or a *Lebensraum,* in which the German master race would rule over a hierarchy of subordinate peoples. The success of that plan for a sphere of influence claimed in the name of security against encirclement gave rise to a broader vision of a hemispheric order which would embrace all of Europe, western Asia and Africa, and finally of a world order which would establish the principles of national socialism all over the globe. Extreme neomercantilism, which received the new name of *Wehrwirtschaft,* was accompanied by cultural autarchy, a resolute hostility against all "Western" thought. The rejection of the West and its standards of justice, law, and reciprocity led also to the proclamation of the official maxim: "Right is whatever profits the German nation; wrong is whatever harms it," which was regarded by Reichsminister Dr. Hans Frank, the head of the Academy of German Law, in an address on December 4, 1939, as the "beginning of national-socialist justice."

National-socialist parties existed outside the Reich everywhere where there was a population of German descent which national-socialist agitation succeeded in organizing for its own aims. According to national-socialist doctrine, loyalty to one's race or blood took precedence over one's loyalty as a citizen. Blood, and not a spiritual decision of allegiance, the doctrine taught, was the decisive factor. Wherever national-socialist propaganda penetrated among people of German descent outside Germany, it tried to fill them with the spirit dominant in

Germany, and to create the same institutions and organizations. Thus the implacable fight against individualism and the bourgeois civilization of the West was being carried directly into democratic countries. National socialism, which started as a purely German movement, produced by conditions and traditions peculiar to Germany, assumed, after twenty years of incessant and successful struggle, a world-wide importance and influenced and determined the course of history on a world-wide scale. Confidently it entrusted its fortunes to the test of war. It lost, under the united pressure of the democracies and of the USSR, which Hitler had brought together by his attack on both; Germany was crushed; Hitler himself and his expectations of a millenium of German mastery were buried in the ruins of the fatherland. National socialism, which had been born in 1919 of defeat, ended twenty-six years later in a defeat and disaster unprecedented in modern history.

Characteristic of the mid-twentieth century is the progressive disintegration of language as an instrument of universally accepted rational concepts. The same words cover different and sometimes opposite meanings, and much confusion is due to the indiscriminate and ambiguous use of words. Besides "democracy," "freedom," and "peace," one significant word that has lately changed its meaning is "war." Until very recently war was regarded, even by Clausewitz and Bismarck, as a strictly circumscribed and exceptional state of affairs. War was an instrument of politics, to be used only as the *ultima ratio*, as a case *in extremis*. Politics was the art of avoiding war, which was considered an abnormality. The effort of statesmen was concentrated upon maintaining the normal life, and the occurrence of war was frequently regarded as a proof of faulty statesmanship, as a bankruptcy of policy. Even Mussolini ended the article which he contributed under the title "Audacity" to the first issue of his *Il Popolo d'Italia* on November 15, 1914, with the words: "This cry is a word which I would never have used in normal times . . . a frightening and fascinating word: War!" In the last years, however, totalitarian philosophy has regarded all history as an unrelenting war, and fascism has proclaimed war the normal state of life, the culmination in which the vital and ethical energies of man reveal themselves at their best. Politics now becomes a preparation for war, receives its direction and meaning from this extreme *Ernstfall.* War ceases to be anything strictly circumscribed and limited; the border lines between war and peace grow more and more fluid, everything becomes part of warfare, actual or potential, and everything may therefore be called peace. Where the whole way of life is dominated by the norm of war, the words "war" and "peace" lose their meaning.

This totalitarian philosophy of war grew up under the influence of two intellectual movements, the roots of which we can trace back to the second half of the nineteenth century. One of them is the belief that the substance of life and history is struggle and conflict. The application of Hegelian dialectic and of Darwinian revolution to the social sciences made war and strife appear as the normal manifestations of all nature, of which man was only part. Soon the accepted Christian or bourgeois moral values were revealed as ill suited to this new conception. The fundamental basis of Hitler's *Mein Kampf* is an interpretation of man according to which he is purely a natural being, biologically determined, and inescapably subject to the "iron logic of nature," which he has to obey as animals do if he wishes to preserve or increase his strength and to be true to his "nature." In such a world strength and success alone count: the "idle dreams" of universal truth and justice disappear in the dust heap of bookishness before the triumphant march of full-blooded men. In the face of this nihilism, this twilight of all moral values, life is exalted as the only and inexorable arbiter of all action and conduct.

World history is the world tribunal: it has always justified the stronger, the fuller, the more self-assured life, has given it the right to existence, whether or not it was regarded as good. It has always sacrificed truth and justice to might and vitality, and doomed those peoples to death who considered truth more important than deeds, and justice more essential than might.

The other movement of ideas, closely connected with the first, is the denial of universal values and truth, their relativization and "nationalization." Thus two enemies facing each other are not united any more by a moral or intellectual community above the battlefields. This lack of common moral or intellectual attitudes is always noticeable, as war in reality is a permanent phenomenon. Even in so-called "peace" times, each class, according to the communists, each nation, according to the national socialists, has its own peculiar thought processes, develops its own science, lives according to its own standards of class or national ethics. All bridges of understanding and communication are destroyed. Nationalism reaches here its extreme manifestation: sovereignty is not only political, it is economic and cultural as well. Not only does all hope of world cooperation become futile: the republic of letters and the oneness of mankind and civilization no longer exist or are "unmasked" as idle cerebral fancies or as hypocritical pretense hiding class interests. Under these circumstances the word "enemy" gains a new meaning. Everybody is a potential enemy, and every enemy becomes a total enemy. The whole of existence is always overshadowed by war. The army becomes the model of life, and its collectivism spreads to all fields of human endeavor and is mistaken for socialism. This new "socialism," which is nothing but the collectivism of an army, is again proof of the strangely ambiguous use of words in our times. It was Oswald Spengler, in his *Prussianism and Socialism,* which he published immediately after World War I, who first identified Prussianism and socialism. This socialism is, according to Spengler, "will to power, struggle for the well-being, not of the individual, but of the whole."

A similar conception of "socialism" was propagated at about the same time by Moeller van den Bruck. For him Prussia meant a nationalistic communism or collectivism on a hierarchical and aristocratic basis. In his *Das Dritte Reich,* in which he demands the complete separation of Germany from the bourgeois West (for "am Liberalismus gehen die Völker zu Grunde"), and the fulfillment of a German mission by a new Germany, of which the frontiers will be those of her mission, he states that each people has its own socialism. This new militaristic collectivism differs, however, in one fundamental respect from its Spartan model, in its emphasis upon productive work and upon the importance of the industrial worker. The achievements of modern industrial society, with its stress upon mechanization, standardization, and disciplined teamwork, are not only fully accepted by the totalitarian regimes, but regimented into a system of a military super-industrialism. The worker becomes a soldier; the border lines between industrial society and army become more and more fluid, until they disappear; the factories become barracks, and the same discipline and devotion are demanded in both. Work becomes an obligation toward the state. The state fixes the compensations and conditions of labor, the freedom of exchange or contract is abolished, and property becomes a fideicommissum. Ernst Jünger created in his *Der Arbeiter: Herrschaft und Gestalt* the apotheosis of a thoroughly mechanized and militarized worker, a modern machine-man, a member in a group closely knit together and pervaded by one spirit, united for higher efficiency and external action. The communist worker fights in such a way on the labor "front" and achieves "victories" of disciplined production. He becomes a "hero" of labor.

In this new philosophy of history as struggle, strategic considerations of soldiery take precedence over economic well-being. The normal and peaceful lives of individuals no longer determine society and its functions; it is the anormal, the exceptional, the *ultima ratio,* which determines and directs the normal. Carl Schmitt, the German political scientist, has best expressed this new attitude: "One can say that here, as elsewhere, precisely the exceptional case has a particularly decisive meaning and reveals the heart of the matter. . . . It is from this most extreme possibility that the life of men gains its specific political tension." In his theory about the origins and legitimacy of right, Carl Schmitt allows right to be determined by the supreme legislator, who has the power to realize and enforce the decision. Ideal justice and positive law are discarded as norms of law-making. Starting from the extraordinary situation, the *Staats-*

notstand ("Not kennt kein Gebot"), where the necessities of history seem to demand the disregard of abstract justice or of the existing positive law, Schmitt applies this "anormal" case to the "normal" course of existence. "Right" is thus always dependent upon the concrete situation and has its source in the decision with which the supreme power authority meets the situation. "Jegliches Recht ist Situationsrecht" (Each law corresponds to a concrete situation). As each situation is unique and concrete, there cannot be any general and abstract norm. Each decision is valid only for its own situation. "Justice" becomes the function of the power which makes the essentially political decision; political and judicial functions are no longer separated, although political decisions continue to be made to appear as judicial ones. But in practice, and frequently in theory, the judicial function is subordinated to the political. In his address to the Deutsche Juristentag in 1936, Rudolf Hess repeated Treitschke's words: "Alle Rechtspflege ist eine politische Tätigkeit" (All justice is political).

Whereas in the Western nations after World War I the war itself was recognized as a great calamity, a very large part of the German people did not regard the war as a tragedy, but the defeat. They blamed all the ills, which the Western nations attributed to the war, on the peace treaties. Whereas the Western nations blamed themselves for having got into the war and having made the peace, the large majority of the Germans blamed only the enemy for having devised the peace. Nationalsocialist propaganda increased this growing estrangement from the West by glorifying the war and the German Army, and by strengthening the already too strong German tendencies to see the source of all their maladjustments, not in their own faults or shortcomings, but in the machinations of "enemies." The inevitable course of history seemed to assure victory to those who fought for the right and infallible cause. Hitler's racial theory had the effect of destroying the remaining sense of reciprocity and responsibility in the German people and of convincing them that because of their superior qualities they are always right and that the heroic warrior ideal which they have cultivated justified their world domination. "The struggle for a German rebirth is a struggle for the assertion of the German hero ideal against the democratic shopkeeper ideal," Rosenberg declared in his contempt for bourgeois capitalism.[4]

In the totalitarian regimes society is entirely subordinated to the state and even destroyed by it. There is no individual or social sphere outside the state. But even the state is not a true state; it is not more than the apparatus of one party which entirely identifies itself with the state and society, absorbing all their functions. The great difference even between Bismarck-Wilhelminian Germany and the state created by national socialism was clearly indicated by the declarations of the respective leaders at the outbreak of the great wars. In 1914 Emperor William II declared that he no longer recognized any parties among the Germans and that he stretched out his hands to all his internal opponents for cooperation and internal peace. At the outbreak of the war in 1939, Chancellor Hitler did not invite the cooperation of any internal opponents, but on the contrary threatened them in terms unusually violent, even for him. The Protestant theologian, Karl Barth, rightly pointed out that the national-socialist state consists in the disintegration of the just or right state, that it is an anarchy tempered by tyranny, or a tyranny tempered by anarchy.[5] The disappearing social order is replaced by an extension and imitation of the order of the army. The terminology of war, warriors, and struggle is applied to every phase of life, even the most civilian. All differences between the military and other walks of life are gradually abolished until the totality of life is subordinated to the set of values of the army, and farmers and teachers, writers, artists and scholars are turned into militant servants and disciplined soldiers of the regime. Professor Karl Alexander von Müller, editor of the *Historische Zeitschrift*, concluded an editorial postscript to the issue published at the beginning of World War II on September 15, 1939:

It is in this battle of souls that we find the sector of the trenches which is also entrusted to the German historical scholarship. It will mount the guard. The watchword has been given by Hegel. The spirit of the universe gave the command to advance; such command will find itself blindly obeyed.

Innumerable are the examples in which all scholarship and all artistic creation in communist society regards and proclaims itself in a state of permanent mobilization in the service of the struggle of the state, of its advances on a road of which it is maintained that it has been unmistakably traced out by history and pointed out by the leader, who in his infallible wisdom is blindly followed.

As in the army, discipline and leadership, the appeal to comradeship and readiness to sacrifice, are stressed in every line of activity. The personality of the leader gets full scope and is elevated by the amorphism of the masses beneath it. He is regarded as infinitely more infallible than any commanding general has ever been by adoring soldiers. The fate of the individual in a nation which has become an army has been formulated in Mussolini's famous words: "In the fascist state the individual is not suppressed, but rather multiplied, just as in a regiment a soldier is not weakened, but multiplied by the number of his comrades." [6] The national-socialist youth exalted as its educational and social ideal the Männerbund, a military order after the model of the Teutonic Knights or the Prussian officers corps. "The principle," wrote Hitler, "which in its time made the Prussian army the most wonderful instrument of the German people, must in the future become the principle of the structure of our whole conception of the state: authority of every leader downwards and responsibility upwards." The totalitarian philosophy of war has been aptly summed up by Carl Schmitt: "War is the essence of everything. The nature of the total war determines the nature and form of the totalitarian state."

The philosophy of war gains even greater importance by the fact that in a war in which a totalitarian nation is involved we do not find one nation fighting against another as equal participants in a common humanity. The totalitarian nation fights inspired by its consciousness of a unique historical mission, which is fulfilled in class or race struggle and invests its fight and victory with an almost sacral character. The people who have the true doctrine represent the realm of salvation invested with all imaginable virtues, while the enemy is charged with all imaginable, and sometimes even unimaginable, vices. One of the weaknesses of this position consists in the fact that whereas the true faith is a constant factor, the enemy is a variable factor, according to the circumstances, the political exigencies of one moment putting up another adversary than those of another moment. This attitude gives to the totalitarian politics at the same time an immense flexibility and, to its own followers, the appearance of a great persistency. Spengler had foreseen this attitude when he defined the new imperialist Caesarism which he saw coming as "that type of government which, in spite of all constitutional and philosophical formulation, is by its inherent nature lacking utterly in defined form." This flexibility allows the substitution of one enemy for another most abruptly and enables the leader to direct the almost mystical totalitarian hatred of his followers against the most diverse objects. That explains the startling change in attitude of the partners in the pact between Germany and the Soviet Union in August, 1939.

The totalitarian army gains its strength not only from the concentration of the whole national and all individual life upon war. It draws its main inspiration from the totalitarian vision according to which each individual war is nothing but a step toward imposing the new way of life upon the whole of mankind. Spengler defined the duty of the German youth:

To work out a new mode of political will and action from the newly formed conditions of the twentieth century, to bring to light new forms, methods, and ideas, which like the ideas of the French Revolution and the customs of the English House of Commons will spread as models from one land to the other, until the history of the coming time progresses in forms whose beginnings will in the future be found in Germany.

The totalitarian army knows itself as the instrument of a collective will, aspiring to the highest goal: to make the nation not only a powerful nation in the Bismarckian sense, but a world nation for which its world day has arrived with the adoption of the new philosophy which is destined to become the faith of mankind. The events of 1945 put an end to these hopes in the case of fascism and of Germany; the very same events gave a new impetus to the similar hopes of communism and of Russia.

XII

COMMUNISM

In the twentieth century communism has been identified with that interpretation of Marxian doctrine which Lenin worked out before and after he and his bolshevik party seized power in Russia in November, 1917, by overthrowing the democratic regime which the Russian Revolution had established in March, 1917.[1] His purpose was from the beginning to spread the system of communism to all parts of the earth in order to establish a world Union of Soviet Socialist Republics. Communism in that sense is only one of the possible interpretations of Marxian socialism, and leading socialists from the beginning have attacked Lenin's theory and its realization in Russia. Many socialists put their faith in an evolutionary development and in democratic means to attain full economic justice and social equality. This attitude has been accepted in the more advanced countries. Communism, on the other hand, regards revolution and an ensuing dictatorship of the proletariat as a necessary period of transition to the future free and equalitarian society in which everyone everywhere would contribute to the common good according to his abilities and receive according to his needs. Lenin in 1917 thought this final goal very near; since then it has receded into a much more distant future and has led to the perpetuation of the revolutionary dictatorship which was formerly regarded as purely transitional.

Lenin's communist interpretation of Marxian socialism goes back to the year 1903, when at its second party congress the Russian social democratic party split into two factions, one representing the majority, and therefore called bolsheviks (which means "majority group"), under Lenin, and a minority group (mensheviks) under Martov. Against his opponents who proposed the formation of a mass party after the example of the German social democrats, Lenin insisted upon the necessity of founding a conspiracy of picked and selected men, entirely devoted to the socialist cause, who would be able to act in revolutionary situations as a closely knit, disciplined, and ruthless group, and to seize power, though they were only a small minority. Thus Lenin's concept sanctified from the beginning the use of violent and conspiratorial methods and accepted the necessity of the guidance of the masses by a ruling elite. Lenin's group opposed any cooperation with bourgeois democratic or moderate socialist parties; during the war of 1914-1918 it assumed an intransigent attitude against any form of "patriotism" and concentrated its efforts on the transformation of the national war into a civil war. After the outbreak of the Russian Revolution in March, 1917, the bolsheviks under the leadership of Lenin were the only group with strict discipline and definite purpose and thus were able to direct the amorphous and leaderless revolutionary discontent of the masses. After having seized power, the bolsheviks established their dictatorship as a dictatorship of the proletariat, renamed the party the communist party, defeated (thanks to the leadership and gift of organization of Leon Trotsky) their adversaries, and kept themselves in power against great initial odds.

According to the communist theory, the social revolution—accomplished in the interests of the proletariat and, after the abolition of class society, of all men—must be conducted by the "proletariat's advance guard," the communist party, because the people as a whole, and even large parts of the proletariat, educated in the presocialist era in the bourgeois concepts of life, are unable to grasp and to realize the new order immediately. The communists insist upon the guided activization of the masses and their growing, though strictly regimented, participation in the establishment of the new order. As the instrument of this participation they accepted originally the workers', soldiers', and peasants' councils (the Russian word for council is "soviet") which had first been formed during the Russian Revolution in 1905. In these soviets only the working classes were represented, not the "capitalists" or "exploiters"; the mode of election was so carefully regulated that only deputies belonging to, or approved by, the party were chosen. Communism believes that true democracy cannot be realized in capitalistic society because of the economic exploitation imposed upon the economically weaker elements of society, and that the generally accepted forms of parliamentary democracy only veil the control of society by capitalists. Therefore the building of the future perfect society proceeds under an autocracy, unbound by any law or ethical consideration of the "bourgeois" age. To this future the happiness of the present generation and the traditions of the past are ruthlessly sacrificed. Theoretically, a classless society of free individuals will emerge as a result of the dictatorship. Marxism regards the state as an organ of class rule; and as the struggle for the emancipation of the proletariat is the last of all possible class conflicts (because after its emancipation there will remain no lower class to be emancipated), the communist state in suppressing the class basis destroys its own basis or, as it has been expressed, the state withers away and a system of complete freedom emerges. What has happened so far in reality, however, is the opposite. The state in Russia under communist dictatorship has not yet begun to wither away, but is the first example of the truly totalitarian state in which no sphere of individual life is allowed to remain outside its all-inclusive grip. In the effort to create a "true" democracy, terror has been ruthlessly employed, humanitarian considerations and individual rights have been disregarded, and the assumption of the class character and economic determination of intellectual and moral life has led to a complete relativization of standards of truth and of ethics.

In its practical application in Russia, communism has passed through several stages. By the end of 1920, after a long struggle against external and internal enemies, the communist power appeared consolidated within Russia. At the same time, it had to abandon the expectations of world revolution which had animated Lenin and his followers in 1917. They had looked upon the Russian Revolution as the first stage of a world-wide process; for them socialism or communism were international movements which could only succeed, and were destined to succeed, on a world-wide basis. In 1919 Lenin had founded the Communist or Third International, but it proved unable to make any serious progress outside Russia, and the several communist parties existing abroad soon became instrumental to the policy of the communist state in Russia.

With the practical abandonment of all hopes for an immediate world revolution and with the complete exhaustion of Russia's resources as a result of the war of 1914-1918 and its own civil wars, Lenin was forced to replace the policy of "war communism" in March, 1921, by the so-called New Economic Policy (NEP). It represented a compromise between nationalized and private economy, an interim providing for the education of the Russian people to that initiative and efficiency which was needed for the functioning of modern industrial civilization. During the NEP period (1921 to 1928), a struggle for leadership in the communist party (after the death of Lenin) developed between Trotsky, his nearest collaborator in the decisive years of the conquest of power, and Joseph Stalin, who as secretary-general had succeeded in bringing the party machine under his control. In this struggle Stalin was victorious. The period of the NEP was followed in 1928 by a renewed drive for the "realization of socialism" in the Soviet Union. This speedy drive toward socialism called for advance planning in all branches of the economic and cultural life of the country. In a poor and backward country like Russia the excessive tempo of the planning, the lack of managerial and engineering talent and of skilled labor, naturally resulted not only in frequent maladjustments and tremendous waste, but could be financed only by a general reduction of the standard of living. The "advance toward socialism" proceeded on three lines: industrial, agricultural, and educational. In the first field the Five-Year Plan was devoted to the better exploitation of natural resources and to the building up of heavy industry; in the second field, to the collectivization of individual farms and to the introduction of machinery and more efficient methods of cultivation; in the third field, to the fight against illiteracy and traditionalism and to a change of the ways of life and thought habits of the population.

The failure of the world proletariat to follow Moscow's call in the years after 1917 led to a change of emphasis and direction in communism under Stalin. Much greater stress was put on Russia as the only genuine leader and representative of communism. Thus the movement presented after 1935 more and more an amalgam of Lenin's world-revolutionary communism with the historical traditions and aspirations of the Russian Empire and of the Russian people. Communism had shown itself the new form in which these aspirations had vitalized and organized the masses of the empire to active participation. Within this framework communist policy underwent several fundamental and sometimes sudden changes, according to the true or supposed needs of communist success and Russian interests. The flexibility of Soviet policy was perhaps enhanced by the ruthless "purges" of 1936-1938, in which Stalin eliminated all those persons, many of them among the oldest and most renowned communists and closest collaborators of Lenin, who could endanger his undisputed and unquestioned leadership. In this process several hundred thousand communists and leading personalities of the political, economic, and military life of the Soviet Union were "liquidated" as "traitors" or "enemies of the people."

This flexibility in policy, though not in communist principles, methods, and goals, showed itself in the sudden change of the "general line" in August, 1939, when the Soviet Union abandoned the principle of collaboration with the democratic nations in the struggle against fascism and lined up side by side with aggressive fascism, which communists had proclaimed until then the mortal enemy of the proletariat, of peace and progress. Until June, 1941, communists everywhere played a rather ambiguous role; nevertheless, they directed all their main attacks against democracy, against Great Britain's efforts to resist fascist aggression, and against the defense program of other democracies, including the United States, to prepare themselves against fascist aggression. The candidacy of Franklin D. Roosevelt for President of the United States in 1940 was violently opposed as that of a "warmonger" in the service of American big-business imperialism. The attitude of sympathy toward Germany and of obstruction to the fight against fascism changed completely, however, with the German attack on the Soviet Union on June 22, 1941.

In the Soviet Union the national patriotic trend, which had been visible already in the preceding years, became more and more pronounced during World War II. Stalin himself took the lead in a message to the Russian people on July 30, 1942. He called upon them to be inspired in this war by "the daring spirit of our great ancestors," and he set as examples heroes of Russia's feudal past. This invocation of the heroic past filled the Soviet youth with a deeply national spirit, different from the international proletarian spirit prevailing in the first years of the Russian Revolution, in which the whole Russian past had been viewed with indifference and even hostility. At the same time communism in Russia mobilized also the patriotic feeling of the Russian church. For the first twenty years of the communist regime, religious education was strictly prohibited, and the government officially sponsored the violent antireligious propaganda of the "Union of the God-less." Now this propaganda completely ceased, and the role of religion in Russian history was positively appraised. In 1943 the Russian Orthodox church was officially recognized, Metropolitan Sergei was elected patriarch for all Russia and installed in a brilliant ceremony in Moscow Cathedral. His successor, Alexei, praised Stalin as "a wise leader, placed by the Lord over our great nation." All churches were ordered to offer prayers "for the health and well-being of the God-sent leader of the peoples of our Christ-loving nation." The Russian church called for the unity of all Orthodox churches under its leadership.

This change from the original proletarianism of Lenin to the emphasis on tradition was carried through in all fields. Like Napoleon in 1804, Stalin after 1940 restored the titles and splendors of the old regime and himself assumed the leadership of this trend by bestowing upon himself the title of marshal and, later, generalissimo. The officers received back their gold-braided uniforms of czarist times, and their style of life distinguished them much more sharply from the rank and file than in any "bourgeois" army. As in czarist days, all officials, even the most inconspicuous civilian ones, received ornate uniforms, and the old militarized bureaucracy reappeared everywhere, even in the schools. Coeducation was abolished in most schools, to take into account the different nature of the two sexes; the boys were trained for a stern soldier's life while the girls were educated for motherhood. The communist parties outside Russia joined in this new trend toward patriotism and emphasis in education on family and authority, on military drill and motherhood. At the end of World War II, this emphasis on patriotism—and with the Russians and other Slav-speaking peoples on the pride and manifest destiny of the Slav race—was combined with a new stress on Leninist doctrine, and a relentless war was waged upon all "deviations" or "heresies." To that purpose, after World War II, it seemed necessary to isolate the Soviet Union more strictly from any contact with the outside world than had ever been attempted in Russia before.

This new development of communism after World War II showed two opposite faces: a completely closed society in Russia and, at the same time, the resumption of the original world-wide drive. Summing up Lenin's testament to the party, Stalin declared after the leader's death in January, 1924: "Lenin never regarded the republic of Soviets as an end in itself. He always regarded it as a necessary link for strengthening the revolutionary movements in the lands of the West and the East, as a necessary link for facilitating the victory of toilers of the whole world over capital. Lenin knew that only such an interpretation is the correct one, not only from the international point of view, but also from the point of view of preserving the republic of Soviets itself." Russia's victory in Europe and Asia and the unprecedented expansion of Russian territory and influence, unexpected a decade before, have opened up new horizons for Russian communism, which felt a new aggressive, heroic, and dynamic vitality, the swelling of an immense forward movement which the military and economic disintegration of Europe and

Asia seemed to favor. The situation proved, at least to the faithful of the communist faith, the superiority of communism over disintegrating capitalist democracy and the superiority of Russia over the decadent West. By the middle of the twentieth century, these two myths were thoroughly systematized in Russia and raised to an unassailable religious dogma. On August 13, 1947, *Izvestia* published a lecture delivered by Kovalev before the All-Union Society for the Dissemination of Political and Scientific Knowledge, in which he regarded "the profound understanding of the superiority of the Soviet system" over all others as "a most important peculiarity of Soviet patriotism. It is precisely the peculiarity which, above all, characterizes Soviet patriotism as patriotism of the highest kind." This was also the theme of the report by A. Fadeev, the secretary-general of the Union of Soviet Writers, to the June, 1947, meeting of the plenum of the Union. As Zhdanov had declared that "our literature, reflecting a much higher system than any bourgeois democratic system, and a culture many times higher than bourgeois culture, has the right to teach others the new panhuman morality," so Fadeev singled out "the Soviet man as the bearer of the highest panhuman morality." Yet in its application this universal morality turned out to be most relative: its supreme standard is the good of the Soviet state.

This attitude animates not only Soviet writers and artists, but also communist scientists. Professor A. Palladin, president of the Ukrainian Academy of Sciences, who attended the International Congress of Physiology at Oxford in July, 1947, expressed after his return, in an article in *Literaturnaya Gazeta* his satisfaction with communist superiority. Proudly he reported how he and his colleagues refused to use English or French in reading their scientific papers: these representatives of "internationalism" regarded this usual procedure as a "humiliating treatment of Soviet science and of the Russian language. This, we said, was the language of a great, victorious nation—and of the nation which had created the greatest and most advanced form of state in the world." Thus, the president of the Ukrainian Academy of Sciences went on, "we read our papers in our own language," by which he did not mean Ukrainian—a fact throwing much light on Moscow's nationality policy—but Russian. "This episode"— which the professor qualified as "our victory"—"showed how important it is never for a moment to yield on points affecting our national honor and dignity; nor must we ever tolerate any kind of toadying to the West." The official communist textbook of pedagogy quoted the words which the Russian critic Belinsky wrote in 1840: "We envy our grandchildren and great-grand-children who are destined to see Russia in 1940 standing at the head of the civilized world, giving laws to science and art, and receiving reverent tribute from all enlightened humanity." With great modesty and exemplary self-criticism, the official textbook added: "These remarkable words have been fulfilled."

By the middle of the twentieth century, communism appeared at the height of power. The centenary of the *Communist Manifesto* in 1948 found the communist teachings accepted as the official doctrine of state over the whole of eastern Europe and northern Asia and shared by many millions outside.[2] At the same time the Russian Empire had expanded farther than the most fervent Pan-Slavists of the nineteenth century had expected. The other totalitarian movements of the twentieth century, fascism and national socialism, were decisively defeated; and of their standard-bearers, Italy was grievously weakened and Germany almost destroyed. The communists may hope to realize, some thirty years later, the expectations of Lenin, to create one world of their own, a monolithic world of one faith and one leadership. Such a one world alone will assure, they believe, the certainty of salvation for the whole of mankind and of security for the Soviet Union. Only if the enemies of the true faith are liquidated, or at least rendered harmless, can there be true security and full salvation. In the declaration concerning the formation of the Union of Soviet Socialist Republics which opens the Constitution of 1923, it was stated that since the formation of the Soviet Union the countries of the world have split into two camps, the camp of capitalism, where national oppression, imperialist brutality, and wars are inherent, and the camp of socialism, which brings peace and harmonious collaboration.

These two camps still faced each other, according to communist doctrine, in the middle of the twentieth century. Russia was the leader in the camp of communism; as the result of recent events, the United States of America has become the leader of democracy, of that Western way of life which, according to Russian communism, has been doomed by the march of history.

FORCES OF REINTEGRATION AND REAFFIRMATION

Les Dieux qui ont donné à la plupart des hommes une lâche ambition, ont attaché à la liberté presqu' autant de malheurs qu'à la servitude. Mais quel que doive être le prix de cette noble liberté, il faut bien le payer aux Dieux.— MONTESQUIEU, "Dialogue de Sylla et d'Eucrate."

There is only the fight to recover what has been lost
And found and lost again and again: and now under conditions
That seem unpropitious. But perhaps neither gain nor loss
For us, there is only the trying. The rest is not our business.
                                        —T. S. ELIOT, "East Coker"

Yea and Nay—
Each has his say:
But God He keeps the Middle Way.
                    —HERMAN MELVILLE, "The Conflict of Convictions"

XIII

DEMOCRACY

Democracy is a form of government based upon self-rule of the people and, in modern times, upon freely elected representative institutions and an executive responsible to the people. It is a way of life recognizing and protecting by the majesty of law the equal right of all individuals to life, liberty (including liberty of thought and expression), and the pursuit of happiness. It presupposes an attitude of tolerance, of patience and willingness to compromise, based upon respect for the freedom and the convictions of others. As important as its ends is its method of free discussion by which the various attitudes, interests, and opinions of individuals, groups, and classes try to find a common ground of agreement. Its end is the recognition of each individual as an end in himself, not as material or a means for the purposes of the group or the progress of history. Though democracy has a long and ancient history as the modern fruit of Western civilization and of its two component elements, the Athenian and Roman legacy and the Judaeo-Christian tradition, it is the most delicate form of political organization and the most difficult to achieve. It has therefore come to fruition only with very few peoples and in relatively short periods of history.

Democracy was known in ancient Greece, especially in Athens, but ancient democracy was in several ways fundamentally different from that of modern times. It was direct democracy, in which the whole people formed the legislator and in which the representative system was unknown. This was made possible by the limited size of the ancient state, which was generally confined to a city and its rural surroundings, and almost never included more than 10,000 citizens. In the ancient democracies every citizen was entitled to attend the legislative meetings and to vote. A very large number of the citizens held one of the many elective offices in the course of the years. No division between the legislative and the executive branch existed; both were in the hands of the whole active citizenry; there was no modern party organization. The inability of the ancients to develop a representative system made it impossible for them to create large democratic states. On the other hand, the political life in the ancient democracies was most intense, and all citizens were actively interested in, and highly conversant with, all details of administration. Direct democracy of this kind was the ideal form envisaged by Jean Jacques Rousseau in his *Contrat social,* and it may be found, to a certain extent, in the New England town meetings and in some of the smaller Swiss cantons. The referendum and the popular initiative preserved in several modern democratic constitutions, as in that of Switzerland, can be regarded as elements of direct democracy surviving in the indirect or representative democracy which is the generally accepted form of modern times.

Another difference between ancient Greek democracy and modern democracy does not concern the form of government but the equality of all individuals. Ancient democracy was not only compatible with slavery, it presupposed slavery, which alone permitted the necessary leisure for the citizens to devote themselves to questions of public interest. Modern democracy has tended more and more to abolish all differences and privileges of birth, class, race, and sex, and to broaden its basis so as to become all-inclusive. The ancients had a low estimate of labor, even of highly skilled labor, which was also performed by slaves. Only modern capitalistic civilization, which arose in countries where modern democracy developed simultaneously, produced the new concept of the dignity and necessity of work that helped to break down the barriers of privilege. It should be noted, however, that in Athens slaves were well treated, and that the main difference between their ways of life and those of other citizens of the poorer classes was the lack of political rights. The Stoic philosophy which dominated the Roman Empire and pervaded Roman law, and the emphasis put by prophetic Judaism and early Christianity on the poor and the disinherited and on the equality of all men before God, created the fundamental assumptions on which modern democracy could develop its faith in the essential equality of all human beings.

Toward the end of the Middle Ages, the growing power and capitalistic wealth of the cities, especially in northern Italy, provided the opportunity for a more intense cultural and social life and with it the reappearance of the spirit of individual liberty. Niccolò Machiavelli, in his *Discorsi sopra la prima deca di Tito Livio,* praised the value of liberty and the superiority of republics over states where the will of one man prevails. He emphasized the fact that the commonweal is observed and promoted nowhere better than in a free citizenry.[1] These discourses, replete with the realistic wisdom of a statesman and political thinker, plead for democracy, assert that the people are wiser and more constant than a single ruler or leader, and reject the contrary opinion, adding that this contrary opinion has its origin in the fact that everyone can speak ill of the people, freely and without fear, even while the people rule, while everyone speaks of the princes or dictators only with a thousand fears and a thousand considerations.[2] Renaissance and Reformation helped to prepare the soil for the growth of democracy through their emphasis on the individual and individual conscience and through their return to the sources of classical and biblical antiquity. A new spirit of inquiry grew up; spurred on by the new discoveries and inventions, it raised man's stature in his own eyes and opened before him vast and unknown possibilities. This new spirit found its expression in Francis Bacon's experimental philosophy as well as in René Descartes' rationalism, which proclaimed in his "I think, therefore I am," the sovereignty and maturity of the thinking individual.

From 1640 on, through a number of revolutions, but even more through the unceasing toil, the unsparing efforts, and the spiritual devotion of countless individuals in many countries during the next three centuries, the ideas of liberty and equality gained more and more concrete form. Seventeenth century England was the birthplace of modern democracy. Christian and classical traditions grew there into something new in a soil well prepared by the development of the Magna Carta and of common law, and fertilized by the Renaissance and Reformation. Liberty under law protected there, in a new feeling of security, the growth of wealth and well-being and the daring curiosity of the inquiring mind. With a deeply religious enthusiasm the English Revolution broke the path for liberty in the modern world. The great voice of the age was raised again and again in a passionate plea for liberty: all of John Milton's writings were imbued with the newly awakened sense of freedom—freedom of thought, freedom of the printed word, freedom of education, freedom of personal life and conduct, in addition to freedom of church and state. His outcry against censorship: "Give me the liberty to know, to utter and to argue freely according to conscience, above all liberties" (*Areopagitica*), was matched by his declaration that "no man who knows aught can be so stupid to deny that all men naturally were born free, being the image and resemblance of God himself . . . it being thus manifest that the power of kings and magistrates is nothing else, but what is only derivative, transferred and committed to them in trust from the people, to the common good of them all" (*Defense of the People of England*). Milton identified the English people and their cause with that of individual liberty, freedom of conscience, and the dignity of reason; but this new dispensation was to be universal, the English only preceding other nations, who were soon to follow. Macaulay in his *Essay on Milton* characterized the man and his epoch:

He lived at one of the most memorable eras in the history of mankind, at the very crisis of the great conflict between liberty and despotism, reason and prejudice. That great battle was fought for no single generation, for no single land. The destinies of the human race were staked on the same case with the freedom of the English people. Then were first proclaimed those mighty principles which have since worked their way in the depths of the American forests, which have aroused Greece from the slavery and degradation of two

thousand years, and which have kindled an unquenchable fire in the
hearts of the oppressed and loosed the knees of the oppressors with
an unwonted fear.

The spirit of liberalism, tolerance, and respect for the individual pervading seventeenth century England found its lasting
expression in John Locke's *Letters on Toleration* and *Two Trea-
tises of Government*. They were dominated by the spirit of compromise and the "live and let live" attitude of mutual respect
and toleration within the common frame which characterize
liberalism and democracy. Locke formulated and expounded
two basic principles: that the individual, his liberty, dignity, and
happiness form the foundation of all social life, and that government is a moral trust dependent upon the free consent of the
governed. As a result of the two revolutions of the seventeenth
century, England was the only country in which the power of
absolutism was definitely broken, and though democracy's
growth was slow, its basis had been so firmly established that
England never knew any retrogression. The control of national
affairs had passed into the hands of a parliament with a steadily
growing preponderance of the House of Commons and a steadily
enlarging electorate; the liberties of the community and of the
individuals were protected by a Bill of Rights; judges were independent from the executive power; the abolition of censorship
and the recognition of tolerance became acknowledged principles.

From these roots the tree of democracy grew faster in the
virgin soil of the American colonies than in the mother country.
Locke became "America's philosopher par excellence." The col-
onists struggled with the mother country as Englishmen and on
the basis of their freedom as Englishmen. What was a constitutional conflict within a common heritage of seventeenth century
liberty became the starting point for a new surge of democracy,
not only as a result of the peculiar social conditions of the colonies and the absence of the institutions surviving from the past,
but also from the influence of the new ideas of natural rights,
the rule of reason and the freedom of man, which were then

propagated in France and England. Their spokesman in America was Thomas Jefferson, who had drafted the Declaration of Independence and whose life work in later years was to convert the United States into a democracy under the influence of eighteenth century ideas.

This American Revolution, deeply influenced by the "French ideas," in turn acted upon developments in France. French society idealized the events across the Atlantic. It saw in them the first example of a people which in its eagerness for liberty and justice had thrown off the yoke of an unjust monarchy, and had established a government based upon the enlightened principles of reason. Soon the French people were to find themselves involved in a similar effort. Years of unprecedented turmoil shook not only the foundations of French society, but those of all Europe. The French Revolution introduced the symbols of a new cult of liberty and human rights and coined the three words which expressed the essence of the new goal of democracy: the liberty of every individual, the equality of all men, and the brotherhood of all human beings. In the immense enthusiasm of its beginnings, age-old privileges were abandoned; the new feeling of the dignity of man, of his right to self-expression and self-determination, not only created new political forms, but manifested itself in all fields of public and private life.

Though the new ideas of liberalism and democracy were perverted in France by the totalitarian rules of the Convention and of Napoleon and were finally defeated on the battlefield, and though Europe was apparently returning to the old authoritarian order, democracy was soon to resume its growth. In the century from 1820 to 1920, it gained both in depth and in breadth. The Revolution of 1830, which started in Paris in July and ended in 1832 with the English Reform Bill, reestablished the trend toward constitutional government with guarantees for the rights and liberties of every citizen. Its invigorating influence made itself felt in 1848, the "spring of the peoples." The new ideas penetrated into central Europe and even into Russia, and finally, at the beginning of the twentieth century, started to transform traditional life in the Ottoman Empire and in Persia, in China and in Japan. The victory of the democratic states of western Europe and of the United States of America over the military and conservative monarchies of central Europe, and the Russian Revolution of March, 1917, marked the highest points of development for democracy up to that date. Democracy for the first time seemed about to fulfill its world-wide mission of a liberating message to all classes and to all peoples.

For it is the nature of democracy, in a gradual and orderly process but unceasingly, to broaden and deepen its basis and to include ever new classes and peoples. In their rise liberalism and democracy were connected with the ascendancy of the middle classes and with the growth of industrial civilization. As social phenomena, the English revolutions of the seventeenth century and the revolutions of 1830 and 1848 were largely middle-class movements. Economically, they served the fight against a feudal and rural economy to provide the necessary liberty of development for the rising urban economy of traders and industrialists. This new economy was based on essential liberties removing all the restrictions of the past which had hindered the free development of the individual and had kept him in the station of life to which he had been assigned by birth or tradition. The rise of democracy, with its emphasis upon equality and upon each individual's right to the pursuit of happiness, awakened the masses to the realization of their situation and brought many members of the upper and middle classes to the conviction that the benefits and blessings of democracy must be extended to become real and effective for the masses.

Ultimately, democracy will be determined by its strength as a moral and spiritual factor dominating the public mind. Great democratic statesmen, like William Ewart Gladstone in England, have always understood how to instill some of their own democratic fervor and moral conviction in their people and thus to keep democracy as a live issue. For democracy does not exhaust itself in political techniques or in economic reforms. It is, above all, a fundamental attitude, a scale of values, a definite conception of man and his place in society. Though the institutions and forms of democracy may differ widely, and in fact do so in various countries, there are central values which underlie all forms of democracy and determine what may be called the "democratic way of life." Above all, it is the method of discussion, of open-minded critical inquiry, and of mutual regard and compromise that distinguishes democracy from its twentieth century carica-ture, the "new" or "true" manipulated democracy of the totali-tarian mass states. Democracy presupposes the existence of op-position as a legitimate partner in the democratic process; it accepts a pluralistic view of values and associations, and it rejects any totalitarian or monolithic identification of the state with one party or with one dogma. But discussion and tolerance must always be held within the framework of the democratic faith, and that means the recognition of the fundamental values of individual liberty and of the freedom of the inquiring mind. Tol-erance toward elements which deny the fundamental assump-tions of democracy, and even its right to existence, would not only be theoretically inadmissible, but also practically most dan-gerous to the existence of democracy. Democracy has many shortcomings, some of which are inherent in its nature; they can and must be improved and modified by constant criticism and vigilant opposition; they should not be allowed to foster a spirit of unproductive criticism that in its wish to put something "better" in the place of "inefficiency" or "corruption" or "medi-ocrity" generally is not clear about the alternative which turns out to be some form of old authoritarianism, however stream-lined it may seem. By its own essence, democracy can never be perfect, because that would presuppose a perfect citizenry, highly educated and never swayed by blind emotion or by in-ertia. But with all its imperfections, democracy is so far the most human and humane form devised by the growth of Western civilization which tends to increase the dignity and the creative faculties of every individual. Its intrinsic imperfections make it the most difficult, most daring, and most promising form of human organization.

With the awakening of the masses from apathy to activity, from immaturity to full stature, democracy creates a number of complex problems which have sometimes been summed up in

slogans like "revolt of the masses" or, applied to predemocratic
and preindustrialized peoples, "the revolt of the East." With the
broadening of education, which only a comparatively short time
ago was confined to a tiny minority and today tends practically
everywhere to include everyone, the level of education necessarily had to be lowered, though the gain on the whole has been
great, not only in the breadth of education imparted, but also in
its quality. Since their awakening from traditional inertia, the
masses have been more easily swayed by emotions; the democratic process of the formation of a collective will is cumbersome
and allows the full play of demagoguery and may, in times of
emergency, weaken or confuse the national resolve. All these
difficulties offered to some an excuse for discarding democracy
and for returning to the domination of a selected group, a self-
appointed elite, convinced of its divine-grace mission over "im-
mature" people. Faced by the complexities of modern life, some
wished to take refuge in an apparent scientific or religious "security" by scrapping three hundred years of social and intellectual development. Since World War I a number of movements
of this kind have arisen, motivated partly by a conscious return
to what Oswald Spengler has called "age-old barbarism," an attitude long believed obsolete, and partly by a sense of defeatism,
of frustration, of discouraged cynicism. Democracy had lost its
vigor to a certain extent, had become softened by a preoccupa-
tion with material progress and economic considerations. But the
attacks to which it found itself exposed revitalized democracy
and brought about a rethinking of its fundamental values and
implications.

The totalitarian governments of the twentieth century regarded
democracy as a hypocritical pretense devised in the interests
of certain classes or nations. At the same time they believed
democracy unable to cope with the complexities of modern mass
life. They were convinced that democracy was doomed and that
its methods were obsolete and its adherents decadent. They
expected that it would perish by its own inner tensions, discords,
and conflicts. They opposed to democracy the alleged harmony
of a monolithic society in which class or racial conflicts were

eliminated and which was held together by an allegiance to one class or one race only. While the democratic states were in theory above classes or races, and in any case aimed at harmonizing their various interests, the totalitarian states in theory identified the state with one class or one race and preached the merciless struggle of this class or race against all others. At the end of World War I, democracy seemed to gain everywhere, except in Russia, where Lenin's Revolution of November, 1917, had established the first totalitarian regime. Even in Germany and throughout central Europe, democratic republics replaced conservative monarchies. Japan, under the influence of the general trend, made definite progress toward democracy after 1918. But in Italy fascism under Benito Mussolini followed in many ways the new one-party state of Russia and established between 1922 and 1926 another totalitarian regime which rejected democracy. In the first part of the 1930's, fascist regimes were established in several other countries, notably in Germany. Under their influence, other nations began to waver between democracy and fascism. By their self-confidence, aggressiveness, military preparations, and controlled public opinion, totalitarian powers seemed superior to the democracies, the totalitarian methods more efficient.

Totalitarianism was encouraged by its successes, which were due in a large degree not only to the peaceful character of the democratic peoples, but above all to the unwillingness of the democracies to cooperate in face of a threat to all democracy. After World War I, each democracy thought only of itself and its own supposed interests. Great Britain and France no longer stood together; the United States retreated into an attitude of isolation and recrimination. Thus the democracies had to face again the challenge of an authoritarian bloc based upon unity achieved at the price of freedom. The reluctance of the democracies to establish a close cooperation or a union endangered not only the national security of each democracy, but also the cause of freedom and human worth everywhere. Britain and France found the unity of their strategic interests and predominant way of life only in the moment of supreme danger, too late to save France and almost too late to guarantee Britain's survival.

In that situation in June, 1940, the British government, under the leadership of Winston Churchill, submitted to the French an official proposal for a union of the two countries. The proposed declaration read:

At this most fateful moment in the history of the modern world, the governments of the United Kingdom and the French Republic make this declaration of indissoluble union and unyielding resolution in their common defense of justice and freedom, against subjection to a system which reduces mankind to a life of robots and slaves. The two governments declare that France and Britain shall no longer be two nations but one Franco-British union. The constitution of the union will provide for joint organs of defense, foreign, financial, and economic policies. Every citizen of France will enjoy immediately citizenship of Great Britain, every British subject will become a citizen of France.

This proposal was rejected by the French cabinet in the spirit of defeatism then gripping the nation.

In the pursuance of World War II, victory for the democracies was made possible by the close cooperation, amounting almost to a union in strategic and economic affairs, between the United States and Britain. Such a unity had never been achieved during World War I, not even in its last and most critical stage. It was the deep understanding of General Dwight D. Eisenhower, commander in chief of the armies of the democratic allies, of the need for unity among the democratic nations, based upon a common tradition, which made them such a powerful instrument for victory.

Yet in 1939-1941 the fascist nations were confident of success. They had prepared for the war for a long time and they had mobilized their resources for waging it. They had placed "guns before butter" and had ridiculed the softness and liberties of the democracies. Russia, under her totalitarian regime, fearful of war and distrustful of the outside world, had also for many years been preparing militarily and psychologically for the possibility of approaching conflict. She was supported in it by the immensity of her territory, the vast numbers of her population, and the abundance of her resources. The democracies, on the other hand, were in 1939-1941 neither materially nor psychologically prepared. The democratic peoples did not expect war; in fact they believed it impossible and inadmissible. Their economic life was entirely governed by the requirements of "butter before guns." In spite of this material and psychological unpreparedness, the democracies were able to stand the test and to create mighty armaments, equal in quality to the best produced in the totalitarian countries, where for years many gifted brains had given their full attention to military science and technology. The quantity of output was so great that Britain and the United States could supply Russia with many thousands of tanks and planes and vast amounts of various equipment. In the psychological realm democracy showed an astonishing resilience and unity. Neither in Britain nor in the United States did the nondemocratic elements—the fascists and, during the period of German-Russian friendship, the communists—seriously hamper the war effort or its preparation. Before 1939 the enemies of democracy and some of its pusillanimous friends had expressed expectation that in case of war democracy would be unable to maintain civil and political liberties and would turn totalitarian. Nothing of that kind happened. On the contrary, the war effort invigorated the democratic consciousness and made it more vigilant. In Britain and in the United States the constitutional liberties were maintained. The British House of Commons, the mother of parliamentarianism and democracy, continued to direct national existence and express the will of the people during the most tragic and trying hours of World War II. The rights of minorities and the freedom of opinion and expression remained safeguarded. This example strengthened and inspired democratic elements everywhere. On the whole, the totalitarian attacks against democracy led, by the middle of the twentieth century, to a reappraisal and a reassertion of the fundamental attitudes and values inherent in the democratic position, to a new confidence of the democratic nations, and to an unprecedented readiness on their part to cooperate in the defense of peace and human liberty.

XIV

COOPERATION AND FEDERATION

I<small>N THE</small> first half of the twentieth century, the United States, due to its traditions, its geographic position, its resources, its population, rose to the rank of the foremost Western nation. Thus it fulfilled what many Americans and Europeans had expected as early as the end of the eighteenth century. However, the American mind had difficulty in adapting itself to the changing circumstances, to its new international position. It was woefully unprepared for war when it came, and for peace when it had to be secured. For eighty years, from the fall of Napoleon to the beginning of the twentieth century, the United States needed no foreign policy. These years coincided with the happiest period mankind has known so far, with Britain's undisputed role as guardian of peace and of progressive growth to liberty under law everywhere. America's security was then based on the division of Europe, the backwardness of eastern Asia, and Britain's control of the Atlantic, which made the Monroe Doctrine possible and thwarted the recolonization of the Americas by the Holy Alliance. Americans attributed this long freedom from care, not to the realities of the situation, but to the unique condition of America's moral climate.

The turn of the century ended the happy isolation for Britain and America alike: the Boer and Spanish wars almost coincided. New powers emerged in Europe and Asia: Wilhelm's Germany and a Japan victorious over China. Both dreamed of oceanic expansion, built great fleets, and, as a new, infinitely more dynamic and energetic Holy Alliance, looked for a leading role on the world stage and dreamed ultimately of the recolonization of the Americas. Under the shock of the Boer War, Great Britain awakened from isolationism and Victorian imperialism to the new reality: she looked for allies and began the daring and unprecedented transformation of her empire from trustee-ship to partnership, the greatest school of liberty under law known to history. The United States, outgrowing the pains of adolescence, fought under Theodore Roosevelt against the rough and naïve plutocracy at home and for security in a changing world abroad: far-flung empire bases were created at Puerto Rico and Panama, at Hawaii, Guam, and Cavite. But the people as a whole had hardly the first understanding of the changing situation. The rising power of Germany and Japan threatened not only the security of Britain and America; it also threatened their common conception—derived from Magna Carta, Milton, and Locke—of liberty and of man's place in society. Yet Ameri-cans continued in the happy illusion of their Victorian age, hid-ing reality behind all kinds of moralistic and legalistic screens. Their unique economic advance favored a one-track economic interpretation of social relations, weakening their understanding of the decisive factors in history. Thus they entered the war in 1917 without knowing why.

The United States had in Woodrow Wilson a great war Presi-dent.[1] He understood the threat offered by Germany to the Western concept of liberty. He did it because he was deeply steeped in the American moral tradition. As a statesman and historian he also grasped, though only dimly, the threat which a German victory would present to American national security. By the beginning of 1917, a German victory seemed probable; Russia was facing revolution and chaos; France was saved from mutiny and defeatism only by old man Clemenceau; Britain might have been starved into submission by the submarines; a German domination of Europe and of the Atlantic loomed which could involve a recolonization of the Western Hemisphere. But Woodrow Wilson did not clearly envisage the reasons of Amer-ican security for which the country had to fight. His moralistic reasons were valid but, offered exclusively and overemphasized, they confused the American mind about the issues at stake and did not educate them to realize the interdependence of interests of western Europe and the United States. Even after the United States entered the war, it became only an associate, not an allied nation. Wilson fought the war as a separate war, setting America apart on a high moral pedestal from which he looked down upon, and lectured, mankind and his Allies. "One would have hardly judged from his speeches," Professor H. C. F. Bell writes, "that the Allies knew anything about courage and sacrifice and suffering, or that some of the Allied leaders also had ideas. We Americans, it seemed, were to be freedom's chief, if not first and only champions." Thus Wilson was in no way educating the American people to cooperation with, and a fair understanding of, the Allies. He rather increased their naïve arrogance. Complaining to Colonel House of the imperialistic aims of the Allies, he said: "When the war is over we can force them to our way of thinking because by that time they will, among other things, be financially in our hands." He was prepared to club, by American power, other nations into what he considered righteousness. He was convinced, and he educated the American people in the belief, that the American nation alone was disinterested while all other nations thought only of their interests and greed. When the Germans, clever psychologists in that they appealed to him alone, not to the Allies, asked for armistice terms, he did not consult the Allies at all, but handled the whole matter secretly and by himself. When the Allies hesitated to accept Wilson's dictation, he threatened the conclusion of a separate peace.

Wilson's mystical belief in the mission of the American nation was one of the two fundamental elements of his creed; the other was his mystical faith in the "common man," in the people as opposed to their "wicked" governments, in their immediate ability for self-government, whether in Russia or in Germany, in their innate goodness and peacefulness. His faith was a legacy of Rousseau and of 1848. He had much similarity with Mazzini in his nationalism; his battle cry could have been "God and the People" too. He idolized and idealized the "people" and especially the American people. The Americans were to him "a body

of idealists more ready to lay down our lives for a thought than
a dollar." The people were always right—in theory; in practice
he expected them always to think and act as he did. He never
understood that the American people might be less "idealistic"
than their leader and therefore lost his cause by lecturing
European statesmen instead of educating his own people. He
never understood that European statesmen might be much better and more moderate than their peoples and therefore lost his
cause by appealing to the peoples over the heads of their statesmen. Though he deeply believed in the people, he regarded
himself as their undisputed representative who could voice their
"true" opinions and lead them on the path which their "true"
nature demanded. With desperate earnestness he struggled in
their behalf according to his own light, which he deeply believed to be the universal light. Only after his second return
from Europe, in the memorable speeches of his Western tour
in September, 1919, did he show a full understanding of the
situation. Then it was too late.

Most Americans regarded the war as a generous crusade, not
realizing that it was fought as much for American as for British
or French security, though the Americans, fortunately for them,
paid a much lighter price for victory. Victory in itself was a
tremendous prize. It had seemed most doubtful in the spring
of 1918, when the Russians, under Lenin's leadership, had abandoned the Allies, had concluded a separate peace with the Germans, and made it possible for the latter to throw all their
might against the democracies. At that time victory seemed, at
the best, very distant. It came surprisingly fast in the fall of
1918; it created the condition for America's future security and
made the world safe for American democracy. But because the
Americans had not grasped the threat to their security, victory
itself seemed sterile, the war effort a mistake, and no community of interests with the Allies was recognized. They abandoned them—and with that, the fruits of victory, the hopes for
security and peace—and to quiet their confused conscience, they
accepted the myths about World War I and the Treaty of Versailles, which German and communist propaganda busily spread

and which, more than anything else, made World War II possible.[2] As the result, France, Britain, and the United States could not prevent World War II; they were unprepared in their minds and hearts in that fateful summer of 1940 when Churchill alone, endowed with prophetic ethos and a keen sense of historical realities, turned the tide and gave his people and the Americans the chance to understand, to act, and to survive, a service which, fortunately in a much less dramatic moment, he again rendered in February, 1946. But this time the democracies, especially the leading democracies, were to learn their lesson, which, if it had been learned after World War I, would have prevented World War II.

After World War I the democracies refused to cooperate. A period of "debunking" set in, Western civilization and the tradition of liberty were "unmasked" as pretentious and hollow pretexts for economic interests and national egotism.[3] The most farsighted pacifist, Norman Angell, published in 1918 a book called *The Political Conditions of Allied Success,* in which he pointed out that a union of the democracies was an essential condition for the maintenance of peace and the security of liberty:

The survival of the Western democracies, in so far as that is a matter of the effective use of their force, depends upon their capacity to use it as a unit, during the War and after. That unity we have not attained, even for the purposes of the War, because we have refused to recognize its necessary conditions—a kind and degree of democratic internationalism to which current political ideas and feelings are hostile; an internationalism which is not necessary to the enemy, but is to us. He can in some measure ignore it. We cannot. His unity in so far as it rests upon moral factors, can be based upon the old nationalist conceptions; our unity depends upon a revision of them, an enlargement into an internationalism. . . . Return to the old relationships after the War will sooner or later doom the democratic nations, however powerful each may be individually, to subjugation in detail by a group, inferior in power but superior in material unity —a unity which autocracy achieves at the cost of freedom and human worth.

The unhappy forebodings of Norman Angell were fulfilled. No democratic internationalism, no union of democracies were realized after World War I. Britain refused to continue her alliance with France; the United States cut its ties with both. The democracies returned to national sovereignty, isolationism, and supposed self-interests. They did not understand that in the twentieth century their frontiers were in very distant lands, on the Rhine or in the eastern Mediterranean, in Manchuria or in Ethiopia. To avoid action, many deluded themselves with the thought that the will to peace was overwhelmingly strong everywhere. The low ebb of political thinking which was reached could be seen in statements like that of the Englishman who wrote: "I cannot myself understand how anyone could want to make a third World War." Naturally everybody would heartily concur in such a straightforward and noble way of thinking and feeling. Unfortunately, things are not so simple. The coming of World War II was made possible by the many Englishmen and Americans who similarly could not understand the complexity and nature of the international situation and of the German problem. "As people had set their minds on not seeing what happened, they eagerly listened to those who demonstrated that nothing happened." Nobody wanted World War II. It could have been prevented by the union of the democracies after 1918, which would have made it understood by all potential aggressors and enemies of democracy that their attempts would fail.

The demand for such a union of the democracies was voiced in 1917 by Thorstein Veblen, who also clearly recognized that the United States should enter the First World War, not to save others, but to save itself. Veblen wrote:

America is placed in an extra-hazardous position between the two seas beyond which to either side lie the two Imperial Powers [Germany and Japan] whose place in the modern economy of nations it is to disturb the peace in an insatiable quest of dominion. This position is no longer defendable in isolation, under the later state of the industrial arts, and the policy of isolation that has guided the national policy hitherto is therefore falling out of date. It will be said,

of course, that America is competent to take care of itself and its
Monroe Doctrine in the future as in the past. But that view overlooks
the fact that the modern technology has definitively thrown the advantage to the offensive, and that intervening seas can no longer be
counted on as a decisive obstacle. On this latter head, what was
reasonably true fifteen years ago is doubtful today [1917] and it is
in all reasonable expectation invalid for the situation fifteen years
hence. The other peoples that are of a neutral temper [the Western
democracies] may need the help of America sorely enough in their
endeavours to keep the peace, but America's need of cooperation is
sorer still, for the republic is coming into a more precarious place
than any of the others.

Veblen demanded the formation of a union of the democracies, which he called "pacific nations," and he foresaw in 1917
that Germany and Japan, if balked in their endeavor in the
second decade of the twentieth century, would unite their forces
later to resume their attempt in Europe and in the Far East.
Turning to those who wished in 1916 to help the Allies in their
fight against Germany for humanitarian reasons, Veblen wrote
in January, 1917:

Hitherto the spokesmen of a pacific federation of nations have
spoken of America's share in the project as being that of an interested outsider, a humane solicitude for the well-being of civilized
mankind at large. Now, there is not a little verisimilitude in this conception of America as a tower of strength in the projected federation
of neutral nations, however pharisaical an appearance it may all have
in the self-complacent utterances of patriotic Americans. The American republic is, after all, the greatest of the pacific nations in resources, population and industrial capacity; the adherence of the
American republic would, in effect, double the mass and powers of
the projected league, and would so place it beyond all hazard of
defeat from without, or even of serious outside opposition to its aims.
Yet it will not hold true that America is either disinterested or indispensable. To America, the league is indispensable, as a refuge from
otherwise inevitable dangers ahead; singlehanded, America cannot
defend itself, except at a prohibitive cost; whereas in co-partnership
with these others the national defense becomes a virtually negligible
matter.

Veblen demanded a federation of democracies in which "national interests and pretensions would have to give way to the collective control of military force sufficient to insure prompt and concerted action," and he regarded the participation of the United States and of Britain as indispensable to the success of such a federation. Twenty-two years later, in March, 1939, Mr. Henry L. Stimson put the case not differently from Veblen's:

I believe that our foreign policy cannot with safety be geographically limited to a defense of this hemisphere or of our own continental boundaries. On the contrary, I think that if we should stand idly by without protest of action until Britain, France, and China are either conquered or forced to make terms with militaristic aggressors, our own hemisphere might become economically so affected and militarily so endangered that it would be neither a safe nor happy place to live in, for a people with American ideals of life.

But after World War I, the federation of democracies was not formed. All suggestions for an affirmative policy were countered by the objections that any such step would needlessly antagonize nations with whom otherwise peace could be maintained and that it would represent meddling with distant lands which really did not concern the nation. Pacifism—entirely legitimate as a religious pattern of life, as a witness through sacrifice and martyrdom, and, as such, a salt of the earth and a reminder of the verities—underwent a strange corruption. It began to cater to the egotism and understandable longing for peace of the people, promising them peace and happiness only if they would not declare their readiness for timely action. Thus pacifism, by helping to dull the understanding of the present situation and undermining the will to intelligent and timely resistance and the necessary preparation for it, objectively supported plans of aggression. By a supreme irony the pacifists thus helped the most antipacific force on earth. From this point it was only a slight step to a pacifism asserting that the totalitarians really meant peace, in a more or less veiled way accepting most of their pretexts and excuses, and finally justifying Hitler or Stalin and finding fault with their victims. The principle of nonresist-

ance to evil is a great principle if men carry it out, listening only
to the voice within themselves, and ready to bear all martyrdom
for its sake. It becomes something entirely different if it is transferred to the political scene, over the radio and in mass meetings, not in an absolute earnestness, but in an argument as to
the time when a nation should defend itself, whether in an
unchristian egotism only when its own frontiers are invaded, or
wisely and courageously helping fellow victims of potential
aggression. The principle of nonresistance to evil degenerated
into a denial that evil exists, into an appeal to accept the evil
and to condone injustice. Thus pacifism, instead of bearing witness to the verities, became in the universal crisis one of the
elements which could be used and abused by the aggressor
nations for the destruction of the verities.

Unwittingly, pacifism thus supported the communist and fascist propaganda onslaught on democracy. In the certainty of
possessing the only absolute truth, the communists attacked
indiscriminately and venomously everything which did not
entirely agree with their doctrine and even with its changing
interpretations. They offered a "scientific" explanation for the
democratic "sins" of having entered World War I and of having
concluded the peace treaties of 1919. A little later, fascism rein-
forced this propaganda by insisting upon the imperfections of
democracy and of the democracies. The totalitarians almost succeeded in convincing the Western peoples of their deep-seated
rottenness and their shameful hypocrisy, while communists and
fascists never doubted that they themselves were impeccably
right and that, for moral reasons, they represented the irresistible
wave of the future. Their leaders, to whom they rapturously
listened, educated them to such a misrepresentation of reality.

Great national leaders throughout the times have been severe
critics of their people, calling them to repent and to mend their
ways. In biblical times, as today, the masses liked to listen to
"leaders" and advisers who flattered their instincts and their
feelings of self-righteousness. But these men have been called
by the Bible false prophets, and their words have been forgotten, whereas the violent reproaches and censures of the true

prophets, their diatribes against the predatory instincts and self-indulgent inclinations of their own people, have been reverently preserved as an example of what true national leadership implies. Totalitarian leaders, however, in childish exaggeration, glorify the innate genius and greatness of their peoples and their causes. This unceasing, uncritical, and vociferous self-adulation dulls the critical and moral sense and leads to a complete falsification of all standards. The reading of representative newspapers and periodicals from totalitarian countries will leave the reader with an immense feeling of sadness and depression about the constant distortion of truth, the coarse vulgarity of feeling and language, the one-sided perspective in which everything is presented, always to the praise of everything native and to the vilification of everything alien. In liberal countries statements as silly and degrading may sometimes be heard, but there they can be contradicted and laughed off. No contradiction is possible in totalitarian countries, no discussion nor any satire; the screaming monologue repeats undisturbed the same primitive chant of self-glorification. This leads to the dangerous delusion that all the ills under which totalitarian nations suffer are due to the evil machinations of their enemies. From the dizzy heights to which fulsome flattery has raised the unfortunate totalitarian people, it necessarily views any disagreement with its opinions and any resistance to its "rights" as a crime of which only enemies of mankind are capable. Western man, with his antimetaphysical, rational, liberal, nineteenth century mind, could hardly grasp the essence of the totalitarian movements. He took their arguments at face value and treated national-socialist Germany or communist Russia as if they still were nineteenth century powers with limited goals and the desire for understanding and reciprocity.

Isolation and misunderstanding combined to prevent timely and united actions by the democracies which could have prevented World War II. Wishful thinking—about the nature of totalitarianism—led to easy illusionism; fearful thinking—about the destructiveness of war—led to easy cynicism. Both had the same effect: they obscured reality and excused from a sustained effort against perils which the first denied and the second accepted as invincible. On the one hand, democracy was taken for granted; on the other, it was cynically deflated by comparison with standards of absolute perfection. Americans and British let their ideals and their power fall into disrepute at the very moment when, after 1918, the world needed leadership based upon ideals and power. The great wars of the twentieth century had been wars of ideals and power. A German victory in 1914 or in 1939 would have meant not only the triumph of the German arms and an expansion of German territory, but also of the German *Weltanschauung,* with consequences which would have changed entirely the face of the earth. The same would be true of a Russian victory in mid-twentieth century. Ideas are in many ways the heart of a nation's power. But at the end of the thirties, twenty years after World War I, the Americans and the British were, in idea and power, entirely unprepared.

Nowhere was the confusion greater than in the United States. In the years of 1935 and 1936, when Japan, Italy, and Germany were actively preparing for aggression, Senate investigation commissions reaffirmed officially that American participation in World War I had been a sinful mistake and that wars were caused by big-business interests, Wall Street bankers, munitions makers, and British propaganda. President Roosevelt's administration worked on the perfection of American neutrality legislation and thus informed would-be aggressors that they could go on conquering strategic positions for their final onslaught on the "citadel of liberty." The neutrality legislation abandoned victims of aggression resolutely and righteously to their fate. Comfortable reasons were always found to point out the grievous shortcomings of the prospective victims and thus to excuse the aggressor. The neutrality legislation intensified the belief of the American people that its will to peace and its geographical position guaranteed its security. The democratic nations were prone to criticize the inadequate response of fellow democracies to aggression but rarely recognized the implications of their own refusal to take the risk of cooperation. That became especially clear when Britain and France finally, in 1939, without being attacked, decided to resist German aggression, even in distant parts, where none of their direct interests seemed involved. At that moment public opinion in the United States, which until then had voiced sharp dissatisfaction with British and French "peace-mindedness," shrank from any active cooperation and self-righteously took refuge in its "love of peace." These attitudes increased the mutual distrust and recrimination among democracies and diverted attention from the community of danger. The United States waited until it was attacked itself before it gained clarity and courage to act.[4]

The democracies were not the only ones which persisted in the blindness of national egotism. On January 26, 1934, a ten-year pact of friendship was concluded between Germany and Poland, two nations which had faced each other as bitter enemies since 1918. Five years later, on January 30, 1939, Hitler declared before the German Reichstag: "We have just celebrated the fifth anniversary of the conclusion of our non-aggression pact with Poland. There can scarcely be any difference of opinion today among the true friends of peace with regard to the value of this agreement. One only needs to ask oneself what might have happened to Europe if this agreement, which brought such relief, had not been entered into five years ago. In signing it, this great Polish marshal and patriot rendered his people just as great a service as the leaders of the National Socialist State rendered the German people. During the troubled months of the past year the friendship between Germany and Poland was one of the reassuring factors in the political life of Europe." And at the height of the Czechoslovak crisis, on September 26, 1938, Chancellor Hitler declared in a speech in the Berlin Sportpalast that while democracies were bloodthirsty war agitators, nondemocratic Poland had come to an agreement with national-socialist Germany which "for ten years in the first instance entirely removed the danger of a conflict. We are all convinced that this agreement will bring lasting pacification. A way for understanding has been found; and it will be ever further extended." Less than a year later, Hitler's Germany attacked Poland in spite of the fact that the Polish government under

Colonel Josef Beck was a semifascist government which had always acted in close harmony with Hitler's Germany and had supported the latter in the dismemberment of Czechoslovakia.

A few months after Germany declared her ten-year pact of friendship with Poland void, communist Russia concluded a similar agreement with Germany. The Soviet people welcomed Stalin's policy, which seemed a promise to keep them out of war. It was like the Polish policy, pure opportunism based upon considerations of Soviet national interest, on false assumptions about foreign nations—especially the British, who were expected to conclude a separate peace with Germany—and on miscalculations of the probable course of the war. The Soviet leadership hoped that a long-lasting war and an exhaustion of both sides would make it possible for communism to fulfill its aspirations for which it did not find the soil sufficiently prepared after World War I. When Stalin explained his attitude after Russia found herself involved in the war, his words: "As long as Hitler occupied himself with the rectification of the injustices of Versailles, we could and did support Germany. Now Hitler is striving for world domination. This we cannot tolerate," sounded like an echo of Chamberlain's support for Munich in 1938 and his awakening in March, 1939, when he came to the conclusion that Hitler wished to do more than rectify Versailles. Only Chamberlain and the overwhelming majority of British arrived at this conclusion without Germany attacking their country. Germany had suggested to Poland an alliance against Russia and a common expansion at Russia's expense; when Colonel Beck's government rejected this suggestion, Germany turned to Russia and offered her the partition of Poland. Russia eagerly accepted, and the pact of friendship with Germany was concluded, not only out of the desire for peace, as was the Pact of Munich, but for mutual profit and aggrandizement. As a result, Germany attacked Poland and was supported by Russia, which took her share. World War II had started. When Germany attacked Poland, the Western democracies rightly did not ask whether Poland was a true democracy or had a good government. In the interest of peace and of their own security, they supported the existing Polish government and its resistance to aggression. In the same way British help was given to Greece when Italy attacked her on October 28, 1940, in spite of the fact that Greece had then an outright fascist government under General Joannes Metaxas. Fortunately, in these cases the British government acted and did not debate the worth of the government which it helped against aggression.

These cases of aggression also made clear that by its very essence fascism is not an international movement. Communism is an international movement and all communist parties have to look to Moscow as their center and guide. On the other hand, fascist Germany attacked semifascist Poland and fascist Italy invaded fascist Greece; there was no real coordination between Italy and Germany and Japan even during the war; Italian fascists regarded Rome as center and guide; German fascists, Berlin; while Japanese or Spanish fascists would not abandon the primacy of Tokyo and the Japanese imperial house, or of Madrid and Hispanidad to any other embodiment of fascist ideas. Communist countries, by the essence of the movement, are a closely knit unity; fascist countries, by the essence of the movement, stress divergent national self-interest and mission even among fascists; while democracies, if they wish to survive in a world threatened by totalitarianism, are driven in the twentieth century to an ever closer form of cooperation. The framework of national sovereignty has grown too narrow for democracy. With the approach of the middle of the twentieth century, the democratic nations, the guardians of Western civilization, have taken the first steps toward democratic internationalism, toward a union of democracies with full regard for the liberties and diversities, steps which would have seemed unthinkable even in 1945 or 1946. In these steps the American people have taken a courageous lead. Beneath the surface of the alarming news of the day, with its tensions and clashes, there rises a great constructive effort of unprecedented daring. It may bring back to the twentieth century the progress in liberty and the security in peace which the nineteenth century enjoyed, but on a wider

scale and with a greater consciousness of the perils of history
and of the need for sustained effort.[5]

The issues at stake at the end of the 1930's and at the end
of the 1940's were both cast into sharp relief by events in
Czechoslovakia; through its geographical and cultural position,
the country has repeatedly played a symbolic part. The prelude
to World War II was enacted in Bohemia. This prelude was not
the Pact of Munich which Britain and France concluded in
September, 1938, with Hitler's Germany. Though this pact was
objectionable for many reasons—and an influential part of British
public opinion led by Winston Churchill and Anthony Eden
objected to it from the beginning—it could nevertheless be justified. Germany then demanded only the cessation of the Sudeten-
land, a part of Czechoslovakia that was German in feeling,
language, and descent. Hitler could invoke the right of self-
determination, the principles of Woodrow Wilson, in support
of his claims. For very many years liberals and socialists in the
United States and in Britain had bitterly protested the alleged
wrongs of the Treaty of Versailles. Hitler was now out to right
one of these alleged wrongs. Those who should have been the
guardians of the victory of 1918, the democratic peoples of the
United States, of Britain and France, had long abandoned the
guardianship. Materially and psychologically disarmed, they
were unprepared to understand the totalitarian challenge and
much too peace-loving to take it up. Their governments were
unable to think in strategic concepts. It was only Hitler's march
into Prague, in violation of the Pact of Munich, six months later,
that awakened at least the British government of Mr. Neville
Chamberlain and aroused the British people—too late to avert
war, but still in time for Britain to save the liberty of mankind
from Hitler. Hitler's march into Prague was his greatest diplo-
matic mistake; it convinced at least the British that one could
not negotiate and compromise with Hitler. This decision was
arrived at with greatest reluctance, for it ran counter to all the
habits of thought of modern Western civilization and seemed
to doom the hopes of peace.

Hitler's march into Prague in March, 1939, the true turning point in the events immediately preceding World War II, was repeated, with important variations, in the events which happened in Prague in February, 1948, and which resulted in a communist coup taking over Czechoslovakia and imposing a totalitarian dictatorship. This débacle for democracy was preceded by another "Munich," for which again, as for the original Munich, some justification could be found. This new "Munich" occurred in 1944, when President Benes concluded in Moscow, under Stalin's and Molotov's guarantee, an agreement with the communists. At that time the strategic situation was in favor of Stalin, as it had been in 1938 in favor of Hitler. But more important was the fact that the Czech liberals trusted, as Neville Chamberlain had done in 1938 in the case of Hitler, that Stalin would keep the agreement and that the collaboration between communists and liberals was possible. The communists tore up the agreement in February, 1948, as Hitler had torn up the Pact of Munich in March, 1939. They proved that one could not do business with Stalin, and they destroyed the myth that the Czech communists were Czech first and would not act like Russian bolsheviks. In February, 1948, Stalin committed as grave a blunder in Prague as Hitler had done nine years before. But this time the democratic world had learned some lessons at the bitter price of its experiences with the relentless drive of another totalitarianism. Under these circumstances the communist coup in Prague became again a turning point: it awakened the Western world, this time acting so timely that it had the opportunity to prevent World War III by concerted action and to save the liberty of the West without paying the heroic price of war.

In both cases Czechoslovakia, the most democratic state east of the Alps, became a totalitarian state in which respect for the individual, tolerance, and free discussion were replaced by an anti-Western absolutism ruling bodies and souls alike. In both cases the spirit and heritage of T. G. Masaryk were destroyed. For all of Masaryk's life was devoted to one task: to align his people in the spiritual battle between East and West, morally, culturally, and politically, with the West. "In the history of Slav thought, Masaryk's philosophy represented a definite, decisive and triumphant turn towards the West." The decision had not been easy, for the Czechs, a Slav people, have found themselves throughout the centuries surrounded and endangered by the Germans. Thus they turned with sympathy and expectation, which were increased by distance and ignorance, to the greatest Slavic people, the Russians. Leading Czech liberals, who studied Russia closely, warned against illusions about the Colossus of the East. The struggle between East and West always meant to the Czechs, as to the Russians, a confrontation of Europe with Russia. Masaryk's sympathies were entirely with the West and, in Russia, with the Russian westernizers.[6]

In the center of his philosophy stood the Western concept of the dignity of the individual and of the objectivity of truth. His teachers were Descartes and Locke, Hume and Mill. In his great work on Russia and Europe, he regarded Dostoevsky as the true representative of the Russian spirit and of the Russian Revolution. He rejected him as a model and regretted that the Russians had never come under the influence of Kant and his critical spirit. "The philosophical criticism we expect from the Russians will have to return to Hume and to Kant," he wrote in 1913. "It will have to discard uncritical revolutionism." In opposition to the Slavophiles, Masaryk declared: "Through my education I am consciously European; by that I mean that the civilization of Europe and of America suffices intellectually for me."

Masaryk clearly saw that the opposition of the two worlds was not based on economic issues on which a compromise could be easily reached, with good will, but on irreconcilable differences in the interpretation of the nature of man and the meaning of history. Though Masaryk subjected Marxism to extremely sharp criticsim, he was in no way opposed to socialism as long as it respected the dignity of the individual and the objectivity of truth. In the choice between "Jesus or Caesar," Masaryk put himself on the side of Jesus. But he was no absolute pacifist. He recognized that in extreme cases war might be necessary and preparedness indispensable, and he believed that revolutions might be justified under exceptional circumstances when oppression became entirely unbearable. Thus the March Revolution of 1917 in Russia appeared to him legitimate, but the November Revolution of the same year unjustifiable. For Masaryk opposed Lenin's revolution from the beginning. While many Western intellectuals at first hailed the promise of the November Revolution, Masaryk, who knew Russia better than any other occidental and was in Russia during the Revolution, never shared this illusion. At Christmas, 1920, he pointed out that Lenin's revolution was not undertaken in self-defense against an oppressive regime, since Russia was by then on her way to liberty, but that it sprang from a lust to power. He felt the greatest moral horror for the clearly superfluous sacrifice of human life involved. "Degrees of barbarism are always expressed in the way men deal with their own lives and those of others." He regarded bolshevism as determined by Russian backwardness, and Lenin's theory of revolution, in which he found much of Bakunin, as primitive and barbaric. "Uncritical, wholly unscientific infallibility is the basis for the Bolshevik dictatorship," he wrote years ago, "and a regime that quails before criticism and fears to recognize thinking men stands self-condemned." Lenin's revolution destroyed Masaryk's hopes for the Europeanization of Russia. The communist coup in Czechoslovakia of February, 1948, destroyed Masaryk's life work for his own people. It was of almost symbolic value that his closest collaborator and successor and his son died the very same year.[7] But the sacrifice of Czechoslovakia's liberty was not in vain. It awakened the Western world to a realization of the need of unity and vigilance. It created an entirely new spirit throughout the lands of Western civilization. What seemed to many a lost hope, the expectation of peace and the revitalization of democracy, was powerfully rekindled by the new spirit and the new determination which Stalin's coup called forth.

The generation which has lived through World War II has felt in the first years after the victory a sense of impending catastrophe, unknown to the generation which emerged from the turmoil of World War I. After 1945, many came to accept the coming of World War III almost as a certainty. The mounting signs of economic disintegration in vast parts of the globe seemed to predict the breakdown of the capitalistic system—the only one which has so far been able to provide a high and rising standard of living for the masses. But with the approach of the mid-century, it has appeared more and more probable that the prophets of doom may be wrong, that in a close union of the democracies and in a vigilant defense of Western liberty there may be new and justified hope, and that the wishful expectations of the totalitarians and the frantic fears of the friends of liberty may both prove unfounded. They may look different if they are viewed in the perspective of twenty years ago.

In 1928 people not only in the United States but also in Britain, France, and Germany viewed the future with a great sense of security. America was living then through a period of a unique economic boom. Europe had apparently recovered astonishingly fast from the ravages of war. Even Russia, under the New Economic Policy, had then reached a considerable degree of stability and well-being. The Locarno Pact had brought the rapprochement of the former enemies and the promise of growing harmony; the nations of the world signed the Kellogg-Briand Pact in Paris outlawing war, and China, under Chiang Kai-shek's leadership, found national unity for the first time since the overthrow of the Celestial Empire. The generation which had lived through World War I looked forward to a period of peace and prosperity. But the confident dreams of an era of plenty and progress came to nought. Soon the world was to witness economic disintegration and war and the horrors of totalitarianism.

The American people have made great progress in the last twenty years. Their present pessimism, though unfounded, is infinitely healthier than the past optimism, which was equally unfounded. As a result of their optimism, they did not take any precautions, neither against new aggression, which might lead to war, nor against economic overexuberance, which might end in depression. Like the British, they disarmed and gave up military training and thereby encouraged and invited aggression and totalitarian overconfidence. At present the American people in their pessimism are determined to take all the necessary measures to prevent aggression and to avoid depression. They have been forewarned by history and they have learned from history. The study of history is on the whole a saddening experience. Rarely do men and entire nations learn from history and understand its lessons. That that has happened with the American people—not only with some scholars, but with the large majority of average Americans—and in a comparatively short time, is reason for gratitude.

In the elections of November, 1918, at the end of World War I, a Republican Congress was elected while a Democratic administration continued in office. These elections were fought over the issues of foreign policy and of the liquidation of the war. The Republican victory meant the repudiation of the plans for peace advanced by the Democratic President. Woodrow Wilson lost the battle, and the United States withdrew into isolation convinced that they could safeguard their peace by minding their own business. The elections of November, 1946, brought outwardly a result similar to that of twenty-eight years ago. Yet what a difference! This time the foreign policy of the United States was no longer a matter of party advantage or partisan passion: it was the judicious understanding of a mature nation. The growth in stature of men like Senator Vandenberg is one of the most encouraging, and at the same time symptomatic, signs of the progress of the nation.

The American people have lost their sense of security; they have awakened to an understanding of the realities of the world situation and of the verities in the life of nations. They have lost their illusions and shed their wishful thinking. They have freed themselves from disillusionment and cynicism. They are emancipating themselves from the obsession of fear which is conjured by all those who wish to obscure the issues. They are learning to analyze the situation and to face the facts and trends without fear of slanderous or confusing name calling which has been developed to such an art by the oversimplifying, repetitious assertions of the totalitarians and their friends from the right or from the left. As some were not afraid to be called a "red" or a "warmonger" in the late 1930's, they were not afraid to be called a "reactionary" or a "redbaiter" in the late 1940's. They were not frightened into irresolution or confusion, neither by name calling nor by the atomic bomb.

Seeing things in perspective will rid people of the panic created by the atomic war of nerves. Similar wars of nerves were conducted with the fear of Hitler's Luftwaffe before 1939 and had a paralyzing effect on the constructive and courageous thinking of peoples and governments alike. The atomic bomb will certainly have its effects on the art of warfare, and on its frightfulness, as the invention of gunpowder, of the submarine, or the heavy bomber had. But to speak of the "momentous new age" inaugurating an entirely new era seems an unfounded anticipation of history. The fundamentals of international relations, of the nature of man and the nature of things, have not been changed by new inventions. War was an evil before the invention of the atomic bomb; it remains so after it. If the atomic bomb had not been invented, America's problems and her relations with aggressive totalitarianism would be, on the whole, unchanged.

Americans have learned to beware of the hypnotizing power of the incessant incantation of the same oversimplifications. They know now why they fought the two world wars. World War II has reinvigorated democracy. It has shown surprising strength in its mobilization of material and moral resources under full preservation of individual liberty. No serious danger of communism or fascism threatens democratic life in the United States or Britain from within. In the present age nations to survive need not only the armor of weapons, but the inspiration of their ideas. Attractive ideas are a great power in the international world; repulsive ideas are a liability. The Germans lost both wars partly because of their ideas.

The Americans have learned in the last twenty years to free themselves from comfortable isolationism and easy illusionism. They have begun to understand that their frontier is on the Rhine, as they learned in 1940; and in Manchuria, as they learned in 1941; and in the eastern Mediterranean, as they learned in 1947. They are beginning to think in world-wide terms, to consider their responsibilities in an interdependent world society; they are comprehending that this society should be an open society with the barriers of sovereignty lessened and with the free flow of information and goods restored on the largest possible scale; they know that for this end they have to collaborate most closely with the British Commonwealth, with western Europe, and with Latin America.

With the deepening of this education for the world, the twentieth century can yet become one of peace and of the spread of liberty. The new attitude does not imply a wish for American hegemony nor for the imposition of the American way of life on others. Until 1941 no great nation was more reluctant to impose its power or to use it than the United States. There is at present a danger that the American people may fall from this extreme of withdrawal to the opposite one of imposition. They should strive to avoid Scylla as well as Charybdis. The glorious and ancient lands of western Europe would regard Russian domination as the greatest evil which could befall them after the destruction of Germany's similar attempts. But they would regard American control, though to them a lesser evil, with grim apprehension. The United States represents an extension and intensification of the political ideals of Western civilization which, under favorable circumstances, flowered here nearer to realization than anywhere else. The nations on the two shores of the Atlantic belong together in a close community of strategic interests, of moral ideas and political traditions. This belonging together can not express itself through American leadership, but only in a union of the free, in an equal partnership for a common task.

Americans will have to learn that various civilizations and traditions can coexist even in this one world. The wealth of diversity is one of the great elements of history and progress. In the transitional period it will be impossible to develop an all-inclusive world order. Americans are sometimes too fond of clear-cut decisions, of crude alternatives. In 1949, facing Russia,

Americans generally put the dilemma in the way of agreement or war, world order or chaos. Such an approach can only lead to illusions and ultimately to catastrophe. For in the present stage there can be neither agreement nor must there be war. For some time Western mankind will have to live, without agreement and without war, side by side with a closely knit communist world. This demands strength, patience, and a long-range view, but there are no quick solutions, no short cuts, no panaceas. Peace in diversity is only possible under the reign of tolerance, of the "live and let live" of the pretotalitarian period. Diversity is the presupposition of liberty; tolerance is the condition of peace. If the democracies remain united, strong, and vigilant, the totalitarians will lose their fanaticism. Their confident belief that they can impose their faith, sometimes called "true" democracy, upon the "decadent" plain democracy, will wane. Nor will the United States and Russia face each other for a long time as the only two great power centers, a situation which naturally involves great risks. Within a not too distant future a united Europe, a united orderly China, or the revitalized Islamic realm from Morocco to Java may emerge as factors no less powerful, and perhaps more powerful, than the present giants. Until that time, the United States, strong in its understanding of world trends and of its own position through having learned the lessons of history, can help to protect the area of liberty against totalitarianism and the security of peace against aggression. With tact and tolerance, with an open mind and a helpful hand, with firmness and strength, it can steer the ship of state and the ark of Western civilization through the dangerous waters of the unsettled period, which came as the result of the demoralization and devastation caused by warfare and totalitarian revolutions on an unprecedented scale, until the open waters of a settled world are reached. What the American people refused to do twenty years ago, the generation at the turn of the mid-century is willing to undertake. In the Atlantic Pact it has taken the most promising step toward world order.[8] It is fast outgrowing the old notions of sovereignty and segregation. The Atlantic Pact will, by its own nature, develop into an Atlantic Union. The people do not act in blindness; they know the risks involved and prepare for them, but they know that the risks of inactivity and appeasement are infinitely greater. Beyond all the fears and uncertainties of the present, there is the hope that in the closest collaboration possible between western Europe and North America the foundations of a better future are being laid, foundations for a new stage of Western civilization which will outgrow the narrowness of absolute nationalism and restore the faith of Western man in liberty and his armor for peace.

II

By 1957 this policy of cooperation in the North Atlantic Community had begun to bear fruit. The danger of the expansion of the Communist proletarian revolution and of the Russian imperial drive to the Atlantic and the Mediterranean shores, which was very real in 1946, had ended. Thanks to the United States aid program named after its initiator General George Marshall, then United States Secretary of State, and thanks to the North Atlantic Treaty Organization, the economic and moral restoration of Western and Central Europe—even of the former strongholds of anti-Western fascism in the German Federal Republic, in Austria, and in Italy—was accomplished to an unexpected degree within a few years, in spite of the shattering experiences of fascist rule and the tragic devastation of a second great war within the life span of one generation. The German Federal Republic showed a political stability and a sober regard for law unknown to the Weimar Republic, which characteristically had preserved the name of Deutsches Reich with all its dangerous overtones. The center of gravity in Germany had returned to the west and to cooperation with Western Europe after a century which had seen this center steadily shifting to the east and to a rejection of Western standards and political concepts. The Austrian republic which in the first twenty years of its existence, from 1918 to 1938, had lived through a turbulent period of permanent latent or open civil war, has followed since 1945 a policy of successful stabilizing moderation, in which Catholic conservatives and Socialist workers cooperated for the first time in their history and easily defeated all attempts of communism to find a foothold in the impoverished and occupied country. The fierce struggle of Germany, France, and Italy for European hegemony, which did so much to destroy Europe after 1914, has not raised its head since 1945. The initial steps toward the integration of Western Europe have been taken and have been encouraged throughout by the United States.

The consolidation in Western Europe in the middle 1950's contrasted sharply with a growing economic and ideological crisis in the communist realm. The basic identification of Communist revolution and Russian imperialism in which the power of the Soviet Union during the long reign of Stalin was established, was first challenged by the Yugoslav communists under Marshal Tito in 1948, and then by the Polish and Hungarian communists in 1956. In the same year the Chinese communists under Mao Tse-tung and Chou En-lai successfully claimed complete equality with Russian communist leadership. Chou En-lai's visit to Warsaw, Budapest, and Moscow at the beginning of 1957, to mediate with the communist parties of these European countries, testified to the new rank achieved by Asian communism within the world movement. Communism was losing the monocentric and monolithic character which it had possessed under Stalin and seemed to be on the way toward a polycentric development which would allow the communist movements in various countries a certain latitude in methods and principles. At the beginning of 1957 the country most advanced in this direction was Poland. There were new ways explored, under the leadership of Wladyslaw Gomulka —an old-time communist who had been in prison during Stalin's later years—to liberalize the economic and cultural life, to disengage it from the deadening totalitarian grip, and thus to restore some of the economic well-being and intellectual productivity unknown to, and destroyed by, the communist regimes all over central-eastern Europe. Not without some justification the Polish cultural weekly *Przeglad Kulturalny* of November 5, 1956, wrote: "A spectre is haunting Eastern Europe, the spectre of humanitarian socialism."

The free Western world has since the 1930's accepted two premises, dangerous to its safety—that totalitarian indoctrination or education was all-powerful to shape young minds, and that totalitarian regimes could not be shaken by internal upheavals. The year 1956 proved these fears unfounded. In Poland and Hungary attempts were made to break or modify the communist grip on these countries. More important, however, was the fact that these attempts started with the intellectuals and the students in these communist societies, in spite of the fact that the communist regimes have throughout concentrated their efforts on the indoctrination and loyalty of these groups. The youth admitted to the universities was carefully selected by the authorities according to its social reliability: the sons and daughters of proletarians and poor farmers received absolute preference. Throughout its training this youth was ideologically supervised and examined. All totalitarian regimes have always believed that the future is theirs as long as they control the youth and its thinking. The intellectuals in communist countries are a highly privileged class which enjoys economic and social comforts far beyond those of the average good citizen. But these were the groups who revealed themselves unreliable in 1956. Boredom engendered by the prohibition of independent thought and by the insistence on non-problematic conformism led to revolt as soon as a window to the free West was slightly opened. Western liberty exercised an unsuspected power of attraction even on students who were too young to have had personal experience of Western freedom. The Polish and Hungarian movements for greater independence also revealed a serious weakness in the mighty Russian communist strategic position which had seemed so impregnable in 1947: the central-eastern European countries which had been an asset to Russian economy through their merciless exploitation and the lowering of their standards of living had become a liability; now they urgently needed Russian help in order to survive economically; the armies of these countries had proven themselves unreliable, and thus again turned from an asset to a liability for Soviet military operations in Central Europe; moreover, it had become apparent that in case of such operations, the Soviet high command would be faced with a difficult task in assuring the safety of its lines of communication.

The death of Stalin on March 5, 1953, had removed the one undisputed autocrat whose ruthless tyranny had kept the economic and intellectual discontent in the vast communist Russian empire under tight control. After his death his successors were forced to take this discontent into consideration. They raised the demand for de-Stalinization, which found its climax in the long and passionate indictment of Stalin's tyranny by Nikita Khrushchev in his speech before the Twentieth Congress of the Communist Party of the Soviet Union in February, 1956. Khrushchev castigated the lawless crimes which Stalin had committed against fellow communists; he did not mention with equal emphasis the even more brutal violations of all human laws committed by communism against the Russian and other peoples under its domination. But Stalin's successors were forced to make concessions to these peoples and to try to relieve by a number of means the economic misery and the intellectual stagnation of the population in the communist lands. In their foreign policy the new leaders stressed the rapprochement with non-Stalinist lands—with Tito's Yugoslavia, which Khrushchev visited in May, 1955, with Asian nations which witnessed the triumphal reception to Khrushchev in India and Burma at the end of 1955, and with some Arab countries, especially Egypt, which were willing to enter into contact with Russia after they had appealed in vain to the Western powers for economic and military aid and for the removal of bitterly felt grievances.

Stalin's successors had not abandoned communism in the least: de-Stalinization did not mean a compromise with liberty but the return to Leninism—to Lenin's interpretation of Marx. Marx was convinced that the Western civilization of his day was doomed by the approaching class war between the industrial working class and the then more and more dominant middle class; he saw the rise of the proletariat as a repetition of the struggle between aristocracy and middle class which was still going on in Europe during the first half of the nineteenth century. The revolt of the proletarian masses in the industrialized middle class countries would destroy, Marx proclaimed as the supposedly inescapable course of history, the social and intellectual texture of Western society and establish an entirely new society and way of human life—the fulfillment of all utopian hopes of mankind. Lenin supported this thesis even in 1918 when he declared in Moscow before the Sixth Congress of Soviets: "A complete victory of the socialist revolution is unthinkable in any one country. It requires at least the cooperation of several advanced countries, and Russia is not one of them. . . . We can see already how the revolutionary fire has broken out in most countries—in America, in Germany, in England." At the same time, November, 1918, Jakob Sverdlov, one of Lenin's closest collaborators, declared that within six months Soviet rule would triumph in Austria and Germany, in France and Britain. This has not happened. Contrary to the expectations of Marx, the advanced industrialized countries showed an astonishing impregnability to communist penetration. What Marx had not expected, happened. In the first half of the twentieth century Western society solved its most urgent problem which seemed insoluble in the nineteenth century: to integrate labor fully into its political, social, and cultural texture, to make it share the benefits of a rapidly expanding economy, and to turn a proletariat threatened by, and revolting against, its exclusion from property and security into members of the middle class. In the advanced Western countries—in the United States, in Britain and Scandinavia, in the Low Countries and in the German Federal Republic—the worker lost his feeling of being a mere object of exploitation and gained the consciousness of being a co-master of his life and of his nation's destiny.

Rarely has there been in history a more rapid and thorough change in status and economic well-being than that between the conditions of the Western working class around 1900 and those of half a century later. The Western socialist and labor parties recognized it and discarded Marxist ideology as obsolete, as manifestly being in complete discrepancy with the existing reality. Around 1900 observers had shown an inclination to compare modern Western civilization in the twentieth century with the Roman world of the fourth century, and to predict a similar fall of the West—a return to primitive barbarism as had befallen Europe fifteen centuries before. To that end they pointed to the danger of the "internal proletariat" in the Western lands, to the impending revolt of the masses. This revolt for which Marx and Lenin had hoped, did not happen. In its stead, the proletarians were integrated and absorbed into Western society. In the 1950's none of the advanced countries in the Western community is threatened by class war or revolution.

On the contrary, the free Western nations have shown a

remarkable cohesion and an ability to adapt themselves to changing circumstances. In 1889, when the Second Socialist International was founded, the eight-hour working day seemed a far-off ideal. In 1900, for the first time, the Labor Party entered the British House of Commons; its strength then amounted to two members. Less than a half century later, in 1945, this young party had a decisive majority in the House of Commons and carried through a thorough social reform similar to that which the New Deal had accomplished in the United States in the 1930's. More important, however, was the fact that the Conservative government which followed the Labor Party in power in Britain and the Republican administration of 1952 in the United States continued and in many ways broadened the measures which changed an underprivileged part of the population into equal partners. This solution of the chief social problem of the modern Western world not only has strengthened the West; it has terminated the communist hope of destroying the West by subversion.

Yet Lenin was not only a Marxist: he was a Russian, deeply steeped in the traditions of a country of vast backward peasant masses, of a land geographically and socially situated between Europe and Asia. Not by accident did Lenin become the first socialist to pay close attention to the then only beginning rise of nationalism in Asia and to its implications. Already in 1905 he was convinced that the Russian revolution of that year—which had made almost no impression on the workers in the West— had decisively influenced the Asian masses, and that it was among them that Russia could find the necessary allies to win the fated struggle against the West and its capitalism. At the Bolshevik conference in January, 1912, Lenin greeted the Chinese revolution and declared that it was "from our point of view an event of world importance toward achieving the liberation of Asia and the overthrow of European mastery." In 1923, after his hopes for a European revolution had failed, Lenin, in one of his last utterances, lined up Russia and Asia for the impending victory over the West: "The outcome of the struggle for the world depends on the fact that Russia, India, China, and so on, contain the vast majority of the world's population. This majority has progressed more rapidly every year on the road to freedom, and in this sense there can be no shadow of a doubt as to the final outcome of the world's struggle."

But by 1957 it may appear doubtful whether Lenin was not again wrong in his prediction of the inevitable decay and fall of modern Western civilization—an expectation which Russian Slavophilism and Leninist Marxism shared, this time through the cooperation of communism and Afro-Asian nationalism. If Russian communism had been able to mobilize the mounting forces of Asian and African nationalism against the West, the West would certainly have been facing the greatest danger in its history—not only politically and economically but, above all, morally. It would have irretrievably lost its hold on the awakening world public opinion and it would have been led to a policy of repression in contradiction to its own principles. The prospects for a triumph of Leninism seemed in the beginning not unpromising. The Turkish nationalist leader Mustafa Kemal defeated the Greeks and their Western supporters in 1920–1922 only through direct and indirect communist support. A treaty of friendship with the Leninist regime afforded him the necessary backing for his great reform program. Similar communist support allowed the Persians to establish their full independence after the First World War. In the *Izvestia* of October 18, 1925, Grigori Zinovyev, one of Lenin's earliest associates, wrote the words which were widely believed among Asian intellectuals: "The Soviet Union is the great hope of the awakening East. The great Revolution, which has transformed Russia from the graveyard of the peoples to a family of nationalities, all enjoying equal rights, has become a beacon illuminating the path of the oppressed masses in the East. Upon that force the Soviet Union bases its foreign policy and from that it derives its remarkable power." It sounded almost like the confirmation of these words when in the same year, Sun Yat-sen, the leader of the Kuomintang, the Chinese revolutionary nationalist party, addressed from his deathbed a letter to the Central Executive Committee of the Union of

Soviet Socialist Republics, in which he greeted his "dear comrades" as the head "of the union of free republics—that heritage left to the oppressed peoples of the world by the immortal Lenin. With the aid of that heritage the victims of imperialism will inevitably achieve emancipation from that international regime whose foundations have been rooted for ages in slavery, wars, and injustice."

The dying leader adjured his followers to remain true to his teachings by remaining united with communist Russia "in the historic work of the final liberation of China and other exploited countries from the yoke of imperialism." His last words sounded like an echo to the words of the dying Lenin. "Taking leave of you, dear comrades," Sun Yat-sen concluded his letter to the Russian communists, "I want to express the hope that the day will come when the USSR will have a friend and ally in a mighty, free China, and that in the great struggle for the liberation of the oppressed peoples of the world both those allies will go forward to victory hand in hand." This last will of the revered leader goes a long way to explain the lasting impact which communism made on Chinese intellectuals and nationalists, and their final success in 1949.

Marxist-Leninist ideas generally exercised a strong attraction on the minds of Asian and African intellectuals. Though few of them became communists, their thinking was deeply influenced by Leninist thought, especially in the evaluation of the West and in the interpretation of imperialism. The most prominent Asian intellectual of recent times, the Indian leader Jawaharlal Nehru, a man educated at Harrow and Cambridge and deeply steeped in English thought, wrote in his autobiography that though he was repelled by regimentation and violence in communist Russia, he found no lack of violence in the capitalist world either. "Violence was common in both places," he stated, "but the violence of the capitalist order seemed inherent in it; while the violence of Russia, bad though it was, aimed at a new order based on peace and cooperation and real freedom for the masses. . . . Russia, following the great Lenin, looked into the future. . . . In particular, I was impressed by the reports of the great progress made by the backward regions of Central Asia under the Soviet regime. In the balance, therefore, I was all in favor of Russia, and the presence and example of the Soviets was a bright and heartening phenomenon in a dark and dismal world. . . . Russia apart, the theory and philosophy of Marxism lightened up many a dark corner of my mind. History came to have a new meaning for me. The Marxist interpretation threw a flood of light on it, and it became an unfolding drama with some order and purpose, howsoever unconscious, behind it. In spite of the appalling waste and misery of the past and the present, the future was bright with hope, though many dangers intervened."

Communism made little actual progress in the Asian-African world, and the Islamic countries proved especially impervious to it; nevertheless the possibility of a close cooperation between the rapidly awakening non-Western world and Russian communism against the West represents the greatest menace to modern Western civilization in the second half of the twentieth century. This problem can be compared in its gravity to the one which the growing discontent and the rising demands of the proletariat within the Western world presented in the first half of the century. The West can draw justified hope from the fact that out of its own principles of a liberal society it has met the latter challenge with surprising success. Marxist-Leninist hopes for the fall of the West through class struggle have been frustrated. The parallel with the doomed Roman civilization proved in this case unfounded. Internally, the modern West is more secure in 1957 than it has ever been. Yet Rome not only succumbed to social disintegration through the pressure of its internal proletariat, it also succumbed to the ever-expanding inroads by outside "barbarians"—underdeveloped peoples or, as they have been called, an external proletariat. The modern West, applying and expanding its own principles, did solve the great task which faced it in the first half of the twentieth century. The year 1956 has strengthened the hopes that it will be able to solve the even greater task which faces it in the second half of the century. For there can be no doubt that this period will be viewed by future historians as one in which the political, economic, and cultural center of gravity which for three centuries was exclusively located in the West, will become more diffuse and will to a certain extent shift rapidly and irresistibly toward the underdeveloped countries of the earth. Such a shift has become visible in the past year to all through a comparison of the composition of, and the questions raised by, the League of Nations which met two decades ago in Geneva, and the United Nations which is now meeting in New York City.

The accommodation and cooperation necessary in the interests of liberty between the West and the non-Western world are being made more difficult by memories of the recent past, by resentment and pride, by misconceptions of history and by an emotionally colored perspective. Many of these misinterpretations center around the meaning and implications of the word "colonialism." Future historians will recognize that modern Western colonialism, especially British expansion, has done in recent periods on the whole more good than evil to the subject peoples. Empire and colonialism always imply dominion and power; and power, whether exercised by "native" or "alien" governments, has a potency for abuse as probably no other relationship has. Yet Western liberal alien governments—and liberalism means primarily restraint upon, and limitations of, governmental authority—will be more easily controlled by public opinion against abuse of power and thus in the long run will be more beneficial than illiberal "native" governments, be they in Europe—in national-socialist Germany or communist Russia—or in Asia and Africa.

Where immigrant settlers colonized a country and removed the natives from the good land and relegated them to a status of inferiority as in South Africa, Palestine, and Algeria, colonialism has had disastrous effects on the original inhabitants of the land. Where no large-scale immigrant settlement was attempted, however, as in British India or in Malaya, the dependent status has worked to the advantage of the native peoples, who have found themselves, or will soon find themselves, in control of a vastly improved country. There for the first time, native cadres for the administration of a modern country and for all walks of civilized life have come into existence. Many of the new nations, like India, Indonesia, and Ghana, owe their existence and potential cohesion as nations to the colonial regime. The astonishing success of unity and democracy in a vast multi-racial and multi-lingual country like India is entirely due to the training and example of the British administration and the Indian Civil Service. It has been a widespread propaganda slogan that colonialism brought wars, poverty, racial and economic exploitation to Asia and Africa. Yet indigenous colonialism has existed in Asia and Africa since time immemorial, as did wars and poverty and racial conflicts. As far as historical memory goes, one Asian nation or king subjugated other Asian peoples, and African tribes enslaved and exterminated other African tribes.

Great empires have been the pride of Asia and Africa in their long history. European imperialism has had only a brief day in history. For many centuries Asian empires have endangered Europe. In the thirteenth century an accident saved Europe, but not Russia, from Mongol domination. Imperialism and colonialism, meaning one nation's rule over another, are not solely limited to Western relationships with non-Western lands. Within Europe there has been rule of one people over another, even though they were closely akin. Norwegians struggled against Danes, Croatians against Serbs, Slovaks against Czechs, Ukrainians against Russians, Catalans against Castilians—and bitterly resented what they regarded as political dominion, economic exploitation, and relegation to an inferior status; they used the very same words and slogans as do Asian and African nationalists (who have learned their doctrines and tactics from European nationalist movements) against Western colonial powers. Nor will the independence of Asian and African peoples solve the problems of conflicting national and racial aspirations in Asia and Africa. After the achievement of Indian independence, the Dravidian people of the south felt toward the Aryan Brahmins very much as these Brahmins—perhaps with less justification—felt toward the British. "The social exploitation," wrote one of

the leaders of the Dravida Munnetra Kazhagan—the Dravidian
Progressive Federation which works for independence from
Aryan India—"we have endured for so many decades from
Brahminism and the decay of our cultural literature due to this
force is responsible for our attitude. Not only does Brahminism
result in casteism, it has kept us for many a century on the lower
rungs of the social ladder. That is why we say that the poisonous
teeth of the Brahmin snake must be taken out." In the new
Asian nations, movements for national independence continue:
the territorial conflicts between India and Pakistan, between
Pakistan and Afghanistan, the aspirations of the Karens in Burma,
of the South Moluccans and of the inhabitants of other non-
Javanese islands in Indonesia, the bitter feelings between Koreans
and Japanese, the hostility between south and north in the Sudan
and in Nigeria—these are some examples of continuing or growing unrest following the departure of Western colonialism. The
Indian element in East Africa and the Chinese in Southeast Asia
may create difficult racial conflicts and great hardships for the
natives, once Western imperial protection is removed. British
Hongkong has been a unique oasis of liberty and civilized order
in the Far East, entirely owing to British efforts and ideas.
There is no reason to assume that the New Guinean Papuas
would fare better under the administration of Indonesian rulers,
with whom they have no affinity in race, language, or religion,
than under Dutch administration.

With the middle of the twentieth century the tide of Western
imperialism has been definitely receding; its ebbing was due not
primarily to external pressure but to the potency of Western
ideas themselves, especially as represented in their homeland,
modern Britain. Though the brief period of Western imperialism
has witnessed many injustices and cruelties—which however
were in no way worse than the normal happenings in Asia and
Africa before the advent of the white man—it has been on the
whole a period of which the West, and especially Britain, need
not be ashamed. It would be wrong to apply twentieth century
standards and principles of international law to preceding centuries. By doing so—and it should not be forgotten that these new

twentieth century standards were developed by the Western world—the West suffers a bad conscience; the anti-Western propaganda is exploiting these guilt feelings. The extension of European control into American, Asian, and African lands came not as the result of any peculiar iniquity but as the result of a sudden great disparity in cultural energy and economic productivity. Today, largely owing to Western influence, this disparity is vanishing. A difficult readjustment is due today; it will not be helped by clinging—out of national pride or out of a feeling of national needs—to formerly legitimate and now obsolete concepts nor by any feeling of guilt for past deeds which are—and should now be—undone in the light of a new era.

In this respect, too, the events at the end of 1956 and at the beginning of 1957 marked a turning point. They strengthened on the whole the moral position of the West in the non-Western world and lessened the attraction of Russian communism. The Israeli-Franco-British invasion of Egypt and the threat of the occupation and subjugation of Arab territory to non-Arab control aroused protests not only in the non-Western world but throughout the West—in Scandinavia and in Canada, in the United States and among a large section of the British public. French and British action in support of Israeli aggression came without consultation with other members of the North Atlantic Treaty Organization, and this at the very moment when a committee of three foreign ministers—a Canadian, an Italian and a Norwegian —studied ways and means to bring about closer political consultation among all the NATO nations. In its report this Committee of Three stated that there was a widespread suspicion in the non-communist world outside NATO that this North Atlantic Community was tending "to become an agency for the pooling of the strength and the resources of the 'colonial' powers in defense of imperial privileges, racial superiority and Atlantic hegemony under the leadership of the United States. The fact that we know these views to be false and unjustified does not mean that NATO and its governments should not do everything they can to correct and counteract them." The Committee called upon all NATO members "to cooperate fully with other members of the international community in bringing to reality the principles of the Charter of the United Nations."

United States policy in the crucial events at the end of 1956 followed the line proposed by representative spokesmen of the North Atlantic Community. The aggression against Egypt had provided the Russian communists with an "alibi" to act against the freedom movement in Hungary and had given them the opportunity to pose at the same time as a defender of the Arabs, and of Asia and Africa in general, against imperial aggression. Such an aggression in the 1950's could not achieve its aim of overthrowing President Gamal Abdel Nasser of Egypt and of forcing Arab nationalism to accept conditions imposed by force of arms. On the contrary, the invasion of Egypt strengthened Arab nationalism and, at least for the time being, Nasser's prestige. Thus the Iraqi representative, who can in no way be regarded as friendly to Nasser, told the General Assembly of the United Nations on December 6, 1956, that on the Israeli issue "all the Arab world is Egypt and all Arab statesmen are Nassers." By disassociating itself from the invasion of Egypt, the United States not only has joined the large majority of mankind but has restored the moral position and influence of the West in Asia and Africa, and thereby strengthened the North Atlantic Community and the United Nations. Therein the United States was decisively helped by the large part of British public opinion which for practical and moral reasons rejected the invasion of Egypt, and by the dignified and graceful way in which Britain without hesitations or reservations accepted the verdict of the United Nations. As a result, there was a great change in the attitude of the non-Western peoples toward the West on the one hand, and toward the Soviet Union on the other hand. The Russian communist bid for calling a second conference of all Asian-African nations with Russian participation—a conference similar to the one held in Bandung, Indonesia, in 1955—was rejected. At the end of 1956 Jawaharlal Nehru visited Washington and Ottawa, and in the beginning of 1957 influential Arab leaders conferred in Washington. The United Nations, which began as

a most uncertain experiment and has inherited the poor legacy
of the League of Nations, has started by the end of 1956 to take
the first hesitant steps toward fulfilment of the functions of a
world forum where for the first time in human history all races
and all civilizations meet in the difficult attempt to find some
accommodation of conflicting interests and traditions. The Secretary General of the United Nations has emerged as the first international statesman, and the creation of the United Nations
Emergency Force has brought Woodrow Wilson's idea of collective security somewhat nearer to realization. There is still a long
way to go, but for an observer who tries to survey the forty
years since Woodrow Wilson first launched his idea, there has
been some progress. That the new force consists of contingents
of smaller nations from all over the world and not of forces
supplied by the great powers, is a hopeful development.

Future historians may view the second half of the twentieth
century not so much as a power conflict between the Soviet
Union and the United States, but as a period of challenge to the
North Atlantic Community, thrown out by the unexpectedly rapid
rise of non-Western peoples to an ever-growing voice in world
affairs. In the security of the nineteenth century the North
Atlantic peoples could live in isolated national units. In the
twentieth century—faced by the challenges of proletarian unrest,
of communism and fascism, and now of the innumerable multitudes of the non-Western peoples—the North Atlantic nations
must outgrow their nationalism and vitalize and strengthen
their growing sense of community, not in order to dominate the
globe—a goal which in the twentieth century would be as un-
realizable as it would be unethical—but to arrive at an understanding of, and accommodation with, the minds and aspirations of the non-North Atlantic, non-communist and non-fascist
peoples.

These peoples are very different and represent an infinity of
attitudes and civilizations. Latin Americans are Western peoples,
but they harbor, as the Spaniards do, a resentment against modern North Atlantic civilization and feel themselves in many ways
as semi-colonials. The Arabic peoples of the Mediterranean

formed part of the Roman world and are co-heirs with the West of the Greek and Biblical heritage. Yet like the Iberians they have not participated in modern North Atlantic developments. Peoples of Asia are heirs of great and ancient civilizations and through contact with the North Atlantic world have become aware of their own civilization. The Africans south of the Sahara grope, thanks to the influence of the North Atlantic civilization, for a new self-awareness and a new human dignity. All these various multitudes are in the throes of a rapid and uncertain transition, and the reassessment of the North Atlantic relationship to them will be difficult and painful. Yet the North Atlantic Community has shown the power, inventiveness and adaptability—based on its principles of respect for liberty and human dignity—to meet successfully the challenges and crises of the first half of the twentieth century and to solve its own social problems. It must now cooperate in seeking constructive solutions for the new challenge, solutions in harmony with the realities of the twentieth century. As long as the North Atlantic peoples exert the Western virtues of political restraint and public morality, they can hope to turn the destructive and inflammatory passions of twentieth century nationalism and socialism—provided they are not totalitarian—into constructive and civilized channels. The solutions that the North Atlantic Community will seek will also be in harmony with the ideals of the United Nations, which, after all, are only the application of principles of modern Western civilization to an international community in which the West no longer plays the exclusive dominant role but still can act as the guide on the road to the gradual fulfilment of what Cicero called *humanitas*.

WORLD CRISIS AND WORLD CIVILIZATION

> . . . Come my friends,
> 'Tis not too late to seek a newer world. . . .
> Though much is taken, much abides and though
> We are not now that strength which in old days
> Moved earth and heaven: that which we are, we are:—
> One equal temper of heroic hearts
> Made weak by time and fate, but strong in will
> To strive, to seek, to find, and not to yield.
>
> —TENNYSON, *Ulysses*

> . . . Adieu, monsieur; je vous recommande la vérité, la
> liberté, et la vertu, trois seules choses pour lesquelles on
> doive aimer la vie.
>
> —VOLTAIRE, *Questions sur les miracles,* XIe Lettre

XV

THE HISTORIAN IN OUR TIME

T HE HISTORIAN is a man who tries to find out what has happened in the course of time and to correlate the events, within the limits of the available material on the one hand and of his intelligence, imagination, and ethical understanding on the other, into a meaningful sequence. Only when correlated into the pattern of the onrushing and all-inclusive course of time do events become history. Time and its irreversibility is a fundamental and tragic aspect of human life and of history, the source of all ultimate frustration. The escape from time and history into timelessness, into eternity, into the end of history, the *eschata*, the ultimate time, the final day and the final reckoning, is a religious and secular utopian hope for an end to this fundamental tragedy. Such eschatological hopes are a historical fact, but except in their effects, they are not the concern of the historian. He is concerned with survival in the world of human contingency: past events, otherwise lost in the stream of time, are revived by him in the stream of human consciousness and enter into a relationship with our present life either by satisfying our playful curiosity or by enriching our pure knowledge in a disinterested way, or by broadening our understanding and guiding our actions in a utilitarian way.

Writing history, therefore, does not mean to regard events as isolated phenomena but to put them into the context of time. From this point of view everything can become the object of history: the doings of a man or of a nation, the development of our planetary system, the working of any branch of human activity. Though, owing to the limitations of men and material, each historian deals with only a small segment of history—one period, one branch of art, one nation—he must do it in the spirit of universal history, of viewing his segment in the light of what preceded it and at the same time in the context of all other human societies and activities. All writing of history, even of the most minute period or branch, should be part of universal history.

Historical consciousness of this sort is a rather recent phenomenon in the long development of the human species; it distinguishes modern civilization from all the rest of living nature. Prehistoric peoples, aptly called in German *geschichtslose Völker* (peoples without history), lived in the timelessness of natural time. Their stories begin with *"Es war einmal"* ("Once upon a time"), which means, "It will always be so." Perhaps the ancient Hebrews were the first people strongly conscious of history: the past history of their tribe is to them always vividly present and continuous; at the same time tribal history broadens into the context of universal history. Probably it is only at this stage of time-awareness that we meet the phenomenon unknown to the rest of living nature: fear of death and, corresponding to it, the promise of eternal life—of a new birth, of survival. But we should note that the message of comfort brought by Buddha is that of a death which will not be followed by new birth.

In the nineteenth century historical consciousness came fully into its own and became the dominant trait of the period. The revolutionary character of the period which started with the French Revolution and the rapid changes brought about by constant new discoveries and the unprecedented progress of technology created a new consciousness of time as a dynamic and moving force. While the Indian felt at home in timelessness and the Greek believed in the fundamental identity—the *semper idem* —of historical events, modern man became a conscious wanderer through time. Excavations and the interpretation of myths opened to him new dimensions of time. Through the law of evolution everything became subject to time, and thereby to history: religion, language, literature, art, institutions, science. This new historical consciousness came upon man in such a sudden and overwhelming fashion that the Germans developed it into a philosophy of its own, a *Weltanschauung* (historicism), which, in spite of its great achievements, brought great dangers. It led in Hegel and his disciple Marx to a metaphysicization of history. According to this theory the historical process itself is a revelation of the divine; the divine is no longer the law and limit of everything historical but is identical with history. Everything now becomes historically necessary. The German philosopher Martin Heidegger in 1933 greeted the National Socialist totalitarian state as historically inevitable, as *seinsgeschichtlich,* and stressed that the philosopher (*"der Wissende"*) must therefore avoid moral indignation as inappropriate. Lately Heidegger has taken a similar attitude toward Communism.

The other danger, closely connected with the one pointed out, is what might be called the historization of metaphysics, whereby everything becomes relative, valid in itself. Whereas the first attitude raises historical categories to absolutes, the second easily leads to nihilism, to the rejection of any absolute standards or values. Historicism in our time has led to two other consequences: the abuse of the past (often in a misrepresented form) to justify present or future claims of nationalism; and the fascination of prehistory, enticing us to praise instinct and myth at the expense of reasonableness and common sense.

In spite of these inherent dangers, the new historical consciousness and the ensuing historiography have had beneficial effects. History, rightly studied, can sharpen man's critical insight into human relationships and personality; it makes him more conscious of his limitations and therefore more humble but it also teaches him to regard the future as open, containing potentially new developments. True, the present is a product of the past; retrospectively, the historian can show how the present grew out of the past. But the present is also always something new and is itself pregnant with future developments. Though historians can show retrospectively, if without agreement among themselves, how the present has come about so that it almost appears as a necessary outcome of the past, historians at no moment in the past could have predicted the future development tending toward the present. In 1918, for example, there were several possibilities before Germany, but nobody in 1918 could have predicted the course of events of the 1930's. It might have been guessed as a possibility; it could never have been predicted as a certainty. It could have been assumed as a future possibility only in the Germany of 1918, not, for instance, in the United States of 1932 or even the France of 1934, because the past, though it does not determine the future, sets certain limits within which future developments can take place. Though by means of their intelligence, imagination, and moral understanding men at any given moment can decide freely among several possibilities, thereby establishing and affirming their humanity, they decide within the limits of a concrete situation, the result of past developments. Only by recognition of the conditions created by the past and thereby of the true nature of the concrete problem can men find an answer which is neither destructive nor utopian but which is, to use a famous expression of Toynbee, a response to the challenge, a responsible answer to the concrete situation. Such a response demands historical understanding and also ethical standards which are above and beyond all historical understanding but cannot be fruitfully applied without it.

Ranke's famous saying that the task of the historian is to find out and to narrate "how things really happened," *"wie es eigentlich gewesen,"* can be accepted as basic. The first task of the historian is to find out by patient and painstaking research the true facts of the past. From this point of view history is scholarly research and, like all scientific endeavor, carries its reward in itself, in the joy of discovering unknown facts, of finding new interpretations, of shedding light on obscure relationships. Such history serves knowledge and not society. Its responsibility is to find out how it was, not how it should have been. Yet no historian can know the whole past, not even the full story of one man, of one year, or even of one day. From the infinity of facts we are always forced to select within the limits of surviving documentation and those imposed by our intelligence and our intentions. We select according to our set of principles, which, like a searchlight, illumines in the immensity of any past time

THE HISTORIAN IN OUR TIME

that part which seems to us relevant. Therefore no work of history is ever finished, and there can be in the true sense of the word no definitive work of history. History, which in its findings and conclusions is always approximate and tentative, ever to be verified by fresh discoveries and above all by new experiences and insights, is a science and not an art, because art produces definitive creations which no new experience and no new discoveries can alter in their permanent validity.

Yet history—and in this it differs from the sciences—contains an essential element of art too; therefore great books by historians retain their permanent value—and not only for the historian of historiography—even though many single facts and whole interpretations have been found to be erroneous. For history, though it does not serve society, serves man—beyond enriching his knowledge—by equipping him with a deeper understanding of himself, of his fellow men, and of the situations in which men are put. It can tell us as much about man and the human condition as the best novel or the greatest drama. In this way too, then, history has much in common with art. Beyond this function, it should give us a critical awareness of ourselves and of our own time by providing perspective through comparison and distinction. Persons, events, and situations are always different and never the same: but they are never entirely new or unique. That is the truth, the partial truth, in the Greek attitude toward history, which saw in history a morphology of human behavior, or as Florus, the Roman historian of the time of Trajan and a disciple of Livy, put it pithily, *"ut qui res eius legunt, non unius populi, sed generis humani facta discant"* ("so that those who read its story, learn the facts not about one people but about the whole human kind").

This view of the recurrent character of history, revived in our time by Rückert and Danilevsky, Nietzsche and Spengler, has been opposed by the view which sees in history one continuous development. This latter view has been generally accepted in the West since Augustine. The Judeo-Christian understanding of history as a meaningfully directed process of salvation, *Heilsgeschichte*, was secularized in the eighteenth century into the conviction that history is an infinite progress from darkness to ever-greater light, from the night of the past either to the bright day of the present, as the optimistic Enlightenment saw it, or to the even brighter day of the near future, as Marx, overstressing the dark shadows in the picture of the present, later proclaimed. This faith in progress, absolutized and vulgarized in Communism, has lately given way to another mythical interpretation of history, which regards at least modern history not as the story of progress and salvation but as the story of decay and doom. This concept was not unknown in antiquity, when it was immortalized in Hesiod's "Iron Age," and has become fashionable in the last decades, which, in opposition to the promise of the bright day of Enlightenment, glorified the more "profound" view of man groping in the darkness of night and caught in the blindness of myth.

The naïve exaggerations of the men of the Enlightenment have been matched recently by these equally naïve laments of doom from our latter-day prophets. It is remarkable that our age of burning vitality and—in spite of its black spots—manifold promise should give rise to this kind of mournful pessimism. It is fashionable today to speak of an unprecedented "crisis"—a crisis in everything. Historical insight could have tempered the optimism of the eighteenth century; it can help us to see today's crisis in perspective. The historian knows that throughout most of history men have lived in critical times. He might mention only a very few examples and take them from the Middle Ages, to whose supposedly "organic" character many romantics today look back longingly: Francis of Assisi and his followers led a saintly life because they were convinced that the world was sinking in an unprecedented moral crisis, in a morass of corruption, and could not go on in that way. The Black Death which swept Europe in the middle of the fourteenth century destroyed proportionally more lives than atomic bombs would have and left, quite understandably, a feeling of complete insecurity, of total abandonment—*ausgeliefertsein*, as the existentialists call it today. A moral crisis of unsurpassed intensity is revealed to anyone who studies the years when Alexander Borgia was sitting on the papal throne and Savonarola was preaching in Florence. And even in the apparently so quiet late Victorian age, around 1880, the feeling of a deep moral crisis is reflected in the novels and periodicals of the day: the conflict of religion and science, the rise of unskilled labor, the emancipation of women, troubled moral minds. Everything appeared uncertain; foundations seemed to crumble and attitudes to change rapidly, and yet, retrospectively, the period seems blissfully quiet. The unspeakable savagery exercised in some places today by man against man and the frightening moral perversions have been matched in many preceding ages. What makes us speak today of a crisis is not the greater intensity of our suffering compared with that of former centuries but our greater consciousness of it, stimulated by popular journalism and other factors, and, above all, our heightened moral sensitivity. Today we abhor cruelty which other ages accepted without widespread protest.

But a historian is not only a scholar and, to a certain extent, an artist; he should also be a teacher. In fact, most historians are primarily engaged in teaching: teaching not only their students —future historians and future teachers—but trying also to instruct their fellow men; in a democratic age history has become the concern of everybody, and the right teaching of history may be fundamental to the moral and political wisdom of peoples. Historical perspective may help in the rejection of both the utopias of enthusiasm and the utopias of despair; it may help in regarding the present as not too bad and in not expecting too much from the future. In spite of the imperfections and limitations inherent in the nature of man and the nature of things, of which the historian should be painfully conscious, he should nevertheless see that during the relatively short time of three thousand years frail and fallible man has learned much through an ever-renewed and maintained effort, has set lasting examples, and has built a widely accepted ethical tradition. Historians can teach us not to look on nations and classes as isolated phenomena but to see and to judge them in a universal context in the light of this ethical tradition. This tradition continues to grow, and people are always able and sometimes willing to learn from experience. Thus each generation rewrites history, not by adjusting facts to an alleged need of the hour, but by changing its viewpoints, like an old man looking back on some period of his youth, who, though he has achieved no greater factual knowledge, as a result of his experience arrives at a different judgment. If people did not learn from living, life would become useless, but they do learn. Consequently, age has had and should have a greater voice in determining courses of action than youth. Because of this possibility of learning by living, history remains a hopeful process. Past mistakes can be avoided, and new ways can be found.

Two recent examples may illustrate the hopefulness of history. The American people have learned from the experience of the first half of the twentieth century to turn away from isolationism; whereas some years ago a candidate for the presidency had to affirm his rejection of international co-operation, now such a candidate must declare his rejection of isolationism. An understanding of world responsibility and of the nature of a movement as wholly alien as totalitarianism has come to Americans in recent years.[1] But they are not the only ones who have learned by sad experience. After the catastrophe of 1945 German historians started to re-examine German history—a task which they unfortunately had not essayed after 1918, as the Americans had not then turned away from isolationism—to re-examine the trends and ideas dominating the recent German past, the dangerous elements not only in the rise of Hitler but also in Bismarck's triumph and in the generally accepted Germano-centered and state-centered view.[2] German historians are asking themselves whether the path followed by their craft since Ranke has not been wrong, not on account of the facts presented but on account of the value judgments involved. For as historians may find wrong facts, they may also be guided by wrong values; acceptance of either involves great dangers.

Historians have responsibilities, not to nations or classes, to dogmas or creeds, but to truth and to humanity. Their training can help them to understand the genesis of events and movements and to evaluate their relative worth and importance by comparison with similar attitudes in other peoples, climes, and periods. That should make their approach more critical and more cautious, especially as regards their own emotional prejudices and group interests. No sharp distinction is possible between political historians and historians of ideas; ideas and politics are closely interlinked and interdependent. So are facts and values. History, whether as scholarship or as art or as teaching, represents the meeting, the interaction, the interrelationship of objective and subjective factors. The facts of the past present the objective material; the ethos and the personality of the historian present the subjective elements without which the facts of the past and the past itself remain dead.

XVI

IS THE FREE WEST IN DECLINE?

"History's Verdict" in Perspective

OUR time is dominated by a feeling of unprecedented crisis involving every aspect of political, social and intellectual life. The every foundations of modern civilization seem imperiled and the "decline of the West," about which philosophers of history from Spengler to Toynbee have been talking since 1914, is now almost a cant term. But this feeling of crisis, of decay and decline, is scarcely unique. Almost every great age and civilization has had its periods of anxiety and loss of confidence. On the eve of the great era of the *pax Romana,* we find Virgil lamenting in his *Georgics:*

> For here are right and wrong inverted: so many wars in the world, so many fashions of evil; the plough meets not its due honor; our lands, the tillers deported, lie waste, and the crooked pruning-hooks are forged into hard swords. Here Euphrates, there Germany kindles war: even as when from the barriers the chariots burst forth, they gather speed in the course, and the driver, tugging vainly at the bridles, is borne along by the horses and the car heeds not the reins.

The Middle Ages, Renaissance, Reformation, and the period of the French Revolution all had their crises when despairing voices were lifted up to predict the end of the world or the death of civilization. In two respects only, is the present crisis different from all previous ones: it is worldwide, owing to the very nature of modern Western civilization; and it has sucked into its orbit, and given voice to, the hitherto quiescent and "extra-historical" lower classes, who constitute the overwhelming majority of mankind. This "awakening" of the "lower classes" in the Western lands and of the peoples outside of the West to a realization of their human dignity and to a demand for the recognition of their human rights is the unique and great merit of Western liberalism, but it also creates for it situations of unprecedented strain.

Under this strain, the transitory successes of the Nazis, and now those of the Communists, have browbeaten many in the West itself, to a greater extent than they care to acknowledge, into wondering whether Western civilization is faltering and moribund. The "dynamism" of these totalitarian movements has intimidated us, and we have the sinking feeling that they may be the harbingers of a fresh and vigorous, if ruthless, new age which will succeed our failing Western civilization. Along with that often goes the guilty feeling that totalitarianism is somehow our own late-born child. Western society has reached such a point of atomization—many people say—so many classes of people have become rootless wanderers in the anarchy of modern life, that the synthetic, brute unity of the contemporary nationalist and totalitarian movements is the inevitable heir of the bankruptcy of our senile society.

A sober examination of the historical record, I believe, will show that all these gloomy forecasts of a declining West are at the very least premature. The contemporary crisis is not so much a crisis within Western civilization as an attack upon it from without. This attack has come, in our time, from Germany and Russia. These are peripheral areas that in political and social structure never really were full partners of the modern Western way of life, never assimilated fully the ideas and institutions that define it. Liberty understood as the inborn rights of the individual against authority; tolerance based upon the recognition of diversity—the open society; parliamentary government; freedom of inquiry—all these things were never firmly founded in Germany or Russia, Italy or Spain. Communism in Russia, fascism in Italy and Spain, nationalism in Asia have had one thing in common: Politically, they are all a revolt against the leadership of the nations in which modern civilization first took root; spiritually, they represent a rejection of Western values, which are "unmasked" as hypocrisy.

Fascism and communism, to be sure, have themselves claimed to be the true guardians of modern Western civilization and its scientific traditions. In reality, these new movements constitute the latest in a long and hoary line of despotic regimes; they embody the old xenophobia of closed societies and an old adoration of power. And they use the intellectual and social aspirations and achievements of the West, which they interpret in a distorted way, as a weapon against the very spirit of modern Western civilization.

In our modern Western society with its almost unbroken growth from the late seventeenth century to World War I, it is Britain that is both the point of origin and the model. The United States of America is the purest expression of that society's political ideals and strength and thereby its most "Western" member. Germany, on the other hand, never fully accepted either emancipation or enlightenment in its national life. Russia is likewise only a "Westernized" (but not a Western) civilization of the kind that has now spread to Asia.

This "frontier" position of Russia explains the great attraction she lately exercises upon the Orient. The Russo-Japanese War and the Russian revolution of 1905 were the first events to stir the whole of Asia from China to the Red Sea, and the Russian revolutions of 1917 seemed to speak a message directly to the peoples of Asia and Africa, who felt that they were living under conditions similar to those of Russia. Russia's defection from the Allied side in March 1918, when her capital was transferred from westward-looking St. Petersburg back to Moscow in the interior, signalized the growing estrangement of Russia and Asia from the West.

Between Britain, the United States, and parts of Northwestern Europe on the one side, where modern Western civilization maintains itself unchallenged, and Germany and Russia on the other side, where it has never taken real root, stands France—the country in which the Western democratic revolution is forever being fought, without ever being finally resolved. Authoritarianism, whether reactionary or revolutionary, is always threatening to overwhelm French society, and sometimes does, only to be beaten back again by the constantly renewed forces of French liberalism.

The interaction between a common Western spirit and individual national traditions created the West's intellectual and social climate and shaped its political history. The modern Western spirit is strongest in the countries bordering on the North Atlantic, where the social structure and moral and intellectual climate favored its rise. But as it passes eastward its strength declines. Communism and fascism could not come to power in the seats and centers of modern Western civilization —Britain, America, and Northwestern Europe—but only on its periphery.

These movements, and the contemporary crisis, would seem then to express, not the "decline of the West," but the very opposite: the failure of certain nations to be Western enough, to be truly modern. May it not be that what we are witnessing is not the end of Western civilization, due to exhausted energies and decayed institutions, but the growing pains of its youth, a beginning stage in which it still meets checks, frustrations, and temporary reverses?

Considering how recent are the origins of modern Western civilization, how young it actually is, the crisis it now faces is more probably due to the amazing speed with which it has extended its influence and appeal around the world. Modern Western civilization has its roots in the Greco-Roman civilization of antiquity and in the Western Christendom of the Middle Ages. Yet its spirit and outlook were unknown before the seventeenth century, being based upon the new realities of liberty, science, and tolerance. The roots of the modern West go back to Athens, Jerusalem, and Rome, yet it was a new growth that sprang up in London and Amsterdam, Philadelphia and Paris.

In two centuries Western civilization brought about an unprecedented refinement and humanization of customs, a more general participation by all in the opportunities of life, and a great extension of personal liberty and of the impartial rule of law. Step by step, the influence of the West spread beyond Northwestern Europe. Russia and the Balkans began to feel it in the eighteenth century; enlightened rationalism and romantic sentimentalism simultaneously influenced the Scandinavians and the Slavs, the Spaniards and the Greeks. Europe as a cultural unit—from Gibraltar to the Urals, from Bergen to Morea—was a creation of the eighteenth century; it had never existed before. One hundred years later, even this framework seemed too narrow for modern Western civilization, with Asia coming rapidly within its orbit.

Yet under the surface deep and unreconciled differences of civilization persisted, and they began to reassert themselves in the present century. The resistance of Germany, Russia, and the Asian lands to Western influence, the very violence of their rejection of Western civilization and leadership, testifies to the strength and vitality of the West. Western civilization has frequently been attacked from the outside: in antiquity at the time of the Persian Wars and the Germanic invasions; later on when it was threatened by Arabs, Mongols, and Turks. Twice, under Alexander the Great and again at the beginning of the eighteenth century, the West itself took the offensive successfully, not only as a conqueror, but as the bearer of a new and unifying civilization. Now again Western civilization is under attack from the outside. But this time the attack seems to come from within, with the anti-Western forces borrowing their rhetoric, the aims they proclaim, and the machines they use, from their opponent. From their contact with the modern West, they know its weaknesses and exploit them; but because its spiritual core still eludes them or has been only imperfectly assimilated, they cannot grasp its enduring strength.

In flat contradiction with the "theory of decline," where the modern West is oldest it is strongest and most successful. Where we find decline is in the peripheral areas, lapsing from their Westernizing efforts of the nineteenth century into the old intolerance and arbitrary violence. Let us look more closely at

Britain, America, and France on the one side, Germany and Russia on the other, to see these things in the concrete.

The Puritan and Glorious revolutions of seventeenth century England laid the foundations of the new civilization of the West; the Enlightenment, radiating from Holland and France, broadened and universalized its principles. The new trends found their most propitious soil in the English colonies of North America. There the Puritan spirit, surviving the restoration of the monarchy in the mother country, made Locke its philosopher, and the ideal Nature of the eighteenth century *philosophes* promised that better man and that good society impossible of realization in Europe's history-ridden and castle-cluttered landscape. The Anglo-Americans were the first to establish a nation on the basis of the new civilization. Its characteristic features—a pluralistic and open society in place of an authoritarian uniformity of state and faith; reliance on the autonomy of the individual and voluntary association; a rationalistic and humanitarian regard for one's fellow man—gradually asserted themselves as the fruit of a long historical process. In England this type of modern society was the result of a long period of development from the Puritan Revolution to the great Liberal reform administrations; in the United States, it seemed the gift of a benevolent Nature.

But in another important area of the West conditions were markedly different. Eighteenth century France, authoritarian and absolutist (in spite of an older and more polished literature, a more numerous population, fertile soil, and better communications), contrasted unfavorably with a contemporary England strong in its assertion of individual liberty and religious tolerance. The Glorious Revolution and the establishment of parliamentary government in England almost coincided in time with the Revocation of the Edict of Nantes and the zenith of monarchical absolutism in France. A French royal edict of April 1757 reaffirmed the death penalty for authors and printers of unauthorized books. Other royal edicts promulgated between 1764 and 1785 forbade the publication of any discussion of public finances, jurisprudence, or religion. Montesquieu and Voltaire were deeply influenced by the English example; their demands for a reform of government, though ignored by Louis XV and Louis XVI, inspired the enlightened policies of Frederick II of Prussia, Joseph II of Austria, and Catherine II of Russia.

The Revolution of 1789 tried to bridge the gap between rational idealism and absolute reality by adapting English constitutionalism to French conditions. But the absolutist traditions of the French monarchy and Church, and the abstract and uncompromising rationalism of the French intellectuals, prevailed from 1792 on. The Glorious Revolution had united England, in spite of the diversity of opinions and interests, through a spirit of pragmatic compromise; the Constitution of the United States did the same for a people of diversified ethnic origins and religious allegiances; whereas the French Revolution of 1793 split France into two eternally warring camps. Robespierre and Napoleon as little understood the nature of modern civil society as the most reactionary followers of Throne and Altar looking back to the authoritarianism of the *ancien régime*. De Tocqueville noted that in the United States Christianity and liberty seemed to feel at one, whereas in France they were found in opposite camps. The great achievements of 1789—the rights and liberties of the individual, the emancipation of conscience from authority, the open and civil character of society—though they set an example for the entire European continent, were time and again imperiled in France itself. French liberty has been menaced on the left all the way from the Jacobins to the revolutionary syndicalists, from Babeuf to the Communists; on the right, all the way from Joseph de Maistre to Charles Maurras, from Napoleon to Pétain, from Charles X's July Ordinances to the Dreyfus Affair. The French Revolution is "permanent" in the sense that it is always an issue, never having been accepted by significant sections of French society.

But though the achievements of 1789 were never secure in France and had to be defended against periodic attack, they triumphantly reasserted themselves time and again. Their very insecurity and their constant reassertion made nineteenth century France the inspiring exemplar and bulwark of modern Western civilization on the Continent. At the same time, there were always people ready to predict the "decline of the West." Immediately after the war of 1870, Ernest Renan expressed the fear that:

France and even Britain—who at bottom suffer from the same malady [a weakening of the military spirit and the ascendancy of the spirit of commerce]—will soon be reduced to a secondary role; the stage of the European world will be exclusively occupied by a few colossal powers, the Germans and the Slavs, who have preserved the vigor of the military and leadership principles, and whose struggle will fill the future.

But such a fit of pusillanimity did not afflict other French liberals, and Renan himself threw it off when the first shock of the defeat of 1870 had worn off.

Since the eighteenth century, no other great nation on the Continent has had a public opinion so like that of the English-speaking countries as France. Its sense of proportion, respect for reason and practicality, vigilant interest in politics, and distrust of authority repeatedly prevailed over the attraction of the authoritarian theories that the French intellectuals brilliantly formulated, and over the ambitions of military heroes temporarily acclaimed by an enthusiastic populace.

A strong public opinion of this kind has existed neither in Germany nor in Russia. In the eighteenth century, intellectual Germany had been an integral part of Western Europe. But the Enlightenment, which transformed the political and social structure of Britain and France, remained in Germany a purely moral and metaphysical movement. The political and social structure of the German lands was modernized only in the second half of the nineteenth century, when the influence of the Enlightenment's humanitarian individualism and tolerant rationalism was no longer dominant. Powerful tendencies in German thought, arising out of the war against Napoleon, rejected the civil society of England and America and the French Declaration of Rights of 1789, proclaiming instead the superiority of "indigenous" German thought and morality.

Only a few years before, all of Germany's greatest minds—Lessing and Wieland, Klopstock and Herder, Schiller and Wilhelm von Humboldt, Goethe and Kant—despite all their differences, had upheld the pacifism and cosmopolitanism of the Enlightenment. In the same year in which Goethe celebrated America's freedom from the fetters of a feudal past, he spurned the romantic nonsense of Gothicism. "Greek mythology," he declared, "is the most highly conceived embodiment of the best and purest kind of humanity. It merits greater praise than an ugly diabolism and witchery that could only spring from a confused imagination in somber and anxiety-ridden periods. . . ." He regarded French culture as the most vital of his time, and expected it to exercise a great moral influence on the world. With Olympian loftiness he surveyed the civilizations of the world and preferred the ancient Greek and modern French. The intensity and splendor that German intellectual life attained at the end of the eighteenth and beginning of the nineteenth century it attained as an integral part of Western civilization.

But after 1812 an anti-Western attitude began to predominate in Germany. Though the "Westernizers"—to borrow a term from Russian and Asian intellectual life—were always numerous, they were unable to influence decisively the political and intellectual development of Germany. Politically, the center shifted from western Germany, which had once been part of the Roman Empire, to the eastern marches that the Germans had conquered from the Slavs in the later Middle Ages. There, on the exiguous and sandy soil of Brandenburg, a Spartan effort of will and discipline created the great military power of Prussia. Prussian Junkerdom brought the methods of rationalist efficiency to the service of an irrational idolization of power; "reason of state" provided the basis not only for the political but also for the moral and intellectual life of the nation. The supposed necessities of the state became the supreme consideration in domestic and foreign policy. The Prussian state was good, the embodiment of reason and ethics, the argument ran, and thus whatever served the state was good—such was the higher Prussian morality. A number of German intellectuals found in the Prussian army, with its spirit of fellowship and discipline, security and devotion to the common good, the model of a "true" socialism.

This idolization of power and the state—to which the greatest German philosopher (Hegel) and the greatest German historian (Ranke) of the nineteenth century contributed—was supported by the seemingly contradictory "individualism" of German romanticism. "Western" individualism is rational and Christian: in seventeenth century England it based itself on the religious conception of the dignity and equality of all individuals created in the image of God; in eighteenth century France, on the rational conception of the equal rights of all men endowed with a reason that is one for the whole of mankind. Romantic individualism in Germany, however, stressed the unique and exceptional character of the individual, his peculiar endowments and rights. For Goethe personality had meant "to realize within oneself the idea of mankind, the timeless essence of the human race, and to raise oneself to the level of a symbolical representative of eternal humanity." Personality in this sense willingly submitted to universal standards; but in the German romantic meaning, the individual became a law unto himself and his passions and desires, provided they were strong enough, were regarded as self-validating. Later on, the state or the nation, understood as an organic individual of a higher kind, was endowed with the same unique character and rights.

The victories of Bismarck and the triumphs of German arms up to the last months of World War I seemed to confirm this belief in Germany's moral and intellectual superiority over the West. Leading German intellectuals of the period expressed it, men of a generally liberal turn of mind and fully conversant with world history and literature. In 1915, in his *Händler und Helden*, Werner Sombart, one of the greatest representatives of German scholarship at the time, made this comparison of "English shopkeepers" and "German heroes":

German thought and feeling expresses itself first and foremost in a complete rejection of everything that even approaches English or West European thought and feeling. With complete antipathy, with the deepest disdain, the German spirit rises up against the English-born ideas of the eighteenth century. German thinkers have at all times rejected all forms of utilitarianism and eudaimonism. The German heroic concept lays emphasis on duty; it looks on the state not as a contrivance for securing happiness, but as an organism, a spiritual whole.

In 1917 Thomas Mann approached this same German-Western antagonism from a different side. Writing on Dostoevsky, whom he regarded as the representative of the true Russia (which is why he was convinced that Russia after the democratic revolution of March 1917 could not become a democratic and socialist republic on the Western pattern), Mann pointed out, in his *Betrachtungen eines Unpolitischen,* the common opposition of Germany and Russia to the West:

Has anybody ever understood the human meaning of nationalism in a more German way than the greatest Russian moralist? Are not the Russian and German attitudes towards Europe, the West, civilization, politics, and democracy closely akin? Haven't we Germans also our Slavophils and Westernizers? If spiritual affinity can be the basis and justification of political alliances, then Russia and Germany belong together; their agreement now, their union in the future, has been since the beginning of this war the desire and dream of my heart. It is more than a desideratum: it is a political and spiritual necessity if the Anglo-American alliance should endure.

The unexpected defeat of 1918 only deepened the crisis of Western civilization in Germany. For disillusioned German youth, the Western values so eagerly opposed and almost vanquished only a short while ago offered no foundation on which to build a new life. Those of the older generation who upheld the ideals of the West lacked the strength to act upon them under the difficult conditions that prevailed. The English novelist D. H. Lawrence, traveling in Germany in 1928, wrote to a friend:

Immediately you are over the Rhine, the spirit of the place has changed. . . . It is as if the life had retreated eastwards. As if the Germanic life were slowly ebbing away from contact with Western Europe, ebbing to the desert of the East. And there stand the heavy, ponderous round hills of the Black Forest . . . you look at them from the Rhine plain, and know that you stand on an actual border, up against something. . . . So must the Roman soldiers have watched these black massive round woods. A fear of their own opposite. . . . Something has happened. The old spell of the old world has broken, and the old bristling savage spirit has set in, a still older flow has set in. Back, back to the savage polarity of Tartary, and away from the polarity of civilized Christian Europe. . . . Not that the people are actually planning or plotting or preparing. I don't believe it for a minute. Something has happened to the human soul, beyond all help. The human soul recoiling from unison, and making itself strong elsewhere. The ancient spirit of prehistoric Germany coming back, at the end of History.

Three years later the German philosopher Karl Jaspers declared, in *The Spiritual Situation of Our Time*, that Germany—following Kierkegaard, Nietzsche, and Spengler—felt itself face to face with nothingness.

People are coming to believe that everything is breaking down; there is nothing that can't be questioned; nothing that is real stands the test; it is an endless whirl that consists in cheating others and oneself by means of ideologies.

Faced with this nihilism—the roots of which went back to the Romantics and Hegel, to historicism and materialism, to thinkers and movements in no way nihilistic themselves—the Germans turned away completely from Western civilization and sought an absolute security in the unconsciousness of the blood and of past history, of the soil and of dogmatic faith.

But when the new war against the West again ended in disastrous defeat, the Western spirit was still a strong enough element in the German tradition to awaken in many Germans a desire to return to Goethe—the name signifying not so much the man and the poet in his unique greatness as a temper and state of mind. The outward conditions for a Western reorientation of Germany seemed auspicious: Prussia no longer existed as a state, the wish that the Prussian Herder had expressed in 1769—"States like Prussia will never be happy until they are divided up"—having been fulfilled; and Germany's center of gravity had shifted back to the West where it had been during most of her history. Many elements in Germany which for a hundred years had sneered at the moral and spiritual debility of the civilization of the West, now seek Germany's salvation in a revival of that spirit inside her borders. For this venture to succeed, Germany must break with the precedents of 1813, 1848, and 1870, and place individual liberty above the power of a unified nation-state.

The situation was different in Russia. Peter I had tried to overcome by force the inertia and backwardness which he found among the Russians. A century later, after the Napoleonic Wars, Western ideas began to penetrate more deeply into the consciousness of the small educated class. The discrepancy that was revealed between Western ideals and actual conditions in Russia led to a quest for the meaning of Russian history and an examination of Russia's relation to Europe. Unfamiliar with the social and political realities of the West, judging it irresponsibly as a purely intellectual entity, as an idea and only as an idea, many Russians began to view Europe with a critical eye that caught the weaknesses but missed the strength. The Russian intelligentsia's greater remoteness from the West, their extremist disdain of common sense and "bourgeois" attitudes, caused them to exceed the Germans in their superiority feelings and apocalyptic expectations. Thomas G. Masaryk, who knew Russia better than any other contemporary thinker, deplored the unself-critical boastfulness and lack of moderation in much of Russian thought. He found the Russian rationalists as mystically inclined as the Orthodox theologians; in turning away from traditional Orthodoxy they had only changed the object of their faith. A century ago Alexander Herzen saw the underlying affinity between the

Russian autocratic government and the Russian revolutionary movement:

It has been remarked that an opposition leading a frontal attack upon a government always has, in an inverted form, something of the character of its antagonist. I think there is some justification for the fear that the Russian government is beginning to have of Communism: Communism is the Russian autocracy turned upside down.

The word "nihilism" was first popularized in the early 1860's by Ivan Turgenev in his novel *Fathers and Sons*, which described a younger generation that finds not "a single convention of our present-day existence, in family or social life, that does not call for complete and ruthless rejection." The "nihilists" called themselves "new men" or "thinking realists"; but they were as unrealistic and absolutist in their materialism and negativism as the older generation had been in its idealism and Slavophilism. An extreme optimism inspired the Russian youth and their teacher, Nikolai Gavrilovich Chernyshevsky: "We are still ignorant, but we shall learn—we shall become brothers and sisters." But through the dialectics of extremism they arrived at the very opposite of liberty: "After having started from unlimited liberty," Shigalev says in Dostoevsky's *The Possessed*, "I finally arrived at unlimited despotism."

Yet in spite of all the difficulties, Western influence was slowly gaining in Russia, and Russian society underwent a transformation after 1880. The demands put by World War I upon the Russian economy and government machinery and the ensuing defeat of the Russian armies made the reform of Russian society an immediate necessity before the Russian people were ready for it. The Westernizing revolution of March 1917 was followed only a few months later by a mobilization of the un-Europeanized masses. Masaryk saw from the beginning that Lenin's revolution had destroyed the hopes for the Europeanization of Russia. He regarded Leninism as a product of Russian backwardness, and its theory of revolution, in which he detected much of Bakunin, as primitive and barbaric.

In the second quarter of the twentieth century the unexpected had happened. Modern civilization—based upon the rights of the individual, tolerance of diversity, and freedom of inquiry—lost much of the ground it had gained in the preceding one hundred years. This temporary decline was abetted by the transformation which some fundamental Western concepts underwent in the climate of Central and Eastern Europe and Asia: the nation-state of the West, born out of a struggle by the people for constitutional liberties and the tolerance of opposition, had meant a society of free citizens based on laws; whereas the new nationalism, stressing collective power and national unity, tended to mean independence from foreign domination and a nationalist mystique rather than individual liberty and the security of legal guarantees for all citizens at home.

A disregard of individual rights and an extreme utopian impatience characterized intellectual and economic developments in the extra-Western areas. In the United States, Britain, Switzerland, and Scandinavia—the "capitalistic" countries—social reforms secured a high standard of living for the working class and their participation in political life. In Russia, Italy, Germany, and Spain, the anti-"plutocratic" movements, which were fundamentally anti-Western and represented in varying degree an amalgamation of "nationalism" and "socialism," turned the nation into an armed camp. "Socialism" was expected to beget a new man who would rise triumphant over egotistic "individualism." The emphasis placed on the collectivity instead of the individual, on force instead of compromise, on salvation instead of responsible realism, combined with an overestimation of the possibilities of a rationalized efficiency in the state and economy, encouraged an expectation that utopias could be set up here and now, or at least in the very near future. Existing society and civilization were distrusted and despised. Faith in the magic power of national or social revolution or, as the magic word went, "liberation" and the currency of all sorts of chiliastic sentimentalities led to the invention of new social myths which demanded group loyalty based upon homogeneity of origin, similarity of conditions of life, and supposed identity of interest. Nationalities and classes were set apart and declared to be irrevocably different and antagonistic; to fulfill their destinies they needed the leadership of daring minorities who understood the "mission" with which they had been "entrusted" by history.

In the summer of 1940 Europe seemed lost to Western civilization. The "young" and "anti-capitalistic" nations, under the leadership of Hitler and Stalin, Mussolini and Franco, ruled the length and breadth of the continent, with the exception of the Swiss and Swedish enclaves. The "old" and "decaying plutocracies" seemed routed. Yet Britain held firm, and together with the United States went on to liberate much of Europe. Though Western civilization had lost in geographical extent, it gained in historical self-understanding from the ordeals it underwent. It learned to distrust the hypnotizing power of the incantatory oversimplifications. It had cast off the easy illusions of the nineteenth century. The strength of the forces that always threatened Western civilization was now better understood.

The West's encounter with other civilizations brings not only a threat, it is also an experience that may set free new creative energy. Modern civilization in the nineteenth century believed itself so unchallenged that a smug overestimation of material progress threatened to smother that independence of personality so essential to the Western spirit. This spirit had grown out of a disquiet, an intellectual "inquietude," a pioneering spontaneity of the human mind that was not afraid of loneliness and dissent.

Communism, fascism, and other authoritarian and dogmatic creeds wish to relieve men of this glory and torment of maturity. They may make life "easier" and create a type of "well-adjusted" man, though even this achievement is very doubtful. They may give material and psychological security—though in no country as yet have they shown any real signs of providing either. They may avoid economic crises, though for the most part they create historical ones. But for modern Western man this proffer of regimented bliss holds little attraction, nor does he, except for a small defeatist minority, believe in the imminent doom of total crisis. The events of the twentieth century have destroyed his complacency. They have led him to study and scrutinize the roots, premises, and implications of his intellectual and social attitudes; the humanities and the history of ideas have assumed a new importance. In their light he begins to view the crisis in historical perspective. In the hour of danger he feels the need for a closer unity of the nations bordering on the North Atlantic, the birthplace of modern civilization. He wishes to transcend narrow nationalisms that are inconsistent with the best traditions of the modern West. With all its promises and dangers, modern civilization appears to him as a young and recent venture, the possibilities of which have in no way been exhausted. Far from the West's having passed into its senescence, as all the criers of doom have been telling us, we have good grounds for asserting the conviction that it is only just now entering into the period of its vigorous maturity, able to face the challenge of a rapidly changing world, changing and growing up thanks to the contact with the modern West.

XVII

CIVILIZATION IN CRISIS
A CRITIQUE OF TOYNBEE

Professor ARNOLD TOYNBEE has now published the four con-
cluding volumes of the ten which form his magnum opus, *A
Study of History*. These last four volumes alone are a monu-
mental achievement. They contain more than 2,500 pages and
cover in a panoramic sweep all ages from early historic times to
the present day and all civilizations, even the least familiar ones.
A vast, and today probably unparalleled, learning and an earnest
dedication have gone into the writing of these volumes, and a
somewhat old-fashioned but delightful urbanity of style and mind
enhances the pleasure of reading them. This pleasure is not so
much based on an agreement with Mr. Toynbee's fundamental
position as on the wealth of fascinating details and new vistas
with which the author presents us. Toynbee's work is not clothed
in the cool garb of the detached scholar. It is an intensely personal document, the profession of faith of a great scholar and a
universal mind, and as such it deserves our respect in spite of
doubts and disagreements.

Many years have elapsed since the publication of the first six
volumes; they were years of fateful historical events—the initial
triumph of National Socialism, the Second World War, the
emergence of Communist Russia as a leading world power, and
finally the Asian revival with its passionate nationalism and imperialism. These events have understandably impressed Mr.
Toynbee. His work bears their traces to such a degree that the
Study of History is also a tract for our own age and its predicament. Therein lies part of its value as a human document, as a

witness to the time of our life and its problems, and as such it will remain of enduring interest to all future historians. Yet it is with the tract for our "predicament" that I find myself in disagreement, a disagreement not only with Mr. Toynbee but with the whole and recently rapidly growing school of writers who lament the decay of modern Western civilization and call for a "return to God." Of all these innumerable mournful or gleeful prophets, Mr. Toynbee is by far the most serious and reasonable one. For his approach is distinguished by a broad tolerance and a reasonable empiricism, which belong to the best characteristics of modern Western civilization and which are so sorely missing in the Russian Danilevsky and the German Spengler.

As a student of nationalism, I agree with Mr. Toynbee's position that nationalism in the twentieth century has often degenerated, politically and spiritually, into a danger, and perhaps the greatest danger, to individual liberty and international peace, to the human mind and man's well-being. In my first essay on nationalism which I wrote in 1919, at the end of the First World War, I drew the parallel to which Mr. Toynbee also refers, between the religious wars and intolerance of the seventeenth century and the nationalist wars and intolerance of our time. I then expressed the hope that we might return to an age of Enlightenment which would control the political passions of nationalism as the Enlightenment which started with Locke ended the similar passions of religion. The experiences of the Second World War have led other historians toward a similar hope. In his last work, *Geschonden Wereld,* the Dutch historian J. Huizinga wrote in 1943 that "nationalism, the exaggerated and unjustified tendency to emphasize national interests, produced in our time the abominable fruit of hyper-nationalism, the curse of this century."

In his sweeping condemnation of nationalism, Toynbee disregards, however, the fact that nationalism began in eighteenth century Western society as a striving for the protection of the rights of the individual citizen against the power of government and the dogmatism of religion. In the atmosphere of Enlightenment it was a liberating movement from the fetters of a deadening tradition. From Milton and Locke to Jefferson and Condorcet, this early nationalism helped the growth of man's stature. But in the course of the nineteenth century, when nationalism spread from the shores of the Atlantic eastward, into lands with an entirely different political and cultural tradition and social structure, nationalism turned more and more into a desire for collective power and self-assertion and tended to subject the individual to the political, intellectual, and moral authority of the collectivity.

Professor Toynbee's insistence that the units of history are not nations or continents, not political or geographic areas but civilizations, has always impressed me as a most fertile proposition. Asia for the Asians or Europe for the Europeans makes little sense, for where are the boundaries of these continents? Do they end at the Ural mountains, the Straits of Constantinople, or the Suez Canal? Are Egypt or Tunisia part of the same Africa as the Congo? What is the unifying link between two Asian lands like Islamic Saudi Arabia and Buddhist Burma? Asia is the home of several great civilizations, Islamic, Hindu, Chinese, which have nothing in common but borders which have given rise and may give rise again to violent conflicts. Nor is Europe a cultural unit. The European settlements in North America have been throughout their brief history infinitely closer to Western Europe than to Moscow or Constantinople. We should be grateful to Mr. Toynbee for putting civilization and not nations in the foreground of history. Whereas nations have played a very great role in the events of the last centuries, civilization has been a determining factor for human life and history throughout all ages.

But Mr. Toynbee's approach to civilization demands on our part two reservations. Why does he emphasize so much the fact that Western civilization is not the only one, that it does not tower as the fulfillment over all others, and that no civilization is final or immortal? The Chinese or the medieval Christian might have felt certain about the unique superiority and finality of his own civilization, and modern Western common man might have shared this feeling around 1910 about his own civilization. But I doubt whether any serious thinker in the contemporary West holds such a position. The modern Western intellectual on the whole does not overestimate, he rather underestimates his civilization. And Mr. Toynbee does too. We shall always respect and even envy him for the ecumenical breadth of his thought, vision and knowledge. In that respect he is the foremost and most representative historian of the twentieth century, in which for the first time all issues have become world-wide and demand an ecumenical understanding.

Personally I have always stressed the need for an ecumenical understanding too. Forty years ago I published an essay "Der Geist des Orients" (The Oriental Mind), and a quarter of a century ago a book *A History of Nationalism in the East*. In both I paid my respect to non-Western civilizations. I have been fully aware of the existence, and the right to exist, of other civilizations, of their greatness in the past, their importance in the present, and their potential promise for the future. Yet I cannot share Mr. Toynbee's overcritical attitude to modern Western civilization. I admire the glory that was Greece and the beauty of thirteenth century Western Christianity, the depth of the Upanishads and the wisdom of Chinese sages, but modern Western civilization has set new and to me higher standards of respect for the individual, of social responsibility, of critical inquiry, than any preceding civilization. Though all civilizations are a product of history and enmeshed in temporality, and though each one has its virtues and foibles, there is in modern Western civilization a vital spiritual force which singles it out from preceding civilizations and which in the nineteenth and twentieth centuries has helped to revitalize other civilizations and to enhance their self-awareness.

Toynbee accepts the fundamental faith of the Judeo-Christian religious tradition that history is God's path—a course from God, its source, toward God, its goal. This faith presupposes an encompassing vision of the unity, the rationality, and the purposefulness of all history, a religious vision secularized in Hegel and Marx, which the scholar as scholar cannot accept. He remains ignorant of the final aims, if any, of the Divine in and through history. A meaning and a fulfillment of history are postulates for

the emotional and aesthetic satisfaction of Western man. They are not the subject of historical scholarship. History has no answers concerning its ultimate course and goal; faith alone can supply them. Mr. Toynbee has a strong religious faith and he believes that only a religious revival can save civilization. But Mr. Toynbee shows much greater moral earnestness and historical awareness than the other prophets who call for "a return to God." He sees in the return to institutional orthodoxy a symptom of spiritual cowardice.

A post-Christian Western Society's temptation to seek refuge from the consequences of its own technological handiwork by begging for readmittance into the fold of a conventional Christian orthodoxy was neither morally nor intellectually defensible. . . . Souls that have once had the experience of intellectual enlightenment can never thereafter find spiritual salvation by committing intellectual suicide . . . for the progressive decay of a belief in, and an allegiance to, an ancestral religion, which had been the note of a Western Society's spiritual history since the latter decades of the seventeenth century of the Christian era, had not been due solely to Modern Western Man's perversity nor even solely to his bewitchment by his intellect's entrancing scientific discovery . . . [but to the Western Christian Church having] alienated its long-suffering votaries by its grievous sins of both heart and head.

There would be more respect for all the new seekers of God today, if they would like Mr. Toynbee take a courageous stand not only against the insufficiencies of the prevailing civilization but against the moral iniquities of all institutionalized religion, west and east. In that respect Mr. Toynbee's humanitarian and rationalist Christianity recalls that of other great moral teachers of our time, of Leo Tolstoy and of Albert Schweitzer. A teacher of tolerance, free of all dogmatic exclusiveness, Toynbee even resembles the great mind of the German Enlightenment, Gotthold Ephraim Lessing, who in his play Nathan the Wise told eighteenth century Europe that man's religious beliefs and dogmas are unimportant compared with his actions and his ethical spirit. As Lessing saw in Judaism, Christianity, and

Islam variations on a single theme, so Mr. Toynbee, on the enlarged and world-wide scale of the twentieth century, no longer
regards Christianity as the only possible true religion, but sees
all universal religions—Christianity, Islam, Hinduism, and Buddhism—as equally sharing in their great message to mankind,
the message of unity beyond all ethnic divisions.

In spite of his broad tolerance and his critical insight, Mr.
Toynbee seems to overestimate the moral beauty of the ages of
faith and to underestimate the vigor of modern Western civilization. To quote Huizinga's last book again, written while he himself suffered from the effects of the Second World War, "Has
Christianity ever, even in the period when it found most passionate and general adherence, made the average man better
and wiser?" The Middle Ages were a time of great and sublime
piety but also of unsurpassed cruelty and excessive immorality.
Nor did the poets and writers of the time speak of it without a
critical bitterness which reminds us of some writers of our own
day. In the fourteenth century Eustache Deschamps wrote of

> Temps de doleur et de temptacion,
> Aages de plour, d'envie et de tourment,
> Temps de langour et de dampnacion,
> Aages meneur près du definement,
> Temps plain d'orreur qui tout fait faussement,
> Aage menteur, plain d'orgeuil et d'envie,
> Temps sanz honeur et sanz vray jugement,
> Aage en tristesse qui abrege la vie.

And his British contemporary Langland was equally bitter:

> Loud laughed Life. . . .
> And armed him in haste—with words of harlotry
> And held Holiness for a jest—and
> > Courtesy for a waster,
> And Loyalty a churl—and Liar a gentleman,
> Concience and Counsel—he counted it a folly.

Two centuries earlier John of Salisbury, in discussing Caesar's
times in his *Policraticus*, a treatise on court vanities, wrote words
sounding familiar to readers today:

The picture of that time often comes to mind, when subjects see their every act determined by a tyrant's nod, and however their minds rebel, are forced to condemn themselves to exile or to death. . . . So priests are forced to deny the precepts of divine law, old men forget their wisdom, the judge is ignorant of justice . . . the free citizen despises liberty, and the whole people at last scorn peace and quiet. For when all are at the mercy of the ruler's nod, one and all are deprived of the exercise of free will.

Mr. Toynbee is not the only one to lament the follies, misery, and insecurity of twentieth century Western man. Therein he follows only a broad and fashionable trend among intellectuals today, especially on the European continent. But the outstanding student of history which Mr. Toynbee is, knows well that there have been few ages not suffering from the same predicament. There were of course exceptions, but only two come immediately to one's mind: the Mediterranean world of the second century of our era led by Rome, and the Western world of the nineteenth century led by Britain. A century ago man and people lived in an unusual feeling of security, yet even then sensitive minds felt approaching earthquakes. In any case, the twentieth century Western man was rudely awakened to a realization of the general human condition. This rude awakening gave him the feeling of an unprecedented crisis. Arthur Koestler has, intentionally or not, caricatured this crisis feeling of an approaching total catastrophe in his novel *The Age of Longing*. In it the crowds accompanying a funeral in the streets of Paris, sometime in the early 1950's, are seized by excitement at the sounding of air-raid sirens. "The siren wailed, but nobody was sure if it could have meant the Last Judgment, or just another air-raid exercise." The American heroine of the novel thought, observing the panic-stricken faces, "Thus must medieval crowds have stared at the sky Anno Domini 999, waiting for the Comet to appear." In the age of faith the crowds waited in vain—not only in 999 but also on several later occasions—and the Parisian crowds in Koestler's age of longing waited certainly in vain too. Koestler is not the only one to admire the alleged youth and strength of the new age of faith which has dawned in the East.

It is being contrasted, to the latter's disadvantage, with a sceptical, insecure, decaying, and obsolete West.

This message is not new. We have heard it many times from German romanticists and historicists, from Russian Slavophils, from Hindu spiritualists and nationalists. Mr. Toynbee is too great a historian and too deeply steeped in the spirit of liberty and tolerance of the modern West to accept this oversimplified version of the "apocalyptic" and "crisis" thinkers of our time. Yet he too regards modern Western civilization as an apostasy from Christian Western civilization, as a desertion of modern man from faith into the barren grounds of secularism. He dates the beginning of the modern West from the fifteenth century Portuguese and Spanish discoveries. In reality it began in the seventeenth century, in England and Holland. Mr. Toynbee regards "an elimination of religion, not an introduction of science" as the essence "of the seventeenth century Western cultural revolution." But modern Western civilization was not a negative phenomenon, an elimination of religion, it was an entirely new civilization, a new moral, spiritual, and practical attitude, which can be called post-Christian only in the same sense as Western Christian civilization from the eighth to the seventeenth century can be called a post-Greco-Roman civilization.

What happened in the seventeenth century, in the great crisis of the birth of a new Western consciousness, was the rise of a new civilization. It was affiliated, both historically and in its content, to the Western Christian civilization of the Middle Ages, as the latter was affiliated to the Greco-Roman civilization of Antiquity. Religion was in no way "eliminated." On the contrary, it lost only the dominant and all-encompassing function which it had exercised during the Middle Ages and in the first part of the seventeenth century. Not only a new spirit of scientific inquiry but a new respect for liberty under law, for individual dignity, for freedom of thought, for political and intellectual tolerance, a new concept of human relationship in society and of the rights of the citizen in face of his government were born then. Modern Western civilization is not "old," it is "young," barely three centuries in existence even on the shores of the

North Atlantic. Communism and fascism are not the fruit or result of this modern civilization. They are a rejection of it and of its spirit, though eager to take over its technology and material results. Communism and fascism gained hold only in countries where modern Western civilization had not taken firm root. They were a "return" to the "Middle Ages," in Russia and Italy, Germany and Spain.

Mr. Toynbee underrates the newness and greatness of modern Western civilization. He overstresses, and therein he again follows a fashionable trend, the need for a political unification of the world. Such a demand was understandable in the naïve and hopeful belief, only a few years ago, in the universality of Western civilization. Many people believed then that Western civilization would spread all over the earth and become the only civilization. The Russian Marxists, heirs of this overconfident self-estimation of the bourgeois West, are convinced that their Communism will establish on the basis of its one civilization a unified world. We are today less inclined to disregard the diversity of civilizations and historical traditions. Their diversity and even their antagonism adds to the richness of human experience. Several "worlds" can live together provided that they follow Mr. Toynbee's "unflamboyant virtues" of fortitude and reasonableness—which are in the best Western tradition. What is needed is not the—at least at present impossible—unity of the world which can be based only on at present non-existent common attitudes to liberty and law, but the unity of the nations of modern Western civilization, their growing out of nationalism and parochial loyalties into a loyalty to their common civilization which is for them the spiritual source of their life, as Christianity was for thirteenth century Western man. Such a Western or North Atlantic unity in diversity was not needed before 1914. It is essential now when modern Western civilization has found itself under severe attack from non-Western civilizations or from anti-Western movements like fascism and communism.

Mr. Toynbee is too keen and too broad-minded to emphasize differences between Western Europe and the United States. The United States certainly differs in many ways from Britain, but

so does Britain from France or Switzerland. The present crisis is
a common phenomenon of the whole of modern Western civilization. "Any contemporary critic of American *mores* could silence
the carping West European visitor," Mr. Toynbee writes, "with
a crushing De te fabula narratur." Yet even Mr. Toynbee seems
to believe in a "third way" followed by Britain and Scandinavia
between the apparently dogmatic capitalism of the United States
and the communism of the Soviet orbit. Rightly he praises the
trial and error method followed by Britain since the Glorious
Revolution. But the heritage of the Glorious Revolution is common to Britain and the United States, and John Locke has been
rightly called the "American philosopher." The New Deal of
1933 was as much a peaceful domestic revolution as Britain's
reforms under the Labor government of 1945. Nor is American
isolationism so different from British insularity. The wealth of
diversity, the acceptance of contradiction and criticism, the incessant quest for new frontiers of truth, a profound spiritual
mobility, a permanent social and intellectual revolution—these
are characteristic traits which distinguish modern Western civilization. Naturally they produce a feeling of crisis, insecurity, and
change unknown to other civilizations, but they also form the
modern West's strength and glory.

No short essay can exhaust the riches of Mr. Toynbee's massive
volumes nor note the many points of admiration or of disagreement which every reader will encounter. The details in Mr. Toynbee's work are much more important than the general framework, for history, the totality of human life and experience, is
not a surveyable whole. It is, however, at least in the West, a
continuous chain of tradition. Modern Western man knows, and
gratefully acknowledges, how much he owes to medieval Christianity. But he owes an at least equally great debt to the ancient
world, too. Two great Germans who still lived in the community
of Western tradition—before some Germans adumbrated, with
their interpretations of the struggle against the French, the "war
against the West"—Goethe and Schiller, seeking in a crisis of
Western man for healing forces, turned not to the Christian
Middle Ages but to Greek antiquity:

Und die Sonne Homers, siehe, sie leuchtet auch uns.

Modern Western civilization is a new civilization, an apostasy neither from Christianity nor from Greece. The cosmos of the thirteenth century is as distant from us as Homer's nature or Periclean Athens. But in them, and their continuous life in us, we are rooted. Today we are confronted by the danger that this chain of tradition is being broken. Mr. Toynbee, for whom the Old and the New Testament, the Greek and the Roman classics are a living reality, recalls us to a continuity without which the creativity of our modern civilization must wither. At the same time, however, he does not confine us to our own civilization. He broadens the horizon, as no other historian has done, to include the whole panorama of past and contemporary civilizations. History feeds on the diversity and contrariety of men and civilizations. But the Old Testament tells us at the very beginning that all men descend from Adam and Eve and that they share dreams of a common lost past and hopes for ultimate return to paradise and for salvation from the human predicament. To have stressed, beyond the confines of history, the fundamental oneness of mankind and of the human condition, will be a lasting merit of Mr. Toynbee's work and vision.

XVIII

PERSPECTIVE OF THE 1960s

I

Two-THIRDS of the twentieth century lie behind us. So far it has been, as Nietzsche predicted, a war-like century. The first decade after the conclusion of World War II was one of general apprehension, for many people believed in the probability of a repetition of the 1930s: an economic depression in the capitalist countries; a seemingly higher efficiency of totalitarian regimes; another "Munich;" the coming of another world war. So far none of these fears have been justified. Even in the 1950s the situation was different from that of the 1930s. Though two super-powers faced each other, as if they alone counted in the world and as if heavy armaments represented the only decisive factor in a world-community growing ever more interdependent, peace was, on the whole, preserved. The super-powers have shown a degree of restraint which former times have not known.

The United States did not make use of its atomic power monopoly, and Stalin, though the ruthless omnipotent dictator of the powerful and victorious Soviet Union and of its European satellites, abstained from imposing his will upon the hated "Trotskyite" or "fascist" "renegade" Tito, whose Yugoslav forces were insignificant compared with those of Stalin's war machine. The United States government, contrary to some military advice, refrained from carrying the Korean war, which was essentially a defence of South Korea, into communist China. The Soviet Union gave up its rights of occupation in Austria, which had been a willing partner of National Socialist Great Germany in fighting and devastating Russia. The Soviet Union helped to establish the full independence of Austria and respected its newly found Western democratic character as much as that of Finland, Germany's ally in aggression against the Soviet Union. Lying in the shadow of the Soviet giant, having long common frontiers with the Soviet bloc, Finland and Austria were not attacked or blockaded for following an economic and parliamentary policy totally opposed to that of communism. The communists established here an example of co-existence. Vienna could resume its historical role of a meeting ground of Western and Eastern Europe.

Though the Cold War in the form of co-existence will go on for the foreseeable future—nothing in history goes on for ever or in perpetuity—it has lost by the middle of the 1960s its all-inclusive and dominant character. This is in accord with the experience of all history. Mankind has always been half free and half slave, or rather freedom and unfreedom have always existed in innumerable shades side by side, not only on the earth as a whole but even within each country. In the 1960s three main factors have contributed to the waning of the power of a bi-polarized ideological confrontation. One of them has been the recovery and re-assertion of Europe to a degree which no one expected in 1945. Then the second German war of the twentieth century had left Europe prostrate. Largely through the help of the United States, which held its protective umbrella over the Western European nations (which it did not do after the first German war) and poured many billions of aid into their economies, the European nations have in the 1960s regained prosperity and strength. A paradoxical result of this success of American policy is the fact that NATO, founded by American initiative and now seventeen years old, is threatened in its growth by apathy and disintegration. Under General de Gaulle France follows a supple and emphatically French policy, which in many ways finds itself in contradiction to that of the United States. It is a policy based not on ideology but on the evaluation of changing national and international realities. France—and not only France—wishes to become an independent power-center, politically, economically, and culturally. Should a united Western Europe emerge, it will follow the French example, without accepting French leadership. The Western Europeans, with the exception of some circles in the German Federal Republic who seek a revision of its eastern borders and whose avowed anti-communism coincides with a muted traditional anti-Slavism, no longer overestimate the power, cohesion and aggressiveness of the communist bloc.

This bloc has undergone an even more pronounced fragmentation than the Western world. In 1945 the communist countries and parties formed a strictly monolithic structure which without hesitation accepted directions from Moscow. With the spread of communism—which was due to World War II as the rise of communism in Russia was due to World War I—diversity set in almost by necessity. In 1955 Khrushchev recognized the right of communist Yugoslavia to follow its own road to socialism, independent from that travelled by Moscow. By 1966 very little remains of the former cohesion of world communism. Each communist country and party follows its own line. The COMECON and the Warsaw pact have become even less effective than NATO. The Italian communist party, the largest in a non-communist European country, pioneered under Palmiro Togliatti in the recognition of the principle of polycentrism. Moscow has learned to respect the desire of its former satellites for independent and equal status. From 1963 on, communist Rumania has stressed more and more her "Latin" and non-Slav character and has developed an active foreign policy in line with its national interests. China, the largest and most populous communist nation, and Albania, the smallest, are equally hostile to the Soviet Union; and communist Vietnam is deeply concerned about an extension of the traditional Chinese influence southward.

At the same time Asia, Africa, and Latin America have tried to take their place "in the foreground of the stage of world affairs." [1] The self-assertion on the part of these "under-developed" countries represents the great revolution of the mid-twentieth century, by far surpassing in global importance that of the revolutions of 1789 or of 1917. Like its forerunners—the Young Turk revolution of 1908, the Mexican revolution of 1910-1917, the Chinese revolution of 1911 and finally Lenin's seizure of power in 1917—the global revolution of our days is the response of backward countries to the dynamic challenge of modern Western civilization which in the seventeenth and eighteenth centuries invigorated and transformed the thought and societies of the North Atlantic countries and of which Marx in his "Communist Manifesto" foresaw the world-wide revolutionary implications.[2] It was the historical achievement, though not the intention, of recent Western imperialism to unify the globe, as did Roman imperialism in the Mediterranean *orbis terrarum* of antiquity.

II

The devil theory of conspiracy—whether the "devil" be the Free Masons or the Jesuits, Anglo-Saxon capitalism or Russian communism—hardly explains great historical changes. The 1960s have put an end to the rigidity of the bipolar ideological conflict which marked the early 1950s. In the 1960s a multiplicity of complex and shifting relationships has replaced the over-simplified division of mankind into two camps, originally conceived by communism and elevated to the status of a dogma. The rapprochement of de Gaulle's France and communist China, the passing but nevertheless characteristic flirtations of Castro's Cuba and Franco's Spain, of Islamic Pakistan and atheist China, are only a few random examples of the often rapidly and unexpectedly shifting international scene. In this process no one "third force" is emerging, as formerly has been claimed, but instead many and varying third forces and realignments, in which ideology plays a minor role and sometimes no role at all.

The events leading up to and shaping World War II were also not primarily determined by ideological considerations. Fascist Germany in 1939 did not attack democratic Britain or communist Russia, but—in close cooperation with communist Russia—semi-fascist, anti-democratic, anti-communist, anti-semitic Poland which for over five years had closely collaborated with fascist Germany. Fascist Spain refused its protector Hitler the passage through Spain to attack Gibraltar and occupy North

Africa. In October, 1940, fascist Italy selected as its victim Greece which was then, under General John Metaxas, an outright fascist state, the Third Hellas. When, at the beginning of December, 1941, the Germans stood at the gates of Moscow, their Japanese allies turned not against the Soviet Union, which in this event might have lost the war, but against the United States.

Common to all countries in the 1960s is the growth of nationalism. This fact is perhaps the best safeguard against the control of mankind by one power or group of powers or by one ideology. Global aspirations of a centrally unified and directed order were still pursued in the 1930s by Hitler and the Japanese military oligarchy and in the 1940s by Stalin. In the 1960s they are doomed by the insistence of each nation on being "itself," whatever that may mean in the concrete circumstances. The emphasis on equality of status irrespective of actual power exists today among all nations, strong and weak, old and new, democratic and communist as well as among the very many which are neither democratic nor communist. This nationalism has withdrawn Cuba from the sphere of influence of the United States and has frustrated Russia's age-old aspirations of establishing control in the Middle East, and her and China's new aspirations of gaining a foothold in Africa. Such aspirations still prevailed under Stalin when in 1945 he demanded in vain bases in the Bosphorus, in the Dodecanese, in Eritrea and Libya. Even then communism was far removed from achieving an unbroken sequence of victories—with which many Americans credited it, helping thereby to foster the legend of communist superhuman intelligence and strength, thus playing into communist hands. The Soviet Union evacuated Iranian Azerbaijan, although this territory was contiguous with Soviet territory inhabited by the same kind of people. In this evacuation the Soviet Union even sacrificed its local communist satellite government without suffering any serious loss of prestige.

Probably Russia today aspires to become a leading world power. This is a legitimate aspiration, different from that of becoming the dominant world power. In the nineteenth century

Britain was such a leading world power; in the present century the United States is in this position, but no nation can expect to remain such a leading power for ever. Russia or China may one day step into this position, but the day is yet far away. After Napoleon's defeat and throughout the nineteenth century Russian nationalists dreamt of such a position for Russia. Khrushchev promised to catch up with and even overcome the United States by 1970 in economic productivity and the standard of living. The nearer 1970 approaches, the less is heard of this aspiration. It will take a very long time for either communist Russia or communist China to approach the standard of living in Western Europe. But there is no doubt that the communist regimes in Russia and China have greatly strengthened their countries in comparison with their monarchist past and have given their peoples a new sense of dignity and importance. As the 1960s move toward their end, the United States possesses a very great and growing superiority of military and economic power over any other country or combination of countries. But superiority which in responsible hands can be an instrument of peace does not mean, and ought not to mean, supremacy, which is an instrument of domination, of imposing one's will upon others. Nothing is more dangerous to a great power than moralistic self-righteousness and the illusion of omnipotence.

Nations have begun to learn the lesson. In November 1958 Khrushchev put forward an ultimatum demanding a change in the status of West Berlin within six months, yet West Berlin finds itself seven years later as free as in 1958. Stalin's Russia failed to impose her will on Yugoslavia in 1948; Tito remained undaunted in spite of the fact that neither oceans nor armaments protected him. Khrushchev's Russia could not impose her will on a tiny fellow-communist country, Albania, which forced Russia to evacuate her submarines from Valona, or Vlone, on the Adriatic sea, Russia's only military base in the Mediterranean area. On February 24, 1964, Albania seized the Soviet-built and Soviet-owned embassy buildings in Tirana, Albania's capital, and Russia could not, or did not, do more than make a formal protest.

In 1961 France defended her important Mediterranean naval base in Bizerta against a Tunisian take-over and in this struggle killed many hundred Tunisians; two years later the French evacuated Bizerta which then came under undisputed Tunisian control. French international prestige suffered as little by this abandonment of an "indispensable" military position as it did by negotiating the complete independence of Algeria with the Algerian rebel leaders whom a short while before France had refused to recognize. To the contrary, France gained in strength and authority by this policy of "renunciation," and Algeria became as little communist as did Egypt. Military and strategic considerations are losing in importance, and the power of a nation in today's world politics is not based on arms alone. In pursuing his policy, General de Gaulle did not listen to the advice of his own military leaders.

III

What seems needed in the mid-1960s is the patience to negotiate and the openness to discourse which, if practiced over a long time, itself exerts an influence on changing conditions. A psychological change must precede any more far-reaching action; we have witnessed several such psychological changes in recent times. In 1944 Americans regarded the Japanese and the Germans as mortal enemies. Few would then have ventured to predict the present ties of friendship that exist. Within two years, from the Truman doctrine on Greece and Turkey proclaimed in March 1947, to the North Atlantic Treaty of April 1949, public opinion in America adapted to the changing world conditions, turning from the extreme isolationism and deep-seated distrust of "British imperialism" which had predominated into 1946, to an active, perhaps even over-active, participation in world affairs and, in particular, to a close cooperation with "British imperialism."

Recent astonishing changes in the world-wide political configuration demand a revaluation of our response to the challenges of our time. The necessity was emphasized in Senator Fulbright's speech before the Senate on March 25, 1964. He said among other things: "There is much cant in American moralism. It resembles in some ways the religious faith of so many respectable peoples who, in Samuel Butler's words, 'would be equally horrified to hear the Christian religion doubted or to see it practiced.' . . . We are confronted with a complex and fluid world situation and we are not adapting ourselves to it. We are clinging to old myths in the face of new realities and we are seeking to escape the contradictions by narrowing the permissible bounds of public discussion, by relegating an increasing number of ideas and viewpoints to a growing category of 'unthinkable thoughts.' I believe that this tendency can and should be reversed, that it is within our ability, and unquestionably in our interests, to cut loose from established myths and to start thinking some 'unthinkable thoughts'—about the cold war and East-West relations, about the underdeveloped countries and particularly those in Latin America, about the changing nature of the Chinese communist threat in Asia and about the festering war in Vietnam."

In the two years which have passed since Senator Fulbright's call for new thoughts, the war in Vietnam has grown both in size and in intensity; and an oversimplified, all-dominating anti-communism has led the United States to intervene in the Dominican Republic and to support openly reactionary military circles there—a step which certainly did not improve the situation in the Dominican Republic or the image and the influence of the United States in Latin America.[3]

One should beware of drawing apparently "self-evident" conclusions from past experiences. A comparison with "Munich" is of little relevance today. In 1938 the West—the United States and Britain—was disunited, almost completely disarmed, and in the midst of the worst possible economic depression. Today the opposite is true. At no time in history has the West been so prosperous and so well armed as in 1965. In the 1930s, after a lost war, the Germans felt deeply, though wrongly, that they were humiliated and degraded, a "people without space," in need of "living space" and of international prestige based on power. In the 1960s, the Russians, after a war that was imposed upon them and yet which they won against enormous initial odds, feel that they are stronger than ever before in their history, that their prestige has grown, and that they cannot (and do not) complain of being hemmed in. Hitler was an impatient, emotional "romantic" ready to risk a Götterdämmerung. Khrushchev and his successors are shrewd peasants and/or competent administrators, who are unwilling to risk Russia's great and unexpected gains. This is true today of Russian society in general. The Russians are grateful for their visibly rising living standards and insist upon their continuation and growth. Although from the period of Ivan III and Ivan IV onward the Russians expanded as did the United States from 1790 to today—much more than the Germans did—their folk-myth did not glorify military uniforms, war, and the warrior hero as German folk-myth did, at least for the last hundred years. China, still very backward, has for over a century suffered the humiliations imposed by Europe and Japan on the ancient civilization of the leading Asian power. Under its present government, in spite of the primitiveness of Mao's "philosophy," China is regaining, by sustained national effort and by the absence of the former glaring corruption, a new prestige and self-confidence. But whereas Germany was throughout the twentieth century a leading economic and scientific power, perhaps the strongest in the whole of Europe, China will need a long time to reach anything approaching Germany's strength. Whereas for Germany in 1938 the road to eastern conquests was wide open, thanks to the disintegration of the Habsburg empire and the jealousies of the successor states, China is encircled by the overwhelming power of United States' air and naval outposts. Two or three decades of internal development may bring the attitude of Chinese communism closer to that of the Soviet Union today. A more sensible relationship on the part of the West may help to heal some of the deep wounds inflicted in the last century on China and render it more willing to enter into the community of nations.

This community will not be one of ideology but one of diversity, not of friendship but of coexistence. President Kennedy stressed this future in his commencement address at the American University in Washington on June 10, 1963. The full text of his address was published the next day in the *New York Times* and in *Izvestia,* the official organ of the Soviet government. In his speech Mr. Kennedy rejected the concept of a *pax Americana* or a *pax Sovietica.* He demanded the recognition of the possibility of and necessity for living together in a pluralistic world community where nations will pursue their own and often conflicting interests. "Let us not be blind to our differences," he said, "but let us also direct attention to our common interests and the means by which these differences can be resolved. And if we cannot end now our differences, at least we can help make the world safe for diversity." Six weeks later the treaty for a partial nuclear test ban was signed in Moscow. The following day President Kennedy declared to the American people: "Yesterday, a shaft of light cut into the darkness. . . . For the first time an agreement has been reached on bringing the forces of nuclear destruction under international control. . . . It offers to all the world a welcome sign of hope. It is not a victory for one side—it is a victory for mankind. It ended the tests which befouled the air of all men and all nations." Some people in the West doubted that the Soviets would honor the pact; similar doubts about the West were probably expressed in communist circles. At the beginning of 1966 it can be said that to date the treaty has been adhered to by both sides. When the Chinese detonated their first atomic weapon, they made a solemn promise never to use nuclear weapons first. Whether this promise will be kept under all circumstances no one knows, but no other power has made a similar promise.

The rapid change in traditional attitudes in the last few years has been best manifested in the Christian churches. The Evangelical Church in Germany (Evangelische Kirche in Deutschland) in a memorandum about the relationship of the German people to its eastern neighbors, published at the end of 1965, started "to cut loose from established myths and think some unthinkable thoughts." This is remarkable in view of the former close connection between German Protestantism and the Prussian-German Reich. Even greater was the revolution started by Pope John XXIII, when he ascended the papal throne in 1958. One has only to compare his encyclical *Pacem in terris* and the second Vatican Council with the *Syllabus errorum* and the first Vatican Council of Pope Pius IX one century ago. The *Syllabus* was the strongest declaration of war on modern civilization and democratic liberty, an unbroken string of condemnations. The first Vatican Council raised the wall which separated the Church from those who were not Roman Catholics even higher. In an entirely different spirit Pope John's encyclical stressed in an unprecedented way human liberty, individual rights, equality of races, and the importance of the United Nations. The second Vatican Council built bridges which in full awareness of fundamental differences would help to open a dialogue with non-Catholics, non-Christians and non-believers, and a cooperation with them in concrete fields of common human interest. The various declarations avoided the former polemical approach and the insistence on Roman Catholic prestige. On December 4, 1965, Pope Paul VI, John's successor, joined in an interfaith prayer with Orthodox and Protestants in St. Paul's Outside the Walls. The Vatican Council accepted the declaration on religious liberty on December 7 by 2,308 votes to 70. Though the Church, naturally enough, deplores atheism, no condemnation of communism was expressed and an amendment pressing for such a condemnation was rejected by a great majority.[4]

Pope Paul VI was the first Pope to visit non-Christian lands and to try to establish contact with their people. In his pilgrimage to the Holy Land he was welcomed both in a Mohammedan kingdom and in a Jewish republic. In Jerusalem he met and embraced the Orthodox patriarch. His second voyage led him to Hindu India. Visits to communist Poland and to Moscow were being discussed at the beginning of 1966. The Pope's appearance before the United Nations on October 5, 1965 was a unique event. In his appeal for peace, the pope threw the moral prestige of the papacy and the Church behind the United Nations during a moment of internal weakness, when several powers, reasserting their national sovereignty, had insisted on solving international problems by one-sided intervention and superior armed forces. Since then the pope has attempted to bring about a cessation of the war in Vietnam. His financial contribution for the victims of that cruel war was distributed equally among the sufferers in North and South Vietnam.

In his address before the United Nations the Pope praised the universality which distinguishes the present world organization from its forerunner, the League of Nations. The latter remained throughout its existence an instrument of French and British policy and was largely confined to "white" nations. It began its activities in 1920 and passed away after a long agony twenty years later. The United Nations, which dates from 1945, entered its twenty-first year in 1966 and carries on, though at present with a diminished vitality. Yet there is a widespread agreement that the United Nations has become indispensable. In stressing its universality, the Pope congratulated it on "having had the wisdom to open this Assembly to the young peoples, to the states which have recently attained independence and national freedom." He called upon the Assembly "to bring back among you any who have left, and seek a means of bringing into your pact of brotherhood, in honor and loyalty, those who do not yet share in it." His demand to bring back could refer only to Indonesia, the only country which had resigned from the United Nations in the first twenty years of its existence. In a similar span of years many countries abandoned the League, often with an open challenge to the principle of international cooperation and peace. When the Pope urged that states still outside the United Nations should be brought into it, he was probably thinking of the Chinese People's Republic and of the two Germanies, Koreas, and Vietnams. The Pope warned against relying upon "offensive weapons, those terrible weapons that modern science has given you," and demanded instead "unanimous trust" in the United Nations and "increasing its authority." [5]

This was no new attitude on behalf of the Pope. More than a a year before, on July 12, 1964, the Pope assured the secretary general of the United Nations, a Buddhist Burmese—a fact which by itself speaks of the unprecedented newness of this world organization and its striving for universality—that the Holy See "considers the United Nations as the steadily developing and improving form of the balanced and unified life of all humanity in its historical and earthly order. The ideologies of those who belong to the United Nations are certainly multiple and diverse, and the Catholic Church regards them with due attention. But the convergence of so many peoples, so many races, so many states in a single organization, intended to avert the evils of war and to favor the good things of peace, is a fact which the Holy See considers as corresponding to its concept of humanity."

The United Nations has grown with the growing unity and complexity of mankind which has developed since 1945. It is the recognized meeting ground for all peoples, civilizations, creeds and ideologies, which in full awareness of their many conflicting interests nevertheless follow the Western parliamentary tradition of discussing them and of trying to find compromise solutions. They enter more and more into an open discourse, in which the small nations can voice their point of view as do the great powers. A world of coexistence safe for diversity may be there in the making. It will take time, patience and self-restraint on all sides before this goal will be in sight. The premise for it—the intensification of destructiveness of weapons and the abolition of distance—has come into existence for the first time in the post-World War II world. This situation demands a new way of political thinking. More than a century ago, Alexis de Tocqueville warned against utopian hopes and cultural despair and faintheartedness: "Let us, then, look forward to the future with that salutary fear which makes men keep watch and ward for freedom, not with that faint and idle terror which depresses and enervates the heart."

NOTES

[1] The poem by John Greenleaf Whittier is called "The Peace Convention at Brussels." See his *Works* (Boston: Houghton Mifflin), seven vols., Vol. III, pp. 318-321.

[2] Victor Hugo's speech at the peace congress of 1849: *Actes et paroles, avant l'Exil, 1841-1851* (Paris: Michel Lévy, 1875), pp. 379-389.

[3] The quotations from Marie Comtesse d'Agoult (1805-1876) are in Daniel Stern, *Histoire de la Révolution de 1848* (Paris: Calmann-Lévy, 1879), three vols., Vol. I, pp. 280, 288.

[4] The quotation from Marx is from his "Zur Kritik der Hegelschen Rechtsphilosophie," Marx-Engels *Gesamtausgabe*, ed. Marx-Engels-Lenin Institute in Moscow (Frankfurt am Main, 1927), Vol. I, Pt. I, pp. 607 f.

[5] Victor Hugo's speech in the Chamber, July 9th, 1849: *Actes et paroles, op. cit.*, pp. 199-212 (under the title "La Misère").

[6] On the German Revolution of 1848, see: Veit Valentin, *Geschichte der deutschen Revolution von 1848-49* (Berlin: Ullstein, 1931), Vol. II, p. 125; Wilhelm Jordan (1819-1904), *ibid.*, pp. 126 f.; Friedrich Christoph Dahlmann (1785-1860), Veit Valentin, *Die erste deutsche Nationalversammlung* (Munich: Oldenbourg, 1919), p. 41.

[7] See J. S. Mill, "Vindications of the French Revolution of February 1848," *Westminster Review*, April, 1849, reprinted in *Dissertations and Discussions, Political, Philosophical and Historical* (London: John W. Parker and Son, 1859), Vol. II, p. 382.

[8] From the poem "Piemonte" (1892):

> Italia, Italia!—E il popolo de' morti
> surse cantando a chiedere la guerra;
> e un re a la morte nel pallor del viso
> sacro e nel cuore
> trasse la spada. Oh anno de' portenti,
> oh primavera de la patria, oh giorni,

ultimi giorni del fiorente maggio,
Oh trionfante
suon de la prima italica vittoria
che mi percosse il cor fanciullo!

Poesie di Giosuè Carducci, 6th ed. (Bologna: Nicola Zanichelli, 1907) pp. 953 f.

⁹ See František Palacký, *Radhost* (Collected Minor Writings) (Prague: Tempsky, 1873), Vol. III, p. 13. See on Palacký (1798-1876), *Not by Arms Alone,* pp. 64-83. On the Slav World in 1848, see H. Desprez, "La Russie et la crise européenne," *Revue des deux mondes,* March 15, 1850. Palacký's attitude changed after 1867, when he despaired of a federal solution for Austria. See Hans Kohn, *Pan-Slavism, Its History and Ideology* (University of Notre Dame Press, 1953); Milan Prelog, *Pouť Slovanů do Moskvy roku 1867* (The Pilgrimage of the Slavs to Moscow in the Year 1867), transl. into Czech by Milada Paulová (Prague: Travaux de l'Institut Slave de Praha, 1931); Julian Klaczko, "Le Congrès de Moscou et la propagande panslaviste," *Revue des deux mondes,* September 1, 1867, pp. 132-181.

CHAPTER II

¹ On Herder and the Slavs, see *Sämmtliche Werke,* ed. B. Suphan (Berlin: Weidmann, 1877-1913), 33 vols., Vol. XIV, pp. 269, 280, 474. See *The Idea of Nationalism,* p. 437 f.

² On Macaulay's Memorandum, see G. Otto Trevelyan, *The Life and Letters of Lord Macaulay* (New York: Harper, 1876), Vol. I, pp. 353 ff. See also Hans Kohn, *History of Nationalism in the East* (London: Routledge, 1929), p. 93 f. and Richmond Croom Beatty, *Lord Macaulay, Victorian Liberal* (Norman: University of Oklahoma, 1938).

³ On Fichte, see Hans Kohn, "The Paradox of Fichte's Nationalism," *Journal of the History of Ideas,* July, 1949.

⁴ On romantic nationalism in India, see Bal Gandaghar Tilak, *His Writings and Speeches,* with an appreciation by Babu Aurobindo Ghose, 2nd ed. (Madras: Ganesh and Co., 1919); D. V. Athalye, *The Life of Lokamanya Tilak,* forword by C. Das (Poona City: Swadeshi Publishing Co., 1922). The words quoted in the text were spoken by Bhawani, one of the names of the goddess Kali, the goddess of destruction and of vital energy, to the Indians, her sons, who

dedicated their lives to her service. In the Bengali revolutionary publication, *Bhawani Mandir*, it was said: "India cannot be destroyed, her race can never die out, for the most brilliant destiny, the most vital to the future of mankind, is reserved for India amongst all the peoples. India must give birth to the future religion of the whole world, the eternal religion, that shall harmonize all religions and sciences and philosophies, and shall unite all in the bond of our common humanity."

[5] On the reforms in Turkey, see *Revolutions and Dictatorships*, pp. 247-277.

CHAPTER III

[1] Goethe, in a poem in 1827, praised the fact that the people of the United States were not looking backward to their various pasts, but were addicted to the present.

> Amerika, du hast es besser
> Als unser Kontinent, das alte,
> Hast keine verfallene Schlösser
> Und keine Basalte.
> Dich stört nicht im Innern,
> Zu lebendiger Zeit,
> Unnützes Erinnern
> Und vergeblicher Streit.
> Benutzt die Gegenwart mit Glück!
> Und wenn nun eure Kinder dichten,
> Bewahre sie ein gut Geschick
> Vor Ritter-, Räuber- und Gespenstergeschichten.

(America, thou art more fortunate than our old continent, thou hast no ruined castles, and no basalts. No useless memories, no vain feuds of the past disturb thee from living in the present. Make happy use of this present. And should thy children start to write poetry, may a kind Providence preserve them from stories of the romantic past.) See Hans Kohn, *American Nationalism, An Interpretative Essay* (New York: Macmillan, 1957).

[2] Carl Schmitt, *Der Begriff des Politischen*, 3rd ed. (Hamburg: Hanseatische Verlagsanstalt, 1933). Schmitt wrote in June, 1937: "War is the essence of everything. The form of total war determines the form and nature of the total state." *Völkerbund und Völkerrecht*, IV, pp. 139 ff. See also Oswald Spengler, *Politische Schriften* (Munich: C. H. Beck, 1933), p. 55: "War is always the highest form

of human existence, and states exist for the sake of war." See "The Totalitarian Philosophy of War," *Not by Arms Alone*, pp. 3-30.

³ On Napoleon, see *Revolutions and Dictatorships*, pp. 38-67.

⁴ On Frederick II, see *The Idea of Nationalism*, pp. 356-363. Of the Prussian state system Lord Acton wrote: "Government so understood is the intellectual guide of the nation, the promoter of wealth, the teacher of knowledge, the guardian of morality, the mainspring of the ascending movement of man. That is the tremendous power supported by millions of bayonets, which . . . was developed . . . chiefly at Berlin; and it is the greatest danger that remains to be encountered by the Anglo-Saxon race." *Lectures on Modern History* (London: Macmillan, 1906), p. 289. On the difference between Western and German political thought, see Ernst Troeltsch, "The Ideas of Natural Law and Humanity in World Politics," in Appendix I to Otto Gierke's *Natural Law and the Theory of Society, 1500-1800*, transl. by Ernest Barker (Cambridge: University Press, 1934), I, pp. 201-222, and Ernest Barker in the Introduction, pp. xlvi-lxxxvii.

⁵ For the judgment by the English historian, see E. L. Woodward, *The Age of Reform, 1815-1817* (Oxford: Clarendon Press, 1938), p. 608.

⁶ For Croce, see *History of Italy, 1871-1915* (Oxford: Clarendon Press, 1929), p. 240.

CHAPTER IV

¹ The phrase "Entzauberung der Welt" was first used by Max Weber, *Gesammelte Aufsätze zur Religionssoziologie* (Tübingen: Mohr, 1920), Vol. I, p. 263.

² The definition of Europe: Paul Hazard, *La Crise de la conscience européenne, 1680-1715* (Paris: Boivin, 1935), Vol. II, p. 287.

³ The pamphlet of Savigny, "Vom Beruf unserer Zeit für Gesetzgebung und Rechtswissenschaft," was translated into English by Abraham Hayward and printed in London by Littlewood and Co. in 1831.

⁴ On Wagner and Nietzsche, see Kurt Hildebrandt, *Wagner und Nietzsche: Ihr Kampf gegen das neunzehnte Jahrhundert* (Breslau: Hirt, 1924). On Wagner, see: Peter Viereck, *Metapolitics:* From the Romantics to Hitler (New York: Knopf, 1941), pp. 90-142; Thomas Mann, *Betrachtungen eines Unpolitischen* (Berlin: S. Fischer, 1920),

pp. 86-91; and Jacques Barzun, *Darwin, Marx, Wagner* (Boston: Little, Brown, 1941). On Nietzsche, see "Symposium on Nietzsche's Centenary," *Journal of the History of Ideas*, June, 1944. The quotations from Nietzsche are from "The Will to Power," 1005 and 462. See also Nietzsche's predictions about the twentieth century: "The time for small-scale politics has passed: the approaching century will bring us a struggle for the control of the globe, the necessity of high politics" (*Beyond Good and Evil*, 208). "There approaches inescapably, hesitatingly and yet terribly like fate, the great task and question: How should the globe as a whole be administered? And to which end should man as a whole, mankind as a whole—no longer one people or one race—be educated and bred?" (*The Will to Power*, 957).

[5] Hegel: *Phenomenology of Mind*, transl. by J. B. Baillie, 2nd ed. (New York: Macmillan, 1931), Vol. I, pp. 341 f.; *Philosophy of Right*, pp. 258, 336, 340, 347; transl. by S. W. Dyde (London: G. Bell & Sons, 1896), pp. 244 ff., 339, 341, 343 f. See also, on national and class ideologies, Hans Barth, *Wahrheit und Ideologie* (Zurich: Manesse Verlag, 1945); Wilhelm Röpke, *Die Gesellschaftskrisis der Gegenwart*, 4th ed. (Zurich: Eugen Rentsch, 1942); Sidney Hook, *Reason, Social Myths, and Democracy* (New York: John Day, 1940).

[6] Georges Sorel, *Réflexions sur la violence*, 4th ed. (Paris: Marcel Rivière, 1919), 3rd Appendix, "Pour Lénine," pp. 437-454.

CHAPTER V

[1] Paul Valéry, "La Crise de l'esprit" (1919) and "L'Européen" (1922) in *Œuvres de Valéry Variété*, Vol. I (Paris: Editions de la N.R.F., 1934), pp. 13-50, transl. by Malcolm Cowley, *Variety* (New York: Harcourt, Brace, 1927), pp. 1-54.

[2] On the Habsburg Empire, see *Not by Arms Alone*, pp. 43-64.

CHAPTER VI

[1] The most characteristic and revealing of Spengler's writings is "Preussentum und Sozialismus," first published in the fall of 1919, reprinted in *Politische Schriften*, pp. 1-105. "A real state existed in Prussia. Here, in the strict sense of the word, private individuals did

not exist. Everybody who lived within the system, which worked with the precision of a good machine, was in some way part of the machine." (*Ibid.*, p. 63). On Hegel: "That which was instinctively felt and naïvely expressed in Machiavelli, now became dressed and sanctified with philosophical reasoning, so that henceforth conscience was quieted, and force and injustice were no longer felt as such. . . . The state has become an end in itself. . . . All individual ethic is rejected." Franz Schnabel, *Deutsche Geschichte im neunzehnten Jahrhundert* (Freiburg: Herder, 1934), Vol. III, p. 17.

[2] The ideal type of the man in totalitarian society is a permanently mobilized proletarian who is worker and soldier at the same time. What Marx had foreseen in his *Communist Manifesto*, when he wrote that modern industry "will organize masses of workers, crowded together in the factory, in military fashion," has been achieved in the militarized collectivism and superindustrialism which has regimented man into disciplined teamwork and mental standardization. This modern machine man, a member of a closely knit group pervaded by one spirit and united for higher efficiency, has been depicted in Ernst Jünger, *Der Arbeiter: Herrschaft und Gestalt*, 2nd ed. (Hamburg: Hanseatische Verlagsanstalt, 1932). See Chap. XI below.

[3] Ferdinand Kürnberger, *Der Amerikamüde*, 2nd ed. (Leipzig: Reclam, 1889), pp. 211 f.

CHAPTER VII

See Hans Kohn, *The Mind of Modern Russia* (Rutgers University Press, 1955), and the chapter on Dostoevsky in *Prophets and Peoples*, pp. 131-160, 198-206.

CHAPTER VIII

[1] Of the Athenians, Diodorus of Sicily wrote: "Did they not invent laws which have changed the common life from a beastly and uncivilized existence into a gentle and civilized community? Have they not been the first to establish the right of asylum for exiles and given in favor of the supplicants laws which were respected by all men?" (*Bibliotheca Historica*, XIII, p. 26). On the other hand, Plutarch said of the Lacedaemonians in his *Lives* (Modern Library Edition,

p. 737): "They, who make it their first principle of action to serve their country's interest, know not anything to be just or unjust by any measure but that." And Thucydides (Bk. V, p. 105): "We must indeed acknowledge that with respect to themselves and the institutions of their own country, the Lacedaemonians practiced virtue in a very high degree, but with respect to their conduct towards the rest of mankind, . . . one may declare that of all men with whom we are acquainted they, most conspicuously, consider what is agreeable to be honorable, and what is expedient, just" (Loeb Classical Library, transl. by Charles Forster Smith, III, p. 169).

[2] Plutarch *Moralia,* transl. by Frank Cole Babbitt (Loeb Classical Library, IV, p. 397 ff. ["De Fortuna Alexandri," I, 6, 329 b, c]).

[3] Claudius Rutilius Namatianus:

> Fecisti patriam diversis gentibus unam;
> Profuit injustis te dominante capi.
> Dumque offers victis proprii consortia juris,
> Urbem fecisti quod prius orbis erat.

[4] Arnold Oskar Meyer, *Deutsche und Engländer* (Munich: Beck, 1935), p. 5.

[5] Orosius, *Historiae Livri VII Adversus Paganos,* VII, 43, transl. by I. W. Raymond, Columbia University Records of Civilization, 26 (New York: Columbia University Press, 1936), p. 396.

[6] On Charlemagne, see *The Idea of Nationalism,* pp. 597 f.

[7] *Monumenta Germaniae Historica: Poetae Latini Aevi Carolini,* II (Berlin: 1884), pp. 559-564.

[8] On Charles V, see *The Idea of Nationalism,* pp. 146-155.

[9] On the character of English nationalism, see *The Idea of Nationalism,* pp. 165-183.

[10] Heinrich von Treitschke, *Politics,* transl. by Blanche Dugdale (London: Constable, 1916), Vol. II, p. 300.

[11] Richard Scholz in *Neue Jahrbücher für deutsche Wissenschaft,* XIII (1937), p. 39.

[12] Paul Joachimsen, "Zur Psychologie des deutschen Staatsgedankens," *Die Dioskuren,* Vol. I (Munich: Meyer & Jessen, 1922), p. 166 f.

[13] Thorstein Veblen: *An Inquiry into the Nature of Peace and the Terms of Its Perpetuation* (New York: Macmillan, 1917), p. 201. See also pp. 83-87, 227-232.

[14] Napoleon: "I wanted to unite all peoples into one strong national

body. When this was done people could devote themselves to the realization of their ideal, at present only a dream, of a higher civilization. Then there would be no more vicissitudes to fear, for there would be only one set of laws, one kind of opinion, one view, one interest, the interest of mankind." Quoted in F. M. Kircheisen, *Napoleon's Autobiography*, transl. by Frederick Collins (New York: Duffield, 1931), p. 230.

<h3 style="text-align:center">CHAPTER IX</h3>

On racialism, see Frederick Hertz, *Nationality in History and Politics* (New York: Oxford University Press, 1944), pp. 52-77; Louis L. Snyder, *Race: A History of Modern Ethnic Theories* (New York: Longmans, Green, 1939); Hans Kohn, "Race Conflict," *Encyclopaedia of the Social Sciences*, XIII, pp. 36-41.

<h3 style="text-align:center">CHAPTER X</h3>

On fascism, see Cecil J. S. Sprigge, *The Development of Modern Italy* (London: Duckworth, 1943); Giuseppe Prezzolini, *Fascism*, transl. by Kathleen Macmillan (London: Methuen, 1926); Gaudens Megaro, *Mussolini in the Making* (Boston: Houghton Mifflin, 1938); G. A. Borgese, *Goliath: The March of Fascism* (New York: Viking, 1937); Herman Finer, *Mussolini's Italy* (New York: Holt, 1935); D. A. Binchy, *Church and State in Fascist Italy* (London: Oxford University Press, 1941); Herbert W. Schneider, *Making the Fascist State* (New York: Oxford University Press, 1928); William Yandell Elliott, *The Pragmatic Revolt in Politics* (New York: Macmillan, 1928).

<h3 style="text-align:center">CHAPTER XI</h3>

[1] On anti-Semitism in Germany, see Waldemar Gurian, "Anti-Semitism in Modern Germany," *Essays on Anti-Semitism*, 2nd ed. (New York: Conference on Jewish Relations, 1946), pp. 218-265.

[2] On some of the forerunners and theoreticians of national socialism, see Edmond Vermeil, *Doctrinaires de la Révolution Allemande (1917-1938)* (Paris: Fernand Sorlot, 1938).

[3] Hitler, *Mein Kampf* (Munich: Eher, 1933), Vol. I, pp. 197-203, 252 f., 129; Vol. II, pp. 439, 421 f., 475 f., 501, 734, 782; Vol. I, pp. 269.

[4] On the mystical character of the race: "Today a new faith awakens: the myth of the blood, the faith that by defending his blood we defend also the divine nature of man. The faith, embodied in scientific clarity, that the Nordic blood represents that mystery which has replaced and conquered the ancient sacraments." Alfred Rosenberg, *Der Mythus des 20. Jahrhunderts,* 37th ed. (Munich: Hoheneichen Verlag, 1934), p. 114. See also pp. 119 and 529.

[5] On the church and national-socialism, see Karl Barth, *The Church and the Political Question of Today* (New York: Scribner, 1939).

[6] On Mussolini's militarism: "The whole nation must be militarized." "Happiness does not exist in life." "I consider the Italian nation in permanent state of war." "Life for me is struggle, risk, tenacity." "The credo of Fascism is heroism." Benito Mussolini, *Scritti e Discorsi* (Edizione Definitiva, Milan: Ulrico Hoepli), Vol. I, p. 283; Vol. II, 230; Vol. V, 238 f.; Vol. IX, 43. "War is to the man what maternity is to the woman. I do not believe in perpetual peace; not only do I not believe in it, but I find it depressing and a negation of all the fundamental virtues of man." *Ibid.,* Vol. IX, p. 98. The preamble to the statute of the Italian fascist party of Dec. 20, 1929, prides itself that "from its beginnings until now, the Party has always thought of itself as in a state of war. Fascism is above all a faith under the impulse of which the Italians work as soldiers, pledged to achieve victory in the struggle between the nation and its enemies."

CHAPTER XII

[1] On Karl Marx, see Isaiah Berlin, *Karl Marx,* 2nd ed. (New York: Oxford University Press, 1948). On Lenin, see David Shub, *Lenin* (New York: Doubleday, 1948).

[2] See also Hans Kohn, "Eastern Europe in 1948," *Current History,* February and April, 1949.

CHAPTER XIII

[1] Bk. II, Chap. 2. See also Bk. I, Chap. 10.
[2] Bk. I, Chap. 58.

CHAPTER XIV

¹ On Woodrow Wilson, see H. C. F. Bell, *Woodrow Wilson and the People* (New York: Doubleday, 1945); Paul Birdsall, *Versailles Twenty Years After* (New York: Reynal & Hitchcock, 1941); E. M. Hugh-Jones, *Woodrow Wilson and American Liberalism* (New York: Macmillan, 1948).

² On the Treaty of Versailles, see T. E. Jessop, *The Treaty of Versailles: Was it Just?* (London: Thomas Nelson, 1942).

³ On the period between the two wars, see R. B. McCallum, *Public Opinion and the Last Peace* (New York: Oxford University Press, 1944); Lindley Fraser, *Germany Between Two Wars* (New York: Oxford University Press, 1944); W. M. Jordan, *Great Britain, France and the German Problem, 1918-1939* (New York: Oxford University Press, 1943); Raoul de Roussy de Sales, *The Making of Tomorrow* (New York: Reynal & Hitchcock, 1942), and *The Making of Yesterday* (Reynal & Hitchcock, 1947).

⁴ On the issues of World War II, see Carl L. Becker, *How New Will the Better World Be?* (New York: Knopf, 1944); Robert Strausz-Hupé, *The Balance of Tomorrow* (New York: Putnam, 1945).

⁵ On the issues of the peace, see Norman Angell, *The Steep Places* (New York: Harper, 1947); Clarence Streit, *Union Now* (New Edition) (New York: Harper, 1949).

⁶ On Masaryk and the differences of East and West, see Masaryk, *The Spirit of Russia* (London: Allen & Unwin, 1919), Vol. II, p. 562; *The Making of a State: Memories and Observations, 1914-1918* (New York: 1927), pp. 180 f.; *Sur le Bolchévisme* (Geneva: Société anonyme des éditions Sonor, 1921). See also Emanuel Rádl, "Masaryk et la philosophie occidentale" in the *Festschrift* to Masaryk's 80th birthday (Bonn: Friedrich Cohen, 1930), pp. 1-5. See also, *Ibid.*, pp. 161 f, 164 f.

⁷ On Beneš and the war, see Eduard Beneš, *Paměti: Od Mníchova k nové valce a k novému vitězství* (Memoirs: From Munich to the New War and to the New Victory) (Prague: Orbis, 1947), especially p. 211.

⁸ At the signing of the Atlantic Pact in Washington on April 5, 1949, the following significant statements were made. President Truman: "It is a simple document, but if it had existed in 1914 and in 1939, supported by the nations who are represented here today, I

believe it would have prevented the acts of aggression which led to two world wars. . . . The nations represented here are bound together by ties of long standing. We are joined by a common heritage of democracy, individual liberty, and the rule of law. . . . We are determined to work together to provide better lives for our people without sacrificing our common ideas of justice and human worth."

Paul-Henri Spaak, Belgium: "The North Atlantic Pact is an act of faith in the destiny of Western civilization. . . . It places in the service of this civilization and of peace the most powerful means of defense that has ever been created."

Lester B. Pearson, Canada: "We are a North Atlantic community of twelve nations. . . . We are strong, above all, in our common tradition of liberty, in our common belief in the dignity of the individual, in our common heritage of social and political thought, and in our resolve to defend our freedoms together. Security and progress, however, like peace and war, are indivisible. So there must be nothing narrow or exclusive about our league; no slackening of our interest in the welfare and security of all friendly people."

Bjarni Benediktsson, Iceland: "We want to make it crystal-clear that we belong and want to belong to this free community of free nations which now is being formally founded. It is a fact that we are unlike each other in many respects, but there are many things which bind us solidly together. We all face the same danger. In this world of ours, where distances have vanished, peace indeed is indivisible. The same disruptive elements are everywhere at their sinister work. Everywhere they are accusing us, who are working for peace, of being warmongers. When we were discussing this Pact in the Parliament of Iceland, those elements tried with force to hinder that venerable institution in its work. Such violence has never before been tried against the one-thousand-year-old Parliament of Iceland. The misguided crowd which tried this, pretended they were shouting for peace. This contradictory behavior of throwing stones with your hands while you are clamoring for peace with your lips, is not in accordance with Icelandic traditions nor is it in conformity with Western culture. We all know where those habits originate, and this mentality certainly is the greatest menace in the world today."

Count Carlo Sforza, Italy: "It is not without reference to the spirit of this Pact, that two of its signatories, the French and the Italian, signed a week ago in Paris a treaty of economic cooperation between our two peoples. Not only would we fail the spirit of the Pact, we would also belittle its force if we considered it only as a protective umbrella. We must pray to God that this Pact will prove to be like the English Magna Carta: on one side intangibles, on the other side a continuous creation."

Halvard Lange, Norway: "As I am about to sign the Pact, I strongly feel that it is a logical sequence to a line which we have followed since the liberation of our country in May, 1945. The five long years of Nazi occupation had given our people a new and deeper conception of freedom, law, and democracy. . . . With great faith and hope the Norwegian government has taken an active part in the United Nations conference in San Francisco. . . . We believe today as firmly as ever in the fundamental soundness and necessity of the universal idea of the United Nations. We cannot close our eyes, however, to the fact, that for reasons which we all know, the United Nations today cannot give us or any other nation the security to which we had confidently looked forward. . . . The logical solution for Norway was to join the North Atlantic Pact. We have a longer coastline on the North Atlantic than any other country. Our experience through the centuries has been that the ocean did not separate. On the contrary, for us it has been the highway of commercial and cultural intercourse. . . . The overwhelming majority of the Norwegian people deeply believe that the signing of the Atlantic Pact is an event which may decisively influence the course of history and hasten the day when all nations can work together for peace and freedom."

Ernest Bevin, Great Britain: "We are in the process of enthroning and making paramount the use of reason as against force. . . . At last democracy is no longer a series of isolated units. It has become a cohesive organism, determined to fulfill its great purpose."

Thus, in the signing of the Atlantic Pact, the issue of force or reason, which loomed so large in 1936, has been clearly stated in 1949; the struggle against violent revolutions and dictatorships has been raised to a level where it will not be fought by arms alone, not even mainly by arms, but by intelligent insight into the need of world order, seen in the historical perspective of the growth of Western civilization.

CHAPTER XV

[1] See Hans Kohn, *American Nationalism. An Interpretative Essay* (New York: Macmillan, 1957), Chapter V.

[2] See Hans Kohn, *German History. Some New German Views*

(Boston: Beacon Press, 1954) and Ludwig Dehio, *Deutschland und die Weltpolitik im 20. Jahrhundert* (Munich: R. Oldenbourg, 1955).

CHAPTER XVI

See also M. N. Roy, "Asian Nationalism," *The Yale Review*, autumn 1952, and Hans Kohn, "Reflections on Colonialism," *The Review of Politics*, July 1956.

CHAPTER XVIII

[1] These words were used by President Charles de Gaulle about Latin America at the occasion of his visit to Mexico in March 1964. An even more striking example of the world-wide character of international politics than President de Gaulle's two visits to Latin America in 1964 was the journey of China's Premier Chou En-lai to Africa, which started with his arrival on December 14, 1963 in Cairo to discuss "Asian-African solidarity." In January 1966 a conference met in Cuba to establish foundations for Asian, African, and Latin American solidarity.

[2] Marx wrote in 1848, long before global intercourse had become a reality: "In place of the old local and national seclusion and self-sufficiency, we have intercourse in every direction, universal interdependence of nations. And as in material, so also in intellectual production. The intellectual creations of individual nations become common property. . . . The bourgeoisie, by . . . the immensely facilitated means of communication, draws all, even the most barbarian, nations into civilization. . . . It compels all nations . . . to introduce what it calls civilization into their midst. . . . In one word, it creates a world after its own image." On this global revolution, its roots and manifestations see Hans Kohn, *The Age of Nationalism: The First Era of Global History* (New York: Harper & Row, 1962).

[3] On the Dominican Republic see the important article by Theodor Draper in *Commentary*, December 1965.

[4] Pope John's revolution "was concerned with the two concentric circles beyond that of Catholics themselves—with Christians not in communion with Rome, and still more with those of other faiths and no faith at all, including atheists and communists. To the radi-

cally secular world, John brought tidings of good will: for the first time in papal history he expressed a clear preference for the democratic form of government; he embraced a new concpt of the duties of the state which many would call socialism; he gave his blessing to the United Nations as the embryo of a world authority; he welcomed the new nations of Asia and Africa laying down without qualification that there are no inferior peoples, no inferior races, only a duty incumbent upon those who have to assist those who have not; he condemned nuclear war as an illicit means even for attaining a just end; and to preserve the peace he preached the necessity of extending the hand of understanding to communist regimes. These, he argued, should be judged by their fruits and not by their surface professions; they might teach a false philosophy, but this should not prevent Christians from working with them toward some external good." H. Stuart Hughes, "Pope John's Revolution: Secular or Religious," *Commonweal*, December 10, 1965. See also E. E. Y. Hales, *Pope John and his Revolution* (New York: Doubleday, 1965).

[5] See on the United Nations, Hans Kohn, *Reflections on Modern History* (Princeton: D. Van Nostrand, 1963), pp. 327-345, and *The Age of Nationalism*, pp. 133-167.

INDEX

303

66, 68, 73, 78, 80, 89 ff., 119, 126,
127, 129, 143, 166, 177, 179, 182,
209, 213, 214, 260 ff., 280

Sacco, Nicola, 70
Saint Simon, Claude Henri de, 10
Samarin, Yury Fedorovich, 102,
106
Sand, George, 6
Savigny, Friedrich Carl von, 46
Savonarola, 245
Scharnhorst, Gerhard von, 38
Schiller, Friedrich, 9, 80, 274
Schlosser, Friedrich Christoph, 24
Schmitt, Carl, 35, 167, 170, 291
Schönerer, Georg von, 158
Schopenhauer, Arthur, 47, 48, 79
Schweitzer, Albert, 269
science, 10, 37, 53, 55, 58, 96, 158
Seneca, 58
Sforza, Count Carlo, 299
Shintoism, 141
Slavophile, 26, 27, 28, 52, 83, 99 ff.,
112, 114
Slavs, 15, 17, 21, 22, 38, 100, 105,
158, 179, 213
socialism, 4, 7, 9, 18, 64, 109, 110,
112, 147, 167, 225 f., 262
Socrates, 67, 84
Sombart, Werner, 257
Sorel, Georges, 56
South Africa, 143
Spaak, Paul-Henri, 299
Spain, 123, 154, 156, 262 f.
Sparta, 154, 167, 295
Spencer, Herbert, 37
Spengler, Oswald, 55, 76, 81, 85,
105, 144, 159, 166, 171, 193, 243,
246
Stalin, Joseph, 30, 52, 75, 176 ff.,
209, 212, 222, 223, x, 276
Staszic, Stanislaw, 104
state, concept of, 55, 175, 189
Stimson, Henry L., 204
stoicism, 58, 84, 119, 120, 186
Strauss, David Friedrich, 55
Sun Yat-sen, 227, 228
Sverdlov, Jakob, 225

Tacitus, 28
technology, 3, 10, 42, 96, 130
Tennyson, Alfred, 62
terror, 8, 75, 109, 175
theology of crisis, 42
Thibaut, Anton, 46
Thucydides, 295
Tilak, Bal Gangadhar, 27
Tito, Joseph, 222
Tocqueville, Alexis de, 1, 5, 288
Togliatti, Palmiro, 278
tolerance, 7, 31, 46, 56, 185, 189,
192, 219
Tolstoi, Leo, 27, 95, 106, 269
Tönnies, Ferdinand, 83
totalitarianism, 41, 56, 57, 59, 65, 66,
68, 71, 75, 79, 125, 128, 131, 148,
152, 153, 161, 162, 170, 190, 193,
194, 206, 223, 249
Toynbee, Arnold, 248, 265 ff.
trade, 59, 61, 124, 125, 191
Treitschke, Heinrich von, 125, 168
Troeltsch, Ernst, 292
Trotsky, Leon, 54, 174, 176
Truman, Harry, 300
Tunisia, 282
Turgenev, Ivan, 95, 106, 261
Turkey, 29, 62, 92, 104, 105, 110,
139, 227
Tyutchev, Fyodor Ivanovich, 78,
104, 106, 107

Ukrainians, 180, 181
unemployment, 71, 163
United Nations, 230, 234, 235, 236,
286, 287, 288, 303
United States of America, 5, 29, 32,
35, 39, 66, 67, 68, 86, 96, 114, 124,
125, 138, 182, 190, 197, 198, 199,
203, 207, 210, 215 ff., 225 ff., 246,
250, 274, viii, 276, 283, 291

Valéry, Paul, 63, 64
Vanzetti, Bartolomeo, 70
Vatican Council, 286
Veblen, Thorstein, 129, 202
Versailles, Peace Treaty of, 159, 200,
205, 211

Revised December, 1966

harper ✦ torchbooks

HUMANITIES AND SOCIAL SCIENCES

American Studies: General

THOMAS C. COCHRAN: The Inner Revolution. *Essays on the Social Sciences in History* TB/1140

EDWARD S. CORWIN: American Constitutional History. *Essays edited by Alpheus T. Mason and Gerald Garvey* △ TB/1136

CARL N. DEGLER, Ed.: Pivotal Interpretations of American History TB/1240, TB/1241

A. HUNTER DUPREE: Science in the Federal Government: *A History of Policies and Activities to 1940* TB/573

A. S. EISENSTADT, Ed.: The Craft of American History: *Recent Essays in American Historical Writing*
Vol. I TB/1255; Vol. II TB/1256

CHARLOTTE P. GILMAN: Women and Economics: *A Study of the Economic Relation between Men and Women as a Factor in Social Evolution.* ‡ *Ed. with an Introduction by Carl N. Degler* TB/3073

OSCAR HANDLIN, Ed.: This Was America: *As Recorded by European Travelers in the Eighteenth, Nineteenth and Twentieth Centuries. Illus.* TB/1119

MARCUS LEE HANSEN: The Atlantic Migration: 1607-1860. *Edited by Arthur M. Schlesinger* TB/1052

MARCUS LEE HANSEN: The Immigrant in American History. TB/1120

JOHN HIGHAM, Ed.: The Reconstruction of American History △ TB/1068

ROBERT H. JACKSON: The Supreme Court in the American System of Government TB/1106

JOHN F. KENNEDY: A Nation of Immigrants. △ *Illus.* TB/1118

LEONARD W. LEVY, Ed.: American Constitutional Law: *Historical Essays* TB/1285

RALPH BARTON PERRY: Puritanism and Democracy TB/1138

ARNOLD ROSE: The Negro in America TB/3048

MAURICE R. STEIN: The Eclipse of Community. *An Interpretation of American Studies* TB/1128

W. LLOYD WARNER and Associates: Democracy in Jonesville: *A Study in Quality and Inequality* ¶ TB/1129

W. LLOYD WARNER: Social Class in America: *The Evaluation of Status* TB/1013

American Studies: Colonial

BERNARD BAILYN, Ed.: Apologia of Robert Keayne: *Self-Portrait of a Puritan Merchant* TB/1201

BERNARD BAILYN: The New England Merchants in the Seventeenth Century TB/1149

JOSEPH CHARLES: The Origins of the American Party System TB/1049

LAWRENCE HENRY GIPSON: The Coming of the Revolution: 1763-1775. † *Illus.* TB/3007

LEONARD W. LEVY: Freedom of Speech and Press in Early American History: *Legacy of Suppression* TB/1109

PERRY MILLER: Errand Into the Wilderness TB/1139

PERRY MILLER & T. H. JOHNSON, Eds.: The Puritans: *A Sourcebook of Their Writings*
Vol. I TB/1093; Vol. II TB/1094

EDMUND S. MORGAN, Ed.: The Diary of Michael Wigglesworth, 1653-1657: *The Conscience of a Puritan* TB/1228

EDMUND S. MORGAN: The Puritan Family: *Religion and Domestic Relations in Seventeenth-Century New England* TB/1227

RICHARD B. MORRIS: Government and Labor in Early America TB/1244

KENNETH B. MURDOCK: Literature and Theology in Colonial New England TB/99

WALLACE NOTESTEIN: The English People on the Eve of Colonization: 1603-1630. † *Illus.* TB/3006

LOUIS B. WRIGHT: The Cultural Life of the American Colonies: 1607-1763. † *Illus.* TB/3005

American Studies: From the Revolution to 1860

JOHN R. ALDEN: The American Revolution: 1775-1783. † *Illus.* TB/3011

MAX BELOFF, Ed.: The Debate on the American Revolution, 1761-1783: *A Sourcebook* △ TB/1225

RAY A. BILLINGTON: The Far Western Frontier: 1830-1860. † *Illus.* TB/3012

W. R. BROCK: An American Crisis: *Congress and Reconstruction, 1865-87* ○ △ TB/1283

EDMUND BURKE: On the American Revolution: *Selected Speeches and Letters.* ‡ *Edited by Elliott Robert Barkan* TB/3068

WHITNEY R. CROSS: The Burned-Over District: *The Social and Intellectual History of Enthusiastic Religion in Western New York, 1800-1850* △ TB/1242

GEORGE DANGERFIELD: The Awakening of American Nationalism: 1815-1828. † *Illus.* TB/3061

CLEMENT EATON: The Freedom-of-Thought Struggle in the Old South. *Revised and Enlarged. Illus.* TB/1150

CLEMENT EATON: The Growth of Southern Civilization: 1790-1860. † *Illus.* TB/3040

LOUIS FILLER: The Crusade Against Slavery: 1830-1860. † *Illus.* TB/3029

DIXON RYAN FOX: The Decline of Aristocracy in the Politics of New York: 1801-1840. ‡ *Edited by Robert V. Remini* TB/3064

FELIX GILBERT: The Beginnings of American Foreign Policy: *To the Farewell Address* TB/1200

FRANCIS GRIERSON: The Valley of Shadows: *The Coming of the Civil War in Lincoln's Midwest: A Contemporary Account* TB/1246

---

† The New American Nation Series, edited by Henry Steele Commager and Richard B. Morris.

‡ American Persectives series, edited by Bernard Wishy and William E. Leuchtenburg.

* The Rise of Modern Europe series, edited by William L. Langer.

¶ Researches in the Social, Cultural, and Behavioral Sciences, edited by Benjamin Nelson.

§ The Library of Religion and Culture, edited by Benjamin Nelson.

Σ Harper Modern Science Series, edited by James R. Newman.

○ Not for sale in Canada.

△ Not for sale in the U. K.

American Studies: The Civil War to 1900

American Studies: 1900 to the Present

Anthropology

Art and Art History

Intellectual History & History of Ideas

PHILIP P. WIENER: Evolution and the Founders of Pragmatism. △ *Foreword by John Dewey* TB/1212

BASIL WILLEY: Nineteenth Century Studies: *Coleridge to Matthew Arnold* o △ TB/1261

BASIL WILLEY: More Nineteenth Century Studies: *A Group of Honest Doubters* o △ TB/1262

Literature, Poetry, The Novel & Criticism

JAMES BAIRD: Ishmael: *The Art of Melville in the Contexts of International Primitivism* TB/1023

JACQUES BARZUN: The House of Intellect △ TB/1051

W. J. BATE: From Classic to Romantic: *Premises of Taste in Eighteenth Century England* TB/1036

RACHEL BESPALOFF: On the Iliad TB/2006

R. P. BLACKMUR et al.: Lectures in Criticism. *Introduction by Huntington Cairns* TB/2003

JAMES BOSWELL: The Life of Dr. Johnson & The Journal of a Tour to the Hebrides with Samuel Johnson LL.D.: *Selections.* o △ *Edited by F. V. Morley. Illus. by Ernest Shepard* TB/1254

ABRAHAM CAHAN: The Rise of David Levinsky: *a documentary novel of social mobility in early twentieth century America. Intro. by John Higham* TB/1028

ERNST R. CURTIUS: European Literature and the Latin Middle Ages △ TB/2015

GEORGE ELIOT: Daniel Deronda: *a novel. Introduction by F. R. Leavis* TB/1039

ADOLF ERMAN, Ed.: The Ancient Egyptians: *A Sourcebook of Their Writings. New Material and Introduction by William Kelly Simpson* TB/1233

ÉTIENNE GILSON: Dante and Philosophy TB/1089

ALFRED HARBAGE: As They Liked It: *A Study of Shakespeare's Moral Artistry* TB/1035

STANLEY R. HOPPER, Ed: Spiritual Problems in Contemporary Literature § TB/21

A. R. HUMPHREYS: The Augustan World: *Society, Thought and Letters in 18th Century England* o △ TB/1105

ALDOUS HUXLEY: Antic Hay & The Giaconda Smile. o △ *Introduction by Martin Green* TB/3503

ALDOUS HUXLEY: Brave New World & Brave New World Revisited. o △ *Introduction by Martin Green* TB/3501

HENRY JAMES: The Tragic Muse: *a novel. Introduction by Leon Edel* TB/1017

ARNOLD KETTLE: An Introduction to the English Novel. △
Volume I: *Defoe to George Eliot* TB/1011
Volume II: *Henry James to the Present* TB/1012

RICHMOND LATTIMORE: The Poetry of Greek Tragedy △ TB/1257

J. B. LEISHMAN: The Monarch of Wit: *An Analytical and Comparative Study of the Poetry of John Donne* o △ TB/1258

J. B. LEISHMAN: Themes and Variations in Shakespeare's Sonnets o △ TB/1259

ROGER SHERMAN LOOMIS: The Development of Arthurian Romance △ TB/1167

JOHN STUART MILL: On Bentham and Coleridge. △ *Introduction by F. R. Leavis* TB/1070

KENNETH B. MURDOCK: Literature and Theology in Colonial New England TB/99

SAMUEL PEPYS: The Diary of Samuel Pepys. o *Edited by O. F. Morshead. Illus. by Ernest Shepard* TB/1007

ST.-JOHN PERSE: Seamarks TB/2002

V. DE S. PINTO: Crisis in English Poetry, 1880-1940 o TB/1260

GEORGE SANTAYANA: Interpretations of Poetry and Religion § TB/9

C. K. STEAD: The New Poetic: Yeats to Eliot △ TB/1263

HEINRICH STRAUMANN: American Literature in the Twentieth Century. △ *Third Edition, Revised* TB/1168

PAGET TOYNBEE: Dante Alighieri: *His Life and Works. Edited with Intro. by Charles S. Singleton* TB/1206

DOROTHY VAN GHENT: The English Novel: *Form and Function* TB/1050

E. B. WHITE: One Man's Meat. *Introduction by Walter Blair* TB/3505

BASIL WILLEY: Nineteenth Century Studies: *Coleridge to Matthew Arnold* △ TB/1261

BASIL WILLEY: More Nineteenth Century Studies: *A Group of Honest Doubters* o △ TB/1262

RAYMOND WILLIAMS: Culture and Society, 1780-1950 o △ TB/1252

RAYMOND WILLIAMS: The Long Revolution. o △ *Revised Edition* TB/1253

MORTON DAUWEN ZABEL, Editor: Literary Opinion in America Vol. I TB/3013; Vol. II TB/3014

Myth, Symbol & Folklore

JOSEPH CAMPBELL, Editor: Pagan and Christian Mysteries *Illus.* TB/2013

MIRCEA ELIADE: Cosmos and History: *The Myth of the Eternal Return* § TB/2050

MIRCEA ELIADE: Rites and Symbols of Initiation: *The Mysteries of Birth and Rebirth* § △ TB/1236

THEODOR H. GASTER: Thespis: *Ritual, Myth and Drama in the Ancient Near East* △ TB/1281

C. G. JUNG & C. KERÉNYI: Essays on a Science of Mythology: *The Myths of the Divine Child and the Divine Maiden* TB/2014

DORA & ERWIN PANOFSKY: Pandora's Box: *The Changing Aspects of a Mythical Symbol.* △ *Revised edition. Illus.* TB/2021

ERWIN PANOFSKY: Studies in Iconology: *Humanistic Themes in the Art of the Renaissance.* △ *180 illustrations* TB/1077

JEAN SEZNEC: The Survival of the Pagan Gods: *The Mythological Tradition and its Place in Renaissance Humanism and Art.* △ *108 illustrations* TB/2004

HELLMUT WILHELM: Change: *Eight Lectures on the I Ching* △ TB/2019

HEINRICH ZIMMER: Myths and Symbols in Indian Art and Civilization. △ *70 illustrations* TB/2005

Philosophy

G. E. M. ANSCOMBE: An Introduction to Wittgenstein's Tractatus. o △ *Second Edition, Revised* TB/1210

HENRI BERGSON: Time and Free Will: *An Essay on the Immediate Data of Consciousness* o △ TB/1021

H. J. BLACKHAM: Six Existentialist Thinkers: *Kierkegaard, Nietzsche, Jaspers, Marcel, Heidegger, Sartre* o △ TB/1002

CRANE BRINTON: Nietzsche. *New Preface, Bibliography and Epilogue by the Author* TB/1197

MARTIN BUBER: The Knowledge of Man. △ *Ed. with an Intro. by Maurice Friedman. Trans. by Maurice Friedman and Ronald Gregor Smith* TB/135

ERNST CASSIRER: The Individual and the Cosmos in Renaissance Philosophy. △ *Translated with an Introduction by Mario Domandi* TB/1097

ERNST CASSIRER: Rousseau, Kant and Goethe. *Introduction by Peter Gay* TB/1092

FREDERICK COPLESTON: Medieval Philosophy o △ TB/376

F. M. CORNFORD: Principium Sapientiae: *A Study of the Origins of Greek Philosophical Thought. Edited by W. K. C. Guthrie* TB/1213

F. M. CORNFORD: From Religion to Philosophy: *A Study in the Origins of Western Speculation* § TB/20

WILFRID DESAN: The Tragic Finale: *An Essay on the Philosophy of Jean-Paul Sartre* TB/1030

A. P. D'ENTRÈVES: Natural Law: *An Historical Survey* △ TB/1223

MARVIN FARBER: The Aims of Phenomenology: *The Motives, Methods, and Impact of Husserl's Thought* TB/1291

HERBERT FINGARETTE: The Self in Transformation: *Psychoanalysis, Philosophy and the Life of the Spirit* ¶ TB/1177

PAUL FRIEDLÄNDER: Plato: *An Introduction* △ TB/2017

ÉTIENNE GILSON: Dante and Philosophy TB/1089

WILLIAM CHASE GREENE: Moira: *Fate, Good, and Evil in Greek Thought* TB/1104

Political Science & Government

Psychology

7

ERICH NEUMANN: Amor and Psyche: *The Psychic Development of the Feminine* △ TB/2012
ERICH NEUMANN: The Archetypal World of Henry Moore. △ *107 illus.* TB/2020
ERICH NEUMANN: The Origins and History of Consciousness △ Vol. I *Illus.* TB/2007; Vol. II TB/2008
C. P. OBERNDORF: A History of Psychoanalysis in America TB/1147
RALPH BARTON PERRY: The Thought and Character of William James: *Briefer Version* TB/1156
JEAN PIAGET, BÄRBEL INHELDER, & ALINA SZEMINSKA: The Child's Conception of Geometry ○ △ TB/1146
JOHN H. SCHAAR: Escape from Authority: *The Perspectives of Erich Fromm* TB/1155
MUZAFER SHERIF: The Psychology of Social Norms TB/3072

Sociology

JACQUES BARZUN: Race: *A Study in Superstition. Revised Edition* TB/1172
BERNARD BERELSON, Ed.: The Behavioral Sciences Today TB/1127
ABRAHAM CAHAN: The Rise of David Levinsky: *A documentary novel of social mobility in early twentieth century America. Intro. by John Higham* TB/1028
THOMAS C. COCHRAN: The Inner Revolution: *Essays on the Social Sciences in History* TB/1140
ALLISON DAVIS & JOHN DOLLARD: Children of Bondage: *The Personality Development of Negro Youth in the Urban South* ¶ TB/3049
ST. CLAIR DRAKE & HORACE R. CAYTON: Black Metropolis: *A Study of Negro Life in a Northern City.* △ *Revised and Enlarged. Intro. by Everett C. Hughes*
Vol. I TB/1086; Vol. II TB/1087
EMILE DURKHEIM et al.: Essays on Sociology and Philosophy: *With Analyses of Durkheim's Life and Work.* ¶ *Edited by Kurt H. Wolff* TB/1151
LEON FESTINGER, HENRY W. RIECKEN & STANLEY SCHACHTER: When Prophecy Fails: *A Social and Psychological Account of a Modern Group that Predicted the Destruction of the World* ¶ TB/1132
ALVIN W. GOULDNER: Wildcat Strike: *A Study in Worker-Management Relationships* ¶ TB/1176
FRANCIS J. GRUND: Aristocracy in America: *Social Class in the Formative Years of the New Nation* △ TB/1001
KURT LEWIN: Field Theory in Social Science: *Selected Theoretical Papers.* ¶ △ *Edited with a Foreword by Dorwin Cartwright* TB/1135
R. M. MAC IVER: Social Causation TB/1153
ROBERT K. MERTON, LEONARD BROOM, LEONARD S. COTTRELL, JR., Editors: Sociology Today: *Problems and Prospects* ¶ Vol. I TB/1173; Vol. II TB/1174
ROBERTO MICHELS: First Lectures in Political Sociology. *Edited by Alfred de Grazia* ¶ ○ TB/1224
BARRINGTON MOORE, JR.: Political Power and Social Theory: *Seven Studies* ¶ TB/1221
BARRINGTON MOORE, JR.: Soviet Politics—The Dilemma of Power: *The Role of Ideas in Social Change* ¶ TB/1222
TALCOTT PARSONS & EDWARD A. SHILS, Editors: Toward a General Theory of Action: *Theoretical Foundations for the Social Sciences* TB/1083
JOHN H. ROHRER & MUNRO S. EDMONDSON, Eds.: The Eighth Generation Grows Up: *Cultures and Personalities of New Orleans Negroes* ¶ TB/3050
ARNOLD ROSE: The Negro in America: *The Condensed Version of Gunnar Myrdal's An American Dilemma* TB/3048
KURT SAMUELSSON: Religion and Economic Action: *A Critique of Max Weber's The Protestant Ethic and the Spirit of Capitalism.* ¶ ○ *Trans. by E. G. French. Ed. with Intro. by D. C. Coleman* TB/1131
PHILIP SELZNICK: TVA and the Grass Roots: *A Study in the Sociology of Formal Organization* TB/1230
GEORG SIMMEL et al.: Essays on Sociology, Philosophy, and Aesthetics. ¶ *Edited by Kurt H. Wolff* TB/1234

HERBERT SIMON: The Shape of Automation: *For Men and Management* △ TB/1245
PITIRIM A. SOROKIN: Contemporary Sociological Theories. *Through the First Quarter of the 20th Century* ¶ TB/3046
MAURICE R. STEIN: The Eclipse of Community: *An Interpretation of American Studies* TB/1128
FERDINAND TÖNNIES: Community and Society: *Gemeinschaft und Gesellschaft. Translated and edited by Charles P. Loomis* TB/1116
W. LLOYD WARNER & Associates: Democracy in Jonesville: *A Study in Quality and Inequality* TB/1129
W. LLOYD WARNER: Social Class in America: *The Evaluation of Status* TB/1013

RELIGION

Ancient & Classical

J. H. BREASTED: Development of Religion and Thought in Ancient Egypt. *Intro. by John A. Wilson* TB/57
HENRI FRANKFORT: Ancient Egyptian Religion: *An Interpretation* TB/77
G. RACHEL LEVY: Religious Conceptions of the Stone Age *and their Influence upon European Thought.* △ *Illus. Introduction by Henri Frankfort* TB/106
MARTIN P. NILSSON: Greek Folk Religion. *Foreword by Arthur Darby Nock* TB/78
ALEXANDRE PIANKOFF: The Shrines of Tut-Ankh-Amon. △ *Edited by N. Rambova. 117 illus.* TB/2011
ERWIN ROHDE: Psyche: *The Cult of Souls and Belief in Immortality Among the Greeks.* △ *Intro. by W. K. C. Guthrie* Vol. I TB/140; Vol. II TB/141
H. J. ROSE: Religion in Greece and Rome △ TB/55

Biblical Thought & Literature

W. F. ALBRIGHT: The Biblical Period from Abraham to Ezra TB/102
C. K. BARRETT, Ed.: The New Testament Background: *Selected Documents* △ TB/86
C. H. DODD: The Authority of the Bible △ TB/43
M. S. ENSLIN: Christian Beginnings △ TB/5
M. S. ENSLIN: The Literature of the Christian Movement △ TB/6
JOHN GRAY: Archaeology and the Old Testament World. △ *Illus.* TB/127
JAMES MUILENBURG: The Way of Israel: *Biblical Faith and Ethics* △ TB/133
H. H. ROWLEY: The Growth of the Old Testament △ TB/107
GEORGE ADAM SMITH: The Historical Geography of the Holy Land. ○ △ *Revised and reset* TB/138
D. WINTON THOMAS, Ed.: Documents from Old Testament Times △ TB/85

The Judaic Tradition

LEO BAECK: Judaism and Christianity. *Trans. with Intro. by Walter Kaufmann* JP/23
SALO W. BARON: Modern Nationalism and Religion JP/18
MARTIN BUBER: Eclipse of God: *Studies in the Relation Between Religion and Philosophy* △ TB/12
MARTIN BUBER: For the Sake of Heaven TB/801
MARTIN BUBER: Hasidism and Modern Man. △ *Ed. and Trans. by Maurice Friedman* TB/839
MARTIN BUBER: The Knowledge of Man. △ *Edited with an Introduction by Maurice Friedman. Translated by Maurice Friedman and Ronald Gregor Smith* TB/135
MARTIN BUBER: Moses: *The Revelation and the Covenant* △ TB/837
MARTIN BUBER: The Origin and Meaning of Hasidism △ TB/835
MARTIN BUBER: Pointing the Way. △ *Introduction by Maurice S. Friedman* TB/103
MARTIN BUBER: The Prophetic Faith TB/73
MARTIN BUBER: Two Types of Faith: *the interpenetration of Judaism and Christianity* ○ △ TB/75

9